AHOUND the WORLD
my travels with Oscar

Joanne Lefson

A HOUND
the
WORLD

my travels with Oscar

Published by Zebra Press
an imprint of Random House Struik (Pty) Ltd
Company Reg. No. 1966/003153/07
80 McKenzie Street, Cape Town, 8001
PO Box 1144, Cape Town, 8000, South Africa

www.zebrapress.co.za

First published 2010

1 3 5 7 9 10 8 6 4 2

Publication © Zebra Press 2010
Text © Joanne Lefson 2010

Cover image and photographs © Joanne Lefson

PUBLISHER: Marlene Fryer
MANAGING EDITOR: Ronel Richter-Herbert
PROOFREADER: Beth Housdon
COVER AND TEXT DESIGNER: Monique Oberholzer
TYPESETTER: Beverley Dodd
PRODUCTION MANAGER: Valerie Kömmer

Set in 11.5 pt on 16 pt Adobe Caslon

Printed and bound by Interpak Books, Pietermaritzburg

ISBN 978 1 77020 046 3

Over 50 000 unique African images available to purchase
from our image bank at www.imagesofafrica.co.za

To my parents for giving me the ultimate journey…
and to Oscar for sharing the best part of it with me

Contents

And the Oscar goes to...

No project of this magnitude could have made it around the world with a pooch without a little help from friends – and we sure made (and found) many! In fact, without the generous support of various entities both large and small, far and wide, I have no doubt that Oscar and I would probably still be camping on some remote desert island, wishing on a shooting star that one day we find our way back to the mainland!

So, yes, indeed, we are most grateful to everyone who shared their 'bite' of peace, love and 'yappiness' with us. Whether it was one brief night of complimentary accommodation in the Namib Desert or a flight from Las Vegas to the Grand Canyon, every contribution made a huge difference to both our budget and our experience.

I have listed at the end of the book the websites associated with those who supported the World Woof Tour, but I would place myself firmly in the dogbox if I didn't acknowledge the handful of top dogs that supported the tour before anyone else took a meandering madam and her mutt seriously. In particular, the Big Five: Christelle van Zyl from Animal Travel Services, whose organisational skills (fully opeional despite receiving the occasional midnight phone call from halfway around the world), unwavering experience and endless patience saw my mutt cross borders without the slightest hiccup.

The team at Pedigree South Africa, who provided us with a financial injection that kicked things off. Their yellow cans ensured that Oscar was on a nutritional 'high' throughout the mighty long tour.

Paul Fuller and his team at Rogz – Irené, John and Claire – who so generously provided us with thousands of collars and leads to hand out to the underdogs around the globe. No words can capture the sheer gratitude and appreciation on the faces of the shelter staff and rural populations who so graciously received these 'gifts'. We shall always remain incredibly grateful to Rogz for their unbelievable generosity in allowing us to share 'the world's coolest gear' with almost every corner of it!

Of course all these leads weighed a ton, and without UPS in South Africa – Sharon Watson and Chantal Young – the products wouldn't have travelled much further than my garage in the suburbs of Cape Town.

And then, thanks to my 911 operators, aka my mom and dad: it is so much easier to head off into the sunset knowing that if and when the poop hits the fan, someone will always be on the other side as your lifeline – whether they like it or not! And, even more importantly, thanks for letting me always have a dog in my life – it taught me more about compassion and caring than I could ever have learnt in a Buddhist monastery high up in the Himalayas.

These acknowledgements wouldn't be complete without my also recognising a few other people who really went out of their way to make the roses smell better along our route. Wonderful individuals like Dr Rajput (National Department of Agriculture, Forestry and Fisheries), who assisted with Oscar's tests and tribulations on leaving and returning to South Africa; the agents who helped us around the world, specifically Chinda Siri-Aree at Dynamic Air Cargo in Thailand, who arranged four import permits for Oscar without even one yelp; Puru Timalsena (Above the Himalaya Trekking), who made obstacles 'no problem' and went out of his way to help without any financial gain. He shows the rest of us how God always intended human beings to be.

To those who removed man-made boundaries and allowed a canine to experience bliss, thank you – specifically Rishi Kapoor and Dave Junker, who allowed Oscar to wine and dine at the finest hotel in Asia, the Imperial Hotel, New Delhi, India; and Francesco Galli Zugaro and Dalia Gibu, who permitted Oscar to experience the great Amazon Basin in five-star comfort without being swallowed by an anaconda!

Jumping back in time: to my primary-school teacher, Di Black, who always encouraged me to keep on saving the whales – and anything else, for that matter; and my English college professor, Gordon van Ness, whose passion for writing taught me how to cross my Is and dot my Ts.

To my editor, Ronel Richter-Herbert at Zebra Press, for turning my question marks into exclamation marks; and to one of my best friends, Evelyn Hunter-Jordan, for waking me up and making me conscious of how our daily choices can make or break the world.

To all the shelters that opened their gates to us when we were in town, and to everyone who works to improve the lives of others: you help to transform the world into what it was always meant to become. Thank you for inspiring Oscar and me throughout our journey, and in the miles beyond.

And, finally, to everyone who has ever adopted a dog and to those who will still adopt a dog: you are lifesavers, and Oscar's true heroes.

This brings me back to the very beginning of this story. With enormous gratitude, I acknowledge all the other shelter dogs that have walked into my home, warmed my soul, enriched my life, eaten my socks, irritated my father and inspired my life's purpose. The journey of writing this book would never have been undertaken had it not been for each of you writing a chapter in my heart...

1

Once upon a tail ...

If anyone had told me years ago that I would one day travel around
the world with my adopted dog, I probably would have called the
loony bin and had the person committed. But the truth is, I should
have known that my life was going to be dedicated to something in
the animal kingdom. I'd been trying to save dogs, whales, dolphins
and anything else that moved since the very first time I bunked
school.

I had my first opportunity to save a living creature when I was
seven years old. The 'guinea pig' was a bright-orange butterfly I
named Daisy. I had been walking to school with my little brown
'box', some stale sandwiches squashed inside, when I came across a
butterfly that couldn't fly on the pavement. I figured the problem
lay in some type of mechanical failure, and that the disabled butterfly urgently needed to go to a private hospital. The situation called
for an episode of *Doctor Doctor*, and I was the nursie-nursie who
would coax my patient back to health. I decided to bunk school and
skipped back home, where I stuck Daisy into the intensive care unit –
a small white cupboard in the corner of my room. It wasn't the largest

Funraising for SPCA std 4

hospital by any means. My parents were separated at the time, so my mom was renting a modest apartment in a middle-class suburb of Cape Town within walking distance of my primary school – and the best ice-cream parlour that side of town. For a pup like me, the place was perfect.

I picked grass and rose petals for Daisy twice a day and gave her stale sandwiches when I'd plucked everything from the garden. But Daisy died after three days, and I cried myself into a puddle. Butterflies made the world more beautiful, and I didn't know how I could go on without my flying flower called Daisy to make me happy.

I've since saved a lot more dogs than butterflies in my thirty-eight years on the planet. In fact, from the moment of Daisy's passing, Barbie and boyfriends *never* stood a chance. When it came to winning my affections, it was canines all the way – and there would be many. I always had a dog by my side, licking my toes or humping my foot. Every single one of them I adopted from a shelter. They were all formidable fleabags, lounging legends in the Lefson household, and none had a lineage that anyone could unravel. Without these pavement specials, I have to admit that I would have been a totally different person today. They shaped my personality, moulded my future and inspired my purpose. I can't even recall the exact number of mutts I've had, but three in particular leap to mind.

I rescued Simba from the Animal Welfare Society (AWS) when he was just a few years old. The AWS was located in one of the dodgiest areas of town – I was lucky to have been able to catch a ride there in the first place. When I saw Simba, no one could tell me what the mustard-coloured mixture was, or where he'd come from. Only his mother knew the secret spices, and we weren't ever going to find her.

I liked Simba. He wasn't High Street Kensington, but he didn't have any hang-ups about his ancestry either. What Simba lacked in pedigree, he made up for in a talent that no one except me could tolerate.

Simba could *sing* – and far worse than anything you've ever heard before! He had a voice that would make Susan Boyle boil and Simon Cowell howl! But Simba wasn't seeking a music contract. All he ever wanted was some attention, and the less he got, the more he roared. Once in full throttle, nothing could stop him. It didn't matter  whether Barbara Woodhouse remonstrated or the neighbourhood complained – Simba was born to sing. The neighbours even erected thick hedges around their properties to muffle the sound.

Attention-seeking aside, the dog psychologist suggested that Simba's vocal offerings could be a gesture of gratitude for his rescue. Whatever the reason was, Simba would not be dissuaded from fulfilling his part of the deal.

Not everyone who visited the Lefson household was amused by our tenacious tenor, and we grew accustomed to enjoying Sunday brunch alone. The postman was not averse to sneaking past our postbox when Simba was practising his vocal chords; ditto the hawkers. Ours was the only house in the neighbourhood that was never robbed.

Six months after adopting Simba, the annual SPCA fête rolled around. By this time, Simba's notoriety had spread far and wide and I was persuaded to enter him in one of the most coveted of all divisions, that of 'South Africa's Greatest Barker'. The only problem was that Simba did not so much bark as howl. Would they, I asked sweetly, allow 'opera howling' to be included in the same category as

3

barking? Naively and, I imagine, to their eternal regret, they agreed, provided that I paid the entrance fee.

Not for a moment did the panel imagine that Placido Dogmingo would pose any threat to the noble-pedigreed assemblage in the arena. Great Danes, Jack Russells, German shepherds and Labradors all sat obediently, waiting their turn. When at last the order came, Simba wasted no time – or effort. He opened his jaws and pitched a full-throated holler towards the sky. Chaos immediately erupted. Hands covered ears, and the other contestants fled yelping, dragging their panic-stricken owners behind them.

Not surprisingly, there weren't many left to witness the awards ceremony, but, as with most things, this didn't worry Simba. He had won the first-place hamper and had also earned bonus points in the attention department. The tournament committee warned me never to show up and try to enter my 'mongrel' ever again in their competition. Simba never wanted to defend the title anyway; he just wanted to savour his moment of glory. For just one day, he was the undisputed canine of the show, and I was the proudest mama in the whole wide world.

Simba died of biliary at a ripe old age, a loss that devastated me. I was overseas at the time and never fully forgave myself for not having been at his side when the music died. I had loved that fleabag with all my heart. He had been with me through thick and thin and was present at every high and low point of my teens; he was my diary when my pen ran out of ink.

Simba's wagging tail waved me off to school each morning, and he was in attendance to serenade me when I returned home. He was there to sing some sense into my head when I wanted to ditch school and join Greenpeace, and he supported me when I tried to get my divorced parents back together before my high-school graduation. Given half a chance, he would have been my date to the matric dance! He watched me squeeze my first pimple and was right there when a boy crept into my room for the very first time.

When life got too much, as it sometimes did, I'd run away from home and Simba would always take the lead. Simply put, he was my high-school sweetheart; the best darn friend a girl could ever have.

Mickey hailed from the same adoption centre as Simba. He was a black Staffordshire bull terrier–cross, and he charged onto the scene a few months after Simba's passing. Mickey wasn't interested in the microphone; Mickey was a sprinter. He would sprint absolutely everywhere and, had he had a chance at the Olympics, he would have bumped Carl Lewis into silver.

Mickey's talent did have its benefits: he kept me fit. From the moment we met, he became my personal trainer. His services came free, with a lifetime supply of love and attention. He demanded that I run him all over the show, and when the blisters kicked in, my car had to take over. That worked out much better; the old black Mercedes was much fitter than I was, anyway. Car and driver would fly over the twenty-kilometre speed limit in our housing estate, Mick-ey in hot pursuit, while the neighbourhood kids dived for cover.

But it was only a matter of time before the Merc was forced into retirement and I had to pick up where the smoking engine had left off. I started running Mickey up and down the mountain like a yo-yo every weekend. Thanks to his demanding routine, I'd completed seven marathons since adopting him, so a few sprints in the wilderness was puppy's play!

Wilder than the wind and freer than the birds, one Sunday morning Mickey gave his usual chase after a troop of monkeys on the mountain slope. Ignoring my desperate calls for him to return, he disappeared deep into a bush in hot pursuit of the fleeing animals. When the bush stopped quivering, I knew it was all over – Mickey had died of a heart attack. I recovered his cold, stiff body, which had been suspended in a running motion. For the first time since he was born, his energetic little legs had run out of steam.

After the tears finally dried, it was time for me to return to the Animal Welfare Society. I was becoming such a loyal customer that they offered me two for the price of one! At R135, money could indeed buy love, and it had never been cheaper!

It was impossible to miss Sevi. She was a lazy, fat sausage on legs. Sevi spotted me from her cage the moment I walked down her aisle, and she wouldn't let me go until I had officially adopted her. She knew that she had landed with her derrière very firmly in the butter.

Sevi wasn't interested in singing or sprinting to earn her keep; she knew she didn't have to. Sevi was an eater – an unapologetic, professional pantry cleaner. What was served didn't matter, as long as she could partake more than a dozen times a day! Sevi would have been the perfect candidate for *The Biggest Loser*, but she definitely

would have been the first to be voted off.

While Sevi spent her days expanding, I was spending much more time abroad. Eventually Sevi managed to make the effort to migrate all the way from my side of the house to my dad's, where the sympathy was stronger and the pickings just as good. She ended up dying of natural causes a few days after my dad's seventieth birthday celebrations. But for the savings on that week's grocery bill, it was the saddest week in the history of the Lefson household.

Through the years, I've always had a dog waiting for me to return home from somewhere. I'm not sure why I never considered taking any of my dogs on my trips. Perhaps it was because I never had to, as I had the best, the cheapest and the most exclusive dog-sitting service in the business – otherwise known as 'Dad'. He took over the canine care in my absence. It never happened without an overload of groaning, but I'd listen sympathetically and then flee in apathy! Dad's was an admirable task conducted with great stoicism, especially considering that each of his charges occasionally traded doing their business in the garden for doing it on his favourite carpet. Furthermore, as an unemployable daughter, I didn't ever have the moolah to pay him for his services.

Throughout my teenage years, I spent many weekends away, attending tennis tournaments. When I finished school, I headed off to Texas A&M University, where I studied wildlife and fisheries science courtesy of a fully sponsored golf scholarship. Whenever excessive studying overpowered my ADD, I would go in search of Buddhist monasteries and other spiritual retreats in the Himalayas.

No matter where my camera and takkies took me, I always missed my dog. Most of the time I returned home only so I could visit the hound, and many times I cancelled a trip because of it! When I was away, I would call home every Sunday afternoon just to bark a loud 'hello' down the line. It was never more than a few 'woofs', but I knew my dog appreciated it more than my dad, who by that stage had resigned himself to the fact that his only daughter was, indeed, a stray herself!

Never once did I imagine that all these experiences with my dogs would eventually have a tremendous influence on the direction my life would take.

Their impact on my life began quietly to reveal itself when I fell in love – and it wasn't with another dog. My pets' medical bills had been a bone of contention ever since I'd adopted my very first dog, so I figured I'd win the heart of the next best thing to a hound – a veterinarian!

2

Any doggie home?

I wasn't looking for a husband, which is exactly how these things sneak up on you! While competing in a professional golf tour in Southern California, a friend of mine told me to pop in at Sea World. She knew I'd always wanted to save the whales, and a grey one had just been rescued off the coast. The injured mammal was being rehabilitated at the facility and, more importantly, there was a very cute veterinarian in charge!

Destiny made an early move when I was met at the gate by the very handsome doc. The day swam past like a salmon run, and I don't remember anything other than falling in love with the whale's boss. Six months later, with the groom suitably attired in a penguin suit, and with Sevi the matronly mutt as my proud bridesmaid, we tied the knot in a beautiful Cape Town church with a tipsy priest presiding at the altar.

When the priest finally sobered up and the party was over, we headed back to San Diego to live happily ever after – or so we thought. On paper, the union seemed perfect. We both loved Southern California, Tiger Woods and sipping Starbucks coffee every morning. The most obvious bond was our love for animals, but as time went by, it became clear that we each loved some a little bit more than others!

In fact, it was the animal kingdom that was disrupting true love. I dug dogs more than dolphins, and my husband seemed to want a whale to call 'wife'. The vows were sinking fast. Playing 'flipper' and squeaking all night might perhaps have helped the union to stay afloat a bit longer, but my disguise as a dolphin would have eventually floundered. As for my poor husband, we didn't have space in our modest home to squeeze in a dog. After a tumultuous few years together, we decided to part, on amicable terms.

It didn't take long to find a new pad in the heart of Cape Town. I dragged out all my stored stuff from my father's garage and, after a few weeks, the walls of my new abode were covered with dusted portraits of all my dogs who had gone before. Only one was missing: the one who would make my house a home.

One beautiful Sunday morning, I jumped into my car and headed over to the Grassy Park SPCA. The grass was a brighter shade of green there and the birds were singing merrily; it seemed as if the universe was on my side. Indeed, it was. It would turn out to be a day that would change my life forever.

The Cape of Good Hope SPCA was as familiar to me as a pooper-scooper. When I was young, many of my weekends were spent volunteering at the facility. I had started out behind the front desk, but was expedited to the kennel area after management discovered that I was verbally insulting anyone who walked in with a dog who looked dejected, neglected or abused. Working in the kennels awarded me diplomatic immunity and quality time with the dogs.

Unfortunately, it was also a reality check from hell. It was here that I witnessed dogs being put down for the first time in my life, and it burnt a permanent scar in the very centre of my heart. I watched in disbelief as the corpses of these once healthy animals were placed into black garbage bags and left to pile up until the municipality came to collect them. The killing was happening every single day – on sunny summer days when everyone was laughing and having fun over a game of beach bats, and even on Christmas Day. I just couldn't bear it, and no matter how hard I tried, I couldn't forget it.

I developed a strong desire to rescue as many dogs as I could from this hideous fate. Every time I helped out at the SPCA, a dog got lucky. It became the greatest pleasure in my life. There was nothing more satisfying for me than to know that a life had been saved. It was one more garbage bag that didn't have to be recycled, and one more dog that would inevitably drive my dad bonkers. Admittedly, I was turning my father's home into a permanent boarding house for hounds, but there wasn't a psychologist around who could cure my 'addiction'. Eventually, Dad banned me from volunteering at the pound.

This Sunday was different. I was all on my own. I didn't have to go to Sunday school any more, and I didn't need to worry about Dad's sanity. I had my own home now. I didn't know how to cook or clean, but I knew how to adopt a dog in a democratic society.

There were two long rows of cages to explore, and I didn't need anyone's permission to go walkies. I knew that all seventy of the dogs I was about to meet would win my heart, but there was only one spare key to my front door. I entered Row A and slowly walked along the concrete path in front of the cages. The dogs came running out to greet me as I strolled by. Anxious faces squeezed between the steel bars as they waited for their fate to be determined: either a garbage bag or a leap to freedom. Barking rang out throughout the kennels and behind each cry sat a pair of desperate eyes observing my every move.

A little black Staffie at the end of the first row caught my attention. She reminded me of a mix between my sprinter and my pantry raider. I knew she would make a great Lefson, and she would be my first prize if nothing else leapt into contention. My search continued to Row B. Step by step I passed the cages, trying not to remind myself that the destiny of many of the dogs before me hinged on my decision.

The pressure overcame my resilience, and tears of despair trickled down my cheeks. I hated shelters. I hated being reminded of this pitiful situation. I hated that people were still buying dogs from breeders when all these amazing dogs were already here, dying for that one last chance. Somewhere in my deepest sorrow I knew that because I was here one of them would get a chance at a life, and even I knew that that was one more than none.

When I arrived at cage number B5, I stopped in my slops. There, on the opposite side of my tracks, sat the funniest-looking creature I'd ever seen. It was a mixture of love at first sight and the biggest belly laugh I'd had in ages. His body was too long and his legs too short. His pitch-black ears were too big for his face, and the rest of him was a concoction of colour, ranging from brown to blond.

Nothing seemed to fit, but that's what made him so perfect! Noticing that he had my attention, he didn't waste any time playing out the 'please-take-me-home-I'm-desperate' act. Like Simba, he didn't have any hang-ups about his mysterious ancestry. Instead, he set out to impress me with a routine of his own, rolling onto his back and raising all four paws skywards. I couldn't fathom where he'd learnt this subtle manoeuvre, but his chances of winning an Oscar and a prized lifetime commitment of love and attention were improving rapidly!

The information sheet attached to his cage labelled him as a 'terrier mix'. Not a bad guess, assuming he was a member of the canine species. He had been handed in at the SPCA as a stray, was estimated as being between two and three years old, and was possessed of a good nature. My ex-husband had had plenty of this too, but that hadn't worked out. Could this muppet turn it all around?

I wanted to adopt the little fellow immediately, but first I had to deal with the devil's advocate inside. This dog was not only unusual, but extremely cute as well. I figured that a dog like this would easily find a home. I was quite happy to take the ugliest specimen on the block. I really wasn't fussy – my main objective was simply to give one hound a second chance.

A staff member arrived to put an end to my indecision. She asked whether I'd like to get acquainted with the odd dog in the grassy area outside the kennels. As she opened the cage gate, B5 immediately ran out to visit all the other mutts along Row B, whom he'd heard howling but had never seen. It gave me a chance to ponder the black Staffie I had seen earlier and compare her with this clown-like teddy bear.

I needed a new man in my life who would love, honour and probably not obey me – until death us do part – but it didn't necessarily have to be the cutest darn thing anyone had ever seen! I told the staff member how guilty I'd feel if I adopted an adorable dog instead of a real 'runt', and she was quick to remind me that cute, cuddly dogs are certainly not immune to death row. 'Inside here,' she said, gesturing towards the kennel building, 'not even Lassie can be guaranteed a home.'

Most of the dogs aren't kept for longer than twelve days, and Number B5, she pointed out, had already been resident for fourteen days. She wasn't trying to make me feel bad – she was just being dead honest. 'This dog probably has one more day before we'll have to … Well, unfortunately we just can't keep them all.'

I had heard enough.

'I'll take him!' I yelled.

I ticked all the right boxes on the adoption form in the office, paid the deposit and agreed to allow the inspector permission to pop in the following day to make sure that my pad was pooch-perfect! I drove back home, stopping to buy all the necessities for what would inevitably become the world's luckiest dog! Back at the pound, Number B5 was being sterilised, dipped, microchipped and inoculated against rabies.

Within five days, we were roommates and were nesting into our new home together very nicely. B5 had my bed to snooze in, a bone to chew on and Animal Planet to watch when he wasn't out walking or chasing squirrels in my garden. All that was missing, aside from knowledge of his ancestry, was a name.

I had always liked 'Diesel', but it didn't quite fit this chap. The staff at the SPCA had suggested 'Benji', but that was too much of a crib on the movie-star dog – and my little fellow wasn't going to follow in anyone else's paw prints. He was a one-of-a-kind prodigy, a born leader quite unlike anything that had lifted a leg on the planet before. He had managed to defy some radical odds to make it out of jail alive. There was a sense of destiny running through his stars.

Thinking about the stars, I thought, what about 'Oscar'? I said the name a few times, and, within seconds, I had a windscreen wiper wagging all over my face. 'Oscar', we both agreed, was just perfect.

3

It ain't nothin'
but a pound dog!

I was convinced that my trophy mongrel was a star, and Oscar proved this within weeks of his adoption. The SPCA's Mutt of the Year show rolled into town, a highly anticipated event on the Cape Town social calendar that attracted mixed breeds from all over the Western Cape. The event also drew plenty of reporters, all wanting a piece of the action. The occasion may have been a beauty pageant for mutts, but it was a platform fit for any great dame.

Oscar sailed through the ten elimination rounds without rolling over once, and after four hours of intense scrutiny, he was one of the final three candidates. Minutes later, he won the coveted title of Mr Mutt 2004, having vanquished well over 300 contestants. Covered with confetti from nose to tail, he was the most decorated pooch at the show. I hadn't felt so proud since Simba had howled himself to victory at the SPCA's annual fête. Like John Travolta and Olivia Newton-John in *Grease*, we strutted back to my car with all of my handsome hero's loot!

SPCA FETE 2005
SUN 20 FEB
10h00-16h00

MUTT OF THE YEAR

CONSTANTIA SPORTS CLUB
Tel: 700 4141 • www.spca-ct.co.za

Success followed Oscar faster than fleas did, and life at home was no exception. Getting my new adoptions acclimatised to the Lefson routine in the past had always taken a fair bit of schooling, but right from the start Oscar knew the drill. As long as he didn't fertilise anything indoors, or get his teeth stuck into any of my high heels, he knew he could have it all. The boundaries were established without a glitch, and we were soon an inseparable team.

We went everywhere together. It didn't matter where I was going or what I had to do – just like my lipstick, Oscar always came along. When dogs weren't allowed at any of my stops, he was happy to snore away on the back seat of my car. Whenever possible, I'd just sneak him in. Often we'd disappear for weekend getaways to retreats that wouldn't dream of allowing a pet on their premises. These places were the most exciting to visit. Steadfast in character and stealthy in demeanour, Oscar would lie low in my bag, wedged between my running shoes and a polka-dot bikini as I circumvented reception! We were never caught, but we always left a few paw prints on the Egyptian-cotton percale sheets just to prove that a 'hot dog' had slept there.

Hotel-crashing aside, what was becoming extremely apparent was the amount of attention Oscar was generating. Wherever we roamed, people would stop me to ask what the heck he was. Adored by everyone on sight, he became an instant conversation point, and his wacky appearance and delightful nature alone were enough to raise spirits all round. It mattered not whether he was having a 'ruff' hair day or was groomed to Coco-Chanelian perfection: everyone wanted to know more about this most unusual creature.

One time in particular, as I was racing down the freeway on a Monday afternoon, a really handsome driver pulled up alongside my car and signalled at me to pull over. Being single at the time, I couldn't believe my luck. George Clooney's doppelgänger had finally arrived. Screeching to a halt, I slapped some lipstick on my puckers and leapt out of my car, just as my knight in Ray-Ban armour ambled across.

Tall and handsome, he was simply divine from head to toe. He also had a broad smile. Even before he could ask me out on a date, I had to suppress an emphatic 'YES!'

'Sorry to pull you over like this,' he said politely, as I waited expectantly, 'but what kind of a dog is that?' My dream of finally meeting my Prince Charming on the side of a busy freeway had slammed into a cul-de-sac. 'My daughter saw your dog as we were overtaking,' he continued, 'and she says she wants one just like it.'

I nearly choked on the car fumes. All I wanted was a man like him in my life, and all he wanted was a dog like mine in his! I told him to go to the SPCA and gave him directions, writing my number below the scribbles just in case he ever wanted to know more about Oscar's chauffeur. I never heard from him again, but I'm almost certain that a dog at the shelter did.

Freeway encounters of the doggie kind aside, Oscar was a man magnet, and my girlfriends were catching on fast. They began to call me up to borrow him for their coffee breaks. Oscar was a guaranteed talking point, and he became the means of stirring up 'espresso' dates with male clientele. I rented Oscar out for free on the condition that when anyone asked where he was from, they would give directions to the nearest SPCA!

Oscar loved all the attention, but it wasn't fulfilling. He was always gracious in acceptance, but I think he intrinsically understood that looks don't maketh the dog, although they had certainly saved his life. With the exception of cats, he began to develop a strong sense of social responsibility for man, dog and anything else that shared the planet! I helped him become a registered volunteer for Pets as Therapy, and he'd visit old-age homes, hospitals and the mentally challenged over weekends. Rather perversely, he also jumped into the middle of occasional catfights as a competitor rather than a peacemaker.

When the residents of one of Oscar's favourite sandy sniffing spots called for a ban on dogs, the hairs on his back stiffened. The grumpy resident claimed that there was too much poop left on Camps Bay beach each morning, and thus this messy situation was one that had to be stopped. Incensed, I wrote to the *Argus* on Oscar's behalf. My missive was titled 'Paws for Thought', and it read as follows:

> *I went walkies on Camps Bay beach on Tuesday morning. Forget the poop palaver and banning us from our regular territory! You should sniff out all the human trash that litters the beach every morning. I'm barking for a ban on humans using the beach, except when walking dogs like me. Woof!*

It was politely signed '"Oscar" Lefson, Higgovale'.

Quite a few dogs wrote letters of support, and it looked like it wasn't just the beach that was going to the dogs – it was the headline news as well!

Now a published activist for previously voiceless coastal canines, Oscar aimed his campaign in the direction of his comrades living in housing estates – most specifically, mine! A pack of whining homeowners had decided that the hounds on their domain were in the dogbox. An official circular from the Homeowners' Association warned everyone that those running riot on the estate would be removed and relocated to the local pound.

Oscar found this rather insensitive. Having been to that motel before, he had no intention of returning! He and the other dogs on the estate had always worn their collars and done their business discreetly, out of doors. And, on a much more personal note, as a sterilised pooch, Oscar had personally never indulged in doggie-style activities.

We rounded up all the resident canines to drum up support for Oscar's new party, the Home-Hounders' Association. Their manifesto cut right to the bone in a language that everyone could understand. A circular, sent out on behalf of every barker, insisted that the humans concentrate on their own kind. It was suggested that gentlemen wear collars at all times, and that they should not be permitted to roam around unless in the company of a dog on a leash. Any human who failed to follow suit would be forced to read *Animal Farm*. The circular was signed '"Oscar Mutt" Lefson'. Although it was a wacky idea, the dogs were never hounded again!

Having become the voice of the voiceless, I thought about getting Oscar a companion. I was fostering a mutt called Tina at the time, and the estate rules allowed for only two dogs per household, so it was impossible for me to adopt another.

We therefore decided we would abide by the rules by adopting an alternative species from the SPCA – which is how Pigcasso, a little black piglet, came into our lives. Being more hog than dog, Oscar set about teaching Pigcasso the ropes in every department but one – gobbling. Pigcasso consumed everything – licorice sticks, beer in the bottle, corn on the cob, toilet rolls, carpet cleaners, curtain rods, Mini Coopers and Homeowners' Association circulars – and, if we hadn't got out of the way when he was hungry, humans and hounds would have been on his ever-expanding menu too! Nothing was out of bounds for Pigcasso. He ate non-stop, so much so that we literally watched him grow before our eyes.

The news of Pigcasso's presence spread almost as fast as his belly, throwing the dreaded Homeowners' Association into a panic. As paranoia once again seized the estate, we tried to reason that Pigcasso was merely a mobile version of the ham and bacon that already existed in the kitchens of the worried proletariat. Just because Pigcasso could move did not mean that we had to *re*move him! To our great surprise, the stony-faced custodians of law and order had a sense of humour and we were never bothered again.

On the downside, however, I was forced to admit that my home was actually beginning to look like a pigsty. Newspapers were scattered across my carpeted floor and yesterday's news was nourishing my garden – or what was left of it. My golf bag had long since been digested, and surely it would be only a matter of time before Pigcasso devoured the very foundations of his first home. I eventually had no choice but to find a new home for him – on a wonderful children's farm nearby, where I knew he could oink happily ever after.

Over the years, Oscar and I had done *almost* everything. We'd climbed mountains, walked trails, paddled the oceans and surreptitiously devoured the fruits of Mammon whenever we could arrange the sleight of hand … er, paw. We'd relaxed under cover in both the finest and foulest accommodation in South Africa, dined with a pig and cocked a snook at the long arm of authority! Firmly established as best friends, we hadn't even had a single argument. Life was great and things couldn't have been better.

But not too far away from our perfect existence was the SPCA dog shelter. We couldn't see it, but it nevertheless loomed large in Oscar's and my subconscious. Every single day – as certain as the sun rose – dogs just as cool as Oscar were being destroyed simply because there weren't any homes for them. How could we sail blissfully into the future and simply forget about the tragedy that was happening right in our own backyard? We desperately wanted to do something to help these animals find homes.

Thanks to all the attention that Oscar was attracting on our daily outings, he was already an accomplished ice-breaker and magnificent mythbuster. With every encounter came an invaluable opportunity to change the perception that all shelter dogs were old, mangy mutts with major issues. Oscar had all the right stuff to give people a whole new perspective on the calibre of dogs available at a shelter.

The more people who got to meet my perfect 'role mutt' along the way, the merrier the gospel of dog adoption became. But it wasn't enough to help save the estimated 475 million homeless dogs in the world. Our sermon needed to reach beyond the boundaries of Cape Town, and Oscar and I were both ready to spread our wings in order to champion the greatest canine cause on the planet. After all, if Oscar could make a George Clooney clone screech to a halt on a local freeway and fast-forward him to a shelter, surely he could make every freeway lead to hound heaven?

Oscar had already proven himself as a vehicle for salvation, but how to spread his charm and influence far and wide? It barked out for a unique project that had never been attempted before; an extraordinary mission that would require a world-class performance. Indeed, it would take an Oscar to win the world over.

4

Barking mad

Planning a world tour with my dog had never entered my wildest dreams, of which I've had plenty. Until I met Oscar, my internal GPS had never considered taking any of my dogs further than the city park or the local bar. They had all been talented, exceptional dogs in their own way, but none had oozed the charisma and noble bearing necessary for the key role of 'pet-jetter'.

Simba would have sung his way into custody at the first border crossing; Mickey would have run himself off the edge of the earth and with any luck landed on Pluto; and I doubt whether Sevi would ever have been able to squeeze through the aircraft door, let alone have a seatbelt fit around his waist!

Oscar, the dog with destiny etched into his bones, had it all – the personality, the charm and the character of a champion willing to enlist for a good cause. He'd actually given me the idea of a world tour a few years earlier. Back then, I had thought about the concept, conjuring up book titles such as *Mutt to Manhattan*, *Pooch in Paris* and *Canine to Cairo* to promote pet-adoption awareness.

When the time was ripe to follow through with the concept, it became obvious that a world tour would create much more interest than the odd trip to just a few distant lands. And we would get the adoption message across even better if we linked it to a series of activities that were not within the normal range of your average Airedale.

Sure, exploring Africa would be a wild experience, affording us the added opportunity of educating the more unsophisticated, poorer inhabitants of the continent on the basics of canine care, but it probably wouldn't make Oscar the most travelled dog in history. And Oscar's message certainly wouldn't reach as many ears. But take on the whole world, and we figured we would make a statement with an exclamatory bark at the end of it! We gave the thought the paws-up and immediately dubbed it 'The World Woof Tour'. It would take fourteen months to plan, but from that moment on, there was no turning back.

This would be an extraordinary and unpredictable adventure, although it wouldn't be a unique event. A few famous precedents had already been set in literature and history, from which we could draw a few tips. Snowy was Tintin's white fox-terrier companion, and together they had travelled the length and breadth of Africa, Asia and Europe. They may have been fictional characters, but Snowy and Tintin were just like Oscar and me – inseparable.

Then there was Laika, a stray dog from Moscow, who became the first creature to orbit the earth way back in 1957, blazing the trail for a succession of canine and human astronauts alike. Although we could draw inspiration from such legends, there was still one major difference: neither Snowy nor Laika had ever had to deal with quarantine, airport bureaucracy, speeding tuk-tuks or the Chinese police! For these reasons, Oscar knew that his mission was going to be that much more hound-raising!

During a meeting on top of my bedspread, Oscar and I agreed

that the tour would be a non-profit awareness campaign with two primary objectives. The first would be to use the tour to draw positive attention towards dog adoption. The second would be to keep the top dog alive and happy at all times. If something happened to me along the way, well, that would be rather unfortunate, but the world could carry on without me. If something happened to Oscar, though, I'd be strung up by animal activists or sued for imposing unrealistic expectations on a sentient being for my own self-promoting objectives.

With that in mind, no effort would be spared to ensure Oscar's safety and contentment. Flying would be kept to an absolute minimum, with time on the ground maximised. His travel box for the hold of the aircraft would be designed around Armani's luxurious living-room suite, and its in-house entertainment centre would include great canine classics such as *Lassie*. Placing my frequent-flyer status on the back burner, chartered flights would be considered whenever dodgy airlines lurked in remote areas, and I would undertake training in aircraft hostage techniques just in case the captain refused to check the temperature in the hold upon my request.

I had travelled around the world before, but exploring global travel through the eyes (and needs) of a dog was a whole new bone game altogether. It wasn't as if I could just call a friend or use a lifeline to find an answer. I'd have to figure out much of it from scratch.

Just basic considerations like accommodation came to mind. Would Oscar be allowed inside wherever we roamed, and what if there wasn't any pet-friendly accommodation in the area at all? Did every airline accept a dog aboard an aircraft, and what about taxis, rental cars and trains? Would they be happy to transport a passenger who looked capable of creating a furry car-seat cover en route? And what would he eat?

Oscar was currently living on a diet of free-range chicken mixed with rice and carrots, but that would be impossible to maintain on a world tour. We would already be travelling with more luggage than we could possibly chew, so there wouldn't be a case for packing in some extra tins of Pedigree.

Yes, there were a zillion questions, and the only way to answer them was to start at the top of the list and slowly work our way down, praying that we would have reached the bottom before taking off on the first leg of our journey!

Before plotting the route, we would need to know which countries had quarantine so that they could be scratched from our list right from the start. I knew that the UK and Australia were no-go territories, but what about places like Croatia and Cambodia?

I reached for the *Yellow Pages* and found a multitude of businesses linked to the pet-travel industry. This was good news – people were obviously travelling with their pets. Better yet, out of the maze before me a name emerged that would prove to be our most prized support on Oscar's tour. Our victim? Christelle van Zyl from Animal Travel Services.

I decided to give her a call. Once I had her attention, I outlined our idea and asked for her help in planning a route through the quarantine labyrinth. A brooding silence settled on the receiving end of my call. I repeated myself. Again, I heard nothing. Eventually there was a chuckle from the other side. It was obvious from her reaction that she thought I was some prank caller from the local radio station who was trying to tease her. Christelle wasn't about to become a giggling guinea pig for the entertainment of peak-hour traffic: in perfectly executed professionalism, she politely suggested that I call back once I'd come up with a rough idea of where I wanted to go with my beloved dog.

Oscar and I set to work immediately. He slept on the couch

while I traded my social life for a crash course in geography. We would want to meet up with a number of welfare organisations along the way, and the plan was to contact them well ahead of time to arrange activities that would maximise support for dog adoption in their area. It therefore made sense to source these groups, mark them on a map and chart the course from there.

A few Google searches later, and I had found just the site I was looking for. World Animal Net had an international listing of over 16 000 animal organisations. All I had to do was to check each one, research the work that they did, and then insert the top picks for each country into their respective locations on my world map, otherwise known as my dining-room floor.

A few weeks later, I had both a map and a wooden floor dotted with numbered pins, each one representing a society that we could potentially visit along our route. A country like the United States had more pins stuck in it than there are cars on an LA freeway, while regions like central Africa and South America were almost empty.

After every organisation was pinned in place, Oscar and I took a long, hard look at the world map. We now had to decide which pin would link to the next, and also *how* we were going to get from one to the other. A number of factors would influence this decision. Oscar's welfare would come first, but we were also planning to take along a cameraman to film our experiences as part of a documentary we would produce for television. This would require us to include visits to unique landmarks while experiencing cultural aspects of the region so that we could vary the footage and keep the viewer glued to the screen.

We pinpointed the most interesting places and, using different colours to depict various activities, saw that the route was starting to take shape. It still needed plenty of tweaking, so I thought it an opportune time to pop in to meet Christelle. When Oscar and I arrived bearing a map with a few hundred stab wounds, she nearly fainted. She wasn't exactly expecting to hear from her least favourite radio DJ ever again.

Christelle and I sat down and started chatting. Her mom, Estelle, had started the pet-travel business over twenty years earlier, and it was her family's pleasure and passion to fly pets all over the planet. I immediately knew that we were at the right place. I spread the world out on the office floor and asked Christelle if she thought that a world tour with a previously disadvantaged dog was indeed possible. Would Oscar really be permitted to travel to all the countries that were currently pinned on the map? That was the six-million-dollar question, and we desperately needed the inside scoop before we could proceed any further.

Christelle hovered over the map and gave a few nods of approval here and there. I could tell that she was still a little overwhelmed by the sheer enormity of what was, to date, undoubtedly the most unusual request her business had received! She was still a little sceptical that the whole affair wasn't just a prank, but suggested that I give her a call in a few days' time, once she had had time to investigate the route properly. When I followed up a few days later, I held my breath. If quarantine was indeed the law of most lands, our tour would be finished before it had even begun.

'There are a few countries on your list that may be a problem for Oscar,' Christelle said. 'For example, both Malaysia and Japan require quarantine, and I'm still trying to find out more about entry into Cuba. South Africa also has a very strict quarantine policy. We'll have to give some thought to how we'll get you guys back into the country. I might be able to help you get permission to have the quarantine waived based on the nature of the project, but I can't guarantee anything.' It was sounding as though Christelle was going to be up to the challenge of helping us.

'So the World Woof Tour is possible then, right?' I asked.

Christelle laughed. 'Off the wall, crazy and highly bizarre, Jo, but as you aren't using *my* savings, it's definitely possible!'

It took a few more weeks to narrow down the choices to 100 organisations in thirty-five key countries. A few more meetings with Christelle, and we had rolled out a route favoured by destiny. We would head north to cover eight African countries by aeroplane, before hopping over to Greece from Egypt and continuing through Europe on overnight trains. From there we'd fly to Russia and on to India, from where we'd take bumpy, albeit trusted, overland routes through much of Asia. Flying on to the United States, we'd drive around seven states before eventually wending our way down through the Caribbean and into South America. Five continents and many pit stops later – and assuming that the Force was with us – we would arrive back in Cape Town exactly six months later.

All we needed now was dough. In short, we needed to find a sponsor in the eye of what was one of the worst economic hurricanes in world history. It was a most inconvenient truth for us, but with dogs being dumped at shelters at an alarmingly higher rate than before Wall Street's slide, we couldn't afford to surrender.

I isolated four companies that I strongly believed would jump like fleas to support Oscar's mission. A professional business proposal was drawn up and I set out to put the sweetest smile exactly where my mutt was. It turned out not to be as simple as I had thought it would be, but it wasn't entirely a disaster either.

Rogz, which makes the world's coolest pet gear, promised to give us over 10 000 collars and leads to hand out to the underdogs we would meet on tour. UPS promised to send them off ahead of time, and Pedigree donated a substantial amount of cash with which to kick off our tour.

A good mate of mine at TaylorMade arranged for Adidas to

cover us in their three stripes from top to bottom, and thanks to another charming golfing connection, Vodacom threw in a few cell-phones. They didn't come with 'roam away from home', but we greatly appreciated the kind gesture. I still had ye faithful old credit card with its $50 000 limit, and my apartment was ready to hit the market should I need an additional cash injection. I knew I could always buy some more mortar and bricks, but there was no way I could bring a healthy dog back from the dead.

Besides, I'd been working on the project full time for well over eight months by then. *And* Oscar and I had already made a pledge to the nearly 500 million homeless dogs in the world that we were coming to help them. The crusade would begin on 2 May 2009.

There was absolutely no way we were going to let them down!

5

Bone voyage!

With a week to go till kick-off, my house looked as if Pigcasso had returned with a vengeance. My legs were running around like outboard motors, I didn't have time to eat, and my pantry was emptier than my stomach (Mickey would have been so proud of me, but Sevi would have died if she'd been living in my house). Oscar's travel papers were mounting up, and my cameraman Wally* and I needed twenty-three visas to gain entry to various countries.

Oscar's charming doc, Dr George Koury, gave him his rabies injection exactly ninety days prior to departure, but visits to the doc to check for parasites, vectors or vector-borne disease became a daily occurrence. Between operating as Oscar's personal taxi service and trying to find the time to brush my teeth and wash my hair, I was also plotting and planning on my laptop and topping up my Skype account.

None of my family and friends took the project seriously. As far as they were concerned, this was a young-life crisis. They assumed that I would get over the crazy idea before D-Day arrived. With one week to go before our departure, and with fourteen months of

* Not his real name – disguised to protect me.

planning behind us, everyone was starting to worry that the Weird Woof Tour was actually going to … er … fly! My friends finally blocked out 2 May in their diaries, and my parents scheduled an appointment for me to visit the family psychologist.

But it was too late. I didn't have the time, and besides, I already knew I had a screw loose upstairs. If I wasn't hurting anyone or anything, best I just got on with fulfilling my dream!

Packing would be a nightmare, and I dreaded it. In the past, even a two-day trip meant hours of deciding which pair of ripped jeans to include and which pair of polka dots to reject. Even for a solitary weekend away it was impossible for me to decide on the style or colour of bra I wanted to take along for the ride.

Whenever my travels took me abroad, it was never a case of how much overweight luggage I was checking in, but how many kilos I'd have to check out on my return! Now I had to pack for at least six months, and Oscar's paperwork alone weighed a ton. Luckily we were travelling in a chartered jet for the first two weeks, so if I packed *everything*, I figured that the pilots could just fly back all the stuff I hadn't used when they returned to Cape Town.

Finally, the morning of 2 May arrived. There wasn't time to reflect too much on what and how much this mission meant to us. We knew we'd have plenty of opportunities to get soppy over a bowl of water and a sentimental Celine Dion tune in the days, weeks and months to come. To kick the day off, we went straight back to Oscar's roots: to cage number B5 at the Cape of Good Hope SPCA. It marked the precise spot where Oscar had taken his first steps to freedom almost exactly five years ago, and symbolised the aspirations of every shelter dog alive on the planet. It was also an opportunity to wave goodbye to the dogs and to offer each one a home-made doggie biscuit. Many of these dogs would not live long enough to hear about Oscar's adventures, but if just one found a home because of Oscar's story, then, in our minds, the project could be deemed an astounding success.

We then headed to the Mutt of the Year contest in Camps Bay, just a short drive from the SPCA. This was the event Oscar had won before, but this year it was serving as our launch pad. Dogs from all over the Western Cape joined us in the celebrations and, luckily for all of them, Oscar didn't have time to enter! We had a helicopter waiting for us on the other side of town, and a city sightseeing bus would take us there with a few rowdy fans on board.

We said our goodbyes, gave every adopted dog at the event a Rogz collar and wished everyone a very boring year while we were away. With a whole lot of bubbly paving the way, a group of friends and family boarded the bus and, like a soccer team that had just won the World Cup, we spread the message of dog adoption from the bus top all along the route.

The closest Oscar had ever come to flying was when he'd hung out of the passenger seat of my convertible, his ears flapping in the wind and me trying to hold on to his head while going at 140 km/h. Oscar had never been aboard a helicopter before, but he handled the short flight from the central helipad to Cape Town International Airport like a seasoned pilot!

Oscar and I were by no means celebs with a fat bank account, but to anyone watching, we had to have been high-flying brats. The helicopter landed right next to our private jet. Chartering this 'toy' to transport us to our first five countries had not been part of the original plan – or budget, for that matter. But after navigating our way around the map of southern Africa, it soon became clear that any means of travel other than a private charter would be too risky.

The societies and organisations that we wanted to visit were all situated in remote areas. To fly commercially *and* organise overland transport would have taken us twice as long. I wasn't that familiar with Africa either, and I certainly wasn't keen on taking on the Big Five, potholes, snakes or landing in the line of rebel fire. Add to that a cameraman whose gold teeth were more valuable than our camera equipment, and we were definitely looking for safe rather than sorry in the unpredictable African bushveld.

Our considerable amount of luggage had been packed inside our Beechcraft Super King Air B200 the day before our departure. The world's most popular turboprop would be at our service for the next two weeks. I had, in what felt like a lifetime ago, dated the country singer John Denver, and at the time had grown rather accustomed to stepping out of a limousine onto a runway with a private jet waiting patiently in the distance. A guilty pleasure of delectable proportions, it was one of those indulgences that I absolutely hated to admit that I just loved – even as a genuine, non-materialistic, down-to-earth kinda gal who needed just a dog and a country love song in her life to be happy.

Pilots James Franklin (the captain) and Kobus van Staden bent over to shake our leader's paw and cordially invited his majesty onto the aircraft. They had been warned that their boss was headed for Botswana and beyond, and that he would look more like a dog than a famous country singer with a guitar strapped to his back. The boarding order and seating arrangements were designated according to the pecking order – Oscar boarded first and everyone else followed.

The aircraft was a nine-seater, but our luggage occupied all of the five back seats. It included over 5 000 Rogz collars and leads destined for the societies we'd visit on our African trail. Oscar's dog-box for commercial flights was also in there somewhere, along with our suitcases, cameras, tripod, computers and the World Woof Tour public relations material. I'd also packed a four-leaf clover that I'd found while walking Oscar a few years earlier. I've always believed that you create your own luck, but if some flora could help out, it was worth the extra weight.

Once we were on board, the pilots briefed us on the usual safety procedures. In case of a loss of cabin pressure, we had to make sure that Oscar's mask was securely fastened before taking care of our own. Captain Franklin was most amused with his latest charge, and laughter resounded throughout the cabin. All his years of training and experience had culminated in this moment: flying a previously disadvantaged dog through Africa to visit his homeless relatives in the hope of charming their human friends into adopting as many of them as reasonably possible.

It was a mission he loved, but one that he couldn't believe he was undertaking.

Finally the runway was cleared, the engines were ringing out and, moments later, the aircraft was in full throttle as it hurtled down the mighty tarred track. At last the World Woof Tour took off, twisted in a north-easterly direction and headed straight for the Botswana SPCA. Our wing tips caught the light and glinted in the tranquillity of the most magnificent Overberg Mountain sunset before us. With an average flying speed of 415 km/h, we would be arriving in Gaborone in approximately ninety minutes; for the VIP, a cool ten and a half hours of snoozing in doggie time.

I placed my hand on Oscar's forehead and patted him ever so gently. I pondered where each of us would have been now had I not gone to the SPCA on that fateful day. Where, if anywhere, would Oscar have been right now? My goodness, where would I have been but probably hitting buckets and buckets full of golf balls on some driving range in Cape Town?

Up until fourteen months ago, golf had been my life. I was

playing two to three times a week, writing for a golf magazine and presenting a women's golf slot on a prominent television channel. When Oscar and I had started contemplating ways of creating awareness of dog adoption, I had had to decide in which direction I wanted to swing. I simply didn't have the time to focus on everything – something had to give. That was when I asked myself one very simple question: If I had one week left to live, what would I want to do in that time?

The most profound answer came to mind. Although I didn't know *exactly* what I wanted to do, I certainly knew what I *didn't* want to do: *I didn't want to lift another golf club*. If I had to be honest, I had never really enjoyed golf. But the sport had opened up so many doors for me that I had just kept on playing. Aside from cleaning up after a pig and a few pooches, it was all I knew.

Why, then, I asked myself, was I spending almost 40 per cent of my life doing something I hated? Who was I trying to impress? What was the point? Was playing for my country simply an ego boost and beating the average male merely an adrenalin rush? That moment was truly the beginning of the end of golf for me. I wasn't going to waste any more precious time doing anything other than what I wanted to do – especially if it had heart and was a tiny attempt at making the world a slightly better place.

Now I knew it was the best decision I could ever have made. Sitting in my grey seat high up in the air, there wasn't a single place in the whole wide world I would rather have been, nor anyone with whom I'd rather have shared it …

What an exceptional little creature Oscar was, and how unbelievably lucky I was to have found him. He had made an invaluable impact on me, and had become an incredible inspiration. He didn't have a negative bone in his body; nor did he harbour any greed, hate, aggression or anger in his heart. He just had the coolest combination of unconditional love and dedication for his tempestuous human friend – which was exactly what I needed at high altitude.

Flying wasn't my favourite thing, and claustrophobia came a close second on my personal freak-out list. The cabin was small, and only Oscar could stand up straight without banging his head. Although I hadn't vetted the pilots, they seemed to know what they were doing. They weren't puppies any more and had obviously survived in the air long enough to keep their qualification – and their fleet – afloat.

I also knew that our aircraft was a real trooper. Unlike most jets, the Beechcraft Super King Air could land anywhere and on almost any runway, making emergency landings possible ... especially if we spotted a stray dog in the bush below! It was too dark to see any right then and, besides, it was almost time to touch down and begin to explore our first country of the tour.

Oscar couldn't wait to lift a leg on terra firma and announce that he had arrived!

6

Barking up the right tree

Getting a pet into any of South Africa's neighbouring countries was a rather relaxed and pretty simple procedure. All that was required for Botswana, Namibia and Zambia was an inter-territorial movement permit, which Christelle from Animal Travel Services had arranged for us.

In a moment of weakness, which can be blamed on Oscar looking at Christelle in his cutest and most calculating manner, she had kindly offered to help us throughout the tour – no matter when the poop hit the fan and regardless of the time zone in which it got stuck. Without knowing it, she had just sacrificed every last second of her free time to the movement – not that we were going to say a word. Having the best in the pet-travel business overseeing our strides certainly gave Oscar and me enough confidence to cross borders without our tails between our legs.

From the reaction of the ground staff, it was immediately obvious that the arrival of a dog at an airport in Botswana wasn't your typical occurrence – especially when its tail pops out of the doors of a private jet. The inspector at customs control gave Oscar the raised eyebrow and then had a good look at the two of us. I hadn't brushed my hair for almost a month now, and the differences in appearance between Oscar and me were fast diminishing.

I produced the permit, along with the rabies and microchip records. The inspector's eyes repeatedly jumped all over the documents. I was a little nervous and remained on my best behaviour. A glitch at the first border crossing would cause panic, considering we had another thirty-four crossings to navigate! After a gruelling ten minutes, Oscar was free to walk across the yellow line and exit the airport terminal. The delay had been just long enough for Oscar and me to avoid helping with the luggage!

Adele Ntobedzi and Jenny Stewart of the Botswana SPCA were waiting outside the terminal building to greet us, and they were delighted that we had actually pitched. Despite the correspondence between us, they hadn't been entirely convinced that the tour wasn't a hoax!

The *Gaborone Sun* had kindly offered to accommodate our (human) team on a complimentary basis at a hotel, but Oscar was an uninvited – though adored – out-of-hotel guest. In exchange for some cash, we were more than satisfied to swap their buffet breakfast and complimentary shower cap for an apartment nearby.

There is only one facility that works to help improve the lives of animals in Botswana, and that's the BSPCA. The facility stretches across a large piece of rented countryside, oozing a genuine rustic flavour that is instantly inviting.

The children of the SOS Children's Village arrived at the shelter early the next morning. They were all decked out in WWT T-shirts, which the Botswana SPCA had arranged for them, and they were simply delighted to meet the roaming mutt – even though he hadn't yet banked much in mileage at that point.

Botswana has one of the highest HIV/AIDS rates in the world, and many of the orphaned children who end up at the SOS Children's Village are HIV-positive. But that didn't stop them from having fun, nor did it curb their enthusiasm in choosing who would be Oscar's very first 'Oscar'.

The idea of selecting one dog to become 'Oscar's Oscar' at each society we visited would become both an integral and measurable part of the WWT. It could be any dog that just needed an extra bit of fuss made over it to find itself a home. The 'winner' would receive a Rogz collar and lead, a WWT tag and a coveted Oscar toy, which would, of course, go to the person who was lucky enough to adopt the prized pooch.

The idea itself was great, but manufacturing the soft toy had turned out to be an entirely different story. I had designed the toy to resemble a comic version of Oscar. Cute and cuddly, it was supposed to be just the kind of thing that kids would covet and beg their parents to buy for them. All I would have to do was sell 2 500 of them for R1 000 each and, bingo, the tour's costs would be covered! To save on expenses, I'd sourced a few manufacturers in China that could make the toy squeak at a favourable rate. Inspired by Oscar's good looks and designed to make little girls blow their pocket money at the mere sight of it, the toy was well on track – until the Chinese lost its looks in translation.

Oscar had begun to take on the shape of a fortune cookie mixed with a bit of Yankee poodle. Six months after my drawings of the toy had landed in a Chinese inbox, the finished product docked in Cape Town. The toys weren't perfect, but Oscar was besotted with himself. He didn't care where they had been made or who they were supposed to resemble. As long as the toys weren't made from animal fur and they didn't melt in his mouth, they were cool to remain in his jaws wherever he went. Unfortunately for the WWT, the toys had arrived too late, leaving us with no time to sell them. That's when the 'Oscar's Oscar' concept was born.

Bobbie was the first recipient, and the white-and-black terrier cross wasted no time in accepting his award with the same enthusiasm the children had shown in choosing him to be their star. The festivities continued throughout the day, but somewhere between getting covered in dust during a celebratory walk with Bobbie and being sprayed with some tomato sauce over lunch, the phone rang. Our captain needed us at the airport. If we wanted to make Sossusvlei before nightfall, we had to get a move-on!

The sand dunes of Sossusvlei in the Namib Desert are arguably the highest dunes in the world, and we could almost see them from Eros Airport in Windhoek, where we'd had to land in order to clear Namibian customs. Thereafter it would be a short thirty-minute hop over to the Sossusvlei Mountain Lodge runway – a modest clearing randomly scratched out in the Namib Desert. Without any runway lights, the aircraft had to land in daylight hours.

Captain Franklin had timed our arrival in Windhoek perfectly, but he hadn't factored in missing customs officials, presumably on alcoholic beverage breaks somewhere in Eros Airport. When 'Patience' finally did wobble back into his office, we were more than irritated and demanded our passports back as quickly as possible. Patience stamped the Schengen visas in our passports and wished us a safe trip back to America.

After this two-hour delay, we weren't certain whether we would be able to land in Sossusvlei, but we were ready to buckle up and assume the brace position. Fortunately there weren't any air-traffic officers to fine speeding aircraft desperately trying to beat the twilight zone. And, after all, the aircraft was insured, and a hot-air-balloon ride was scheduled for five o'clock the next morning. There was no way Oscar was missing the chance to try to destroy a balloon that size!

We descended from the heavens as fast as the rapidly failing light allowed. The jackals ran for cover, but without one fatality or oxygen mask being deployed, we managed to touch down safely.

Balloon operators can carry up to ten passengers at a time, and the next morning our balloon was carrying maximum capacity. When told that children under five weren't allowed on the flight, one kid gave vent to a paroxysm of tears. A dog on a mission, however, was welcome. Oscar and I shuffled into the basket, where we were greeted by a rather stiff-looking group of German tourists. They had been guaranteed a sighting of an iconic solitary gemsbok wandering over the desert dunes, but clearly no one had told them that Fido would be barking through the lenses of their precision binoculars.

As the balloon took off, the loud burners erupted in a fiery flare. Oscar's bark followed like a ballistic missile in the heat of battle. Above him was the biggest balloon he'd ever seen, and he wanted to pop it! Our high-flying neighbours were clearly getting irritated. There was nothing I could do about the situation except pretend that Oscar and I didn't really know each other.

But Oscar was on a mission of his own. As far as he was concerned, it was partly because of dogs that we were all up there in the first place. Back in 1783, when hot-air balloons were first invented, all sorts of animals were used in experimental flights, when they were sent up high. Sheep, roosters, ducks and dogs were all propelled towards the heavens in the name of human helium experimentation, which would eventually enable man to fly.

I have to admit that the barking was beginning to give even me a headache. If there had been a gemsbok wandering below our balloon, it sure hadn't stuck around. Even the dung beetles would have rolled their loot underground in a scurry of a hurry by now. Without an end to the noise within earshot, it was decided to bring the balloon down to allow the unruly guest to prematurely disembark. Being a dog lover, I kindly offered to accompany him back to Sossusvlei Lodge.

Whether you are a dog or a human, Sossusvlei has got to be one of the most spectacular places on earth to visit. It may be too hot during the day to do much except carry on planning the finer details of a world tour, but when the late afternoon arrives, be prepared to send your visionary senses into a wonderland of landscape delight. The towering dunes turn golden orange in colour, and the dramatic contrasts between light and shadow are dissected like a snake sliding along the stark crest of each dune.

The palette of different colours is enough to melt a camera lens and to take your breath away – especially if you try climbing the monster dunes. I gave it a bash, but after a few seconds I found myself moving forwards in a downward trajectory. My furry little Einstein wasn't stupid enough to volunteer for a gravity experiment in order for us simply to shoot some footage, so we got back into our vehicle and drove to another gorgeous area within the Namib Naukluft Park: Dead Vlei.

Trees older than the time when dogs were first domesticated stand frozen on a canvas that could inspire Dali back to life. If there was ever a land of contrasts, we were stuck in the middle of it.

Beyond one wave of dunes danced the ocean; on the opposite side lay a thirsty clay pan. In a bizarre way, it emulated the contrast between a shelter dog and its freedom. On one side of the wire lay the endless ocean of wild freedom; on the other, a confinement in purgatory.

Nature had etched perfection in this deserted moonscape before us; the elements had used their magic wand to fire up the earth for us to enjoy, and so we trod softly, careful not to disturb the dead camel-thorn trees that were scattered across the barren stage. Defiant in their awkward shapes, they had survived fire, drought and flood for over 7000 years, and here they still stood, frozen in time and space.

The aroma of burnt bark wasn't much to behold on Oscar's nostril tip, but who was he to discriminate? He raised his watering can above the stage that had been set so many years ago and broke the deafening silence with a fine salute to one of the world's oldest trees.

Whoever said that a dog was barking up the wrong tree couldn't have experienced this kind of history...

7

'Dr Livingbones, I presume?'

In order to get to the Windhoek SPCA, we needed to pass through Eros Airport a second time. Fortunately, this time no alcoholic aromas were hovering anywhere near the terminal, and the manoeuvre into Namibia's capital city was seamless.

The Windhoek SPCA is set on such a steep slope that only those fit enough – or expert enough in hand-brake suspension – will ever get the chance to see a dog inside, let alone qualify to adopt one. My king canine didn't have to worry about such unexpected challenges, and every ounce of energy that he'd saved savouring the comfortable passenger seat was spent on voting for the shelter's 'Oscar'.

Three dogs were in the running, but no one could decide who the winner should be. Each candidate had a story worthy of their nomination; all were deserving of the award. That's when Oscar came to the rescue. Once certain that everyone was watching, he started humping Diego! It was the first time I'd ever seen my pooch in such fine athletic form. In fact, it was the first time I'd ever seen my dog in the mood, which probably explains why he selected the same sex on his first try. Misfortune aside, the Windhoek SPCA had their Oscar, and my porn star had once again proven that he was the top dog – literally.

We boarded the jet exhausted, inspired and smelling rather like dog! If we had known what was waiting for us in Zambia, we would have cleaned up our act in Windhoek. As our jet rolled to a stop at Livingstone Airport, we were instantly surrounded by Zambia's national news team. It was more than Captain Franklin could stand. Mostly for his own amusement, he had treated Oscar as if he were the King of England, and now a TV crew was waiting for him on the runway as if Oscar were the nation's president! I swore on the queen's throne that it wasn't a set-up and that no one had been paid or bribed to get the cameras on the runway, but he didn't buy it.

The news crew wanted to know more about Oscar's mission and what we were planning to do in Livingstone. At the time, we didn't know we'd have a lesson in Survival 101 in the Zambezi River, but the following day the headlines cried out, 'Dog on $2mil Tour Lands in L/Stone'.

I'm not sure where they got the $2 million from, but for the first time I felt as if I'd got a bargain, knowing that the actual cost of the tour was projected to be $250 000!

Feeling rather glamorous after our red-carpet reception, we stood outside the terminal waiting for our limousine to arrive. When the old pick-up truck pulled up, our cover was slam-dunked. We threw the luggage into the back, dived on top of it and raced off to customs, which was situated at a separate government facility protected by steel gates almost as high as the Victoria Falls nearby. Our pet agent, Amos Chomba of Stuttafords, did all of Oscar's paperwork while we gave our bums a break from our luggage seats.

Bringing a 'live animal' into any country is much like bringing in a box of cigarettes – it has to be declared and a value ascribed to its worth. Oscar may have been insured for a million bucks in his home town, but on the road his value dropped to $10 in order to avoid paying duties. My priceless possession's nose was a little out of joint when he saw the value attached to his coat, but having spent the last two hours dispersing every stray cat in the facility, he didn't have any energy left to contest the pitiful evaluation.

Livingstone is famous for the Mosi-oa-Tunya (the 'mist that thunders'), otherwise known as the Victoria Falls, and, lucky for us, we were staying within spraying distance. The David Livingstone Safari Lodge is situated right on the banks of the Zambezi River, just a few paddles up from the falls. The views are spectacular and, after freshening up, we headed down to the bridge that overlooks the falls and acts as a border crossing between Zimbabwe and Zambia.

It is hard to describe what it's like to see the Victoria Falls for the first time, but it is indeed a sight to behold. It may not be the highest or the widest waterfall in the world, but it is the largest. And explorer David Livingstone may have been the first human to have 'discovered' it, but 154 years later, the first explorer dog from South Africa laid claim to the same.

The Scottish missionary and doctor had probably been a lot more excited than my mutt to see the falls for the first time. My 'Dr Livingbones' was viewing the natural wonder from 200 metres up on a slippery bridge, and it was a little scary. We walked halfway across the bridge and stopped once we had stepped over the yellow line that officially marks the great divide between Zambia and Zimbabwe. Without the need for any paperwork or having to deal with intoxicated officials, we were now officially in Zimbabwe.

Seconds later, we were back in Zambia. Robert Mugabe was rumoured to be in town and I didn't want my dog to be hand-grabbed.

Back at the lodge, it was another glorious evening to savour. The

African bush is wildly alive and unpredictably breathtaking in its majesty. There's a smell in the air that's raw with energy, and when the sun begins to set, the lions start to roar and the bar tab begins to soar.

The open deck at the lodge stretched out to the river's edge, crying out for a sundowner on what surely had to be one of the greatest sipping spots on the planet. It looked safe enough, too. There may have been an electric fence between the hotel grounds and the riverbank to prevent a blind date between a guest and a hungry crocodile, but the deck didn't require the same shock treatment. It was perched high and dry, well out of range of any breaching crocodile or high-flying hippo, and strong enough to withstand a tsunami rising upriver.

I sat down at a corner table, turned on my laptop and ordered a double gin and tonic. I quietly immersed myself in the most magnificent moment as the setting sun, a ball of flaming orange, soaked up the sky and gravitated towards the river's horizon. Thoughts of exploration ran through my mind. Livingstone had respected only those who trod passage in regions without any roads.

I imagined what it must have been like to enter virgin territory without a lodge to check into – no room service, no insect repellent, and not one yard of electric fencing to keep you safe from the curious beasts that hadn't smelt anything human before. I got goosebumps just thinking about it, but nothing could match the nightmare of what was about to unfold.

A sudden spurt of shouting shot through the evening peace like a bullet through my heart. Below the deck, a security guard was yelling and gesturing towards the river in a total fit of panic. I couldn't quite make out what he was going on about, but through the frenzy, I heard one word: 'Dog!' My eyes panned towards the river and, in the distance, I saw Oscar, paddling away in the water with no idea of the dangers that lurked beneath his paws.

The Nile crocodile is the most dangerous predator in the Zambezi River and occupies pole position in the food chain. Nothing that this crocodile takes on can come out of the water alive. Nile crocodiles feed on fish, but are known also to enjoy delicacies such as canoes and kids – and dogs stupid enough to practise their 'flea' style in the Zambezi River.

I started yelling at Oscar to return to shore. Over and over, again and again, I screamed for him to come out of the water *immediately*. By now other hotel guests had come out to see what all the commotion was about. It was only our fifth day on the road, and it was looking as if it may be the last for both of us. If anything happened to Oscar, I thought, I'd kill myself.

'Dog meat is the favourite meat of a crocodile,' said the guard as I caught my breath before screaming again. I had no idea how he knew that, but it sure didn't make me feel any better. Again, I yelled and begged, and then I started to cry. Sensing that I was acting a little crazier than usual, Oz made the decision to return to shore. At his own relaxed pace, he turned in my direction and drifted back to the riverbank, where he shook the water off his coat and proceeded to roll all over the grass.

It took me a while to comprehend what had just transpired. It was also a wake-up call for me to be far more alert from that point on. I knew my dog inside out. There were only four reasons that he would ever sway from my side: if he saw water, cats, a dog called Diego or a soccer ball. With the electric fence circling the property, I had assumed he could only be right by my side, but my streamlined swimmer had obviously found a way to slip through it.

When I had finally calmed down after the ordeal, the manager informed me that a five-metre croc had that very afternoon been basking in the exact spot where Oscar had dived in. I also learnt that Nile crocodiles probably kill a couple of hundred people a year, but more accurate estimates put the number of victims in the thousands. It was a miracle, plain and simple, that Oscar hadn't been swallowed for dinner.

By the time we departed Livingstone, it seemed as if the entire town had watched the nightly news. It was 'pooch versus the paparazzi' at the airport as we wove our way through to the departure gate. Cellphone cameras clicked at Oscar's every move and any hair that dropped off our roaming star was quickly retrieved as a prized souvenir.

Once on board the aircraft, I sank back into my seat. As we accelerated down the runway, I felt tremendously relieved that there wasn't anyone missing on board. As the aeroplane turned in the direction of Ndola, the third-largest town in Zambia, my mind drifted back to the riverbank. I thought about the fine line between life and death and how everything can change in an instant. One second we have this great gift we call 'life', and the next it can be snatched away. I leant forwards and gave my dog a hearty hug, whispering softly into his left ear: 'David Livingstone would have been your best friend, my boy.'

Livingstone once said that he would go anywhere as long as it was forwards. It was a conviction he honoured right up until his very last pair of boots, but I'll bet that he never practised his backstroke in the Zambezi River.

Now that Oscar was safely curled up in the pound seat before me, I could smile again. Call David savvy and Oscar stupid, I thought, but at least my 'Crocodile Dogdee' had dared to go where no great explorer had ever dared to dive in before!

We arrived at the Ndola SPCA an embarrassing two hours later than scheduled, but it didn't dampen any of the young spirits that awaited us. One hundred and fifty children from the Simba School were jumping all over the fence in anticipation of meeting Oscar –

and chasing him across Ndola for the chance to shake his paw and pat him on the back! In just one week on tour, we had already experienced some incredible moments; this was one that would remain in our hearts forever.

The Ndola SPCA, under the supervision of Debbie Vrdoljak, has over fifty dogs up for adoption, but in this rural African town, as is true for the rest of the continent, the focus is on education and sterilisation. The people of Africa are poor and a dog's needs are secondary to man's, which is why the SPCA here is so vital in reducing animal suffering. Debbie, her volunteers and the delightful Dr Andrew escorted us to Chipulukusu Township, where they provide free rabies injections for dogs every month.

Here we witnessed a scene that could not exist anywhere in the world but in Africa. In the middle of a dusty old soccer field stood Dr Andrew in his shiny white coat with an endlessly bright smile, his old work table faithfully by his side. From this epicentre, a line of dogs and their owners stretched across the field, occasionally disappearing in a cloud of dust stirred up by a scuffle between canines.

Dog accessories are non-existent here, so when news spread that some whacky foreigners were accepting rusty old wire, home-made rope and plastic 'leads' and 'collars' in return for handing out spanking-new Rogz gear to everyone who brought their dog in for a rabies shot, attendance records shot through the roof!

Dr Andrew had never given so many injections, nor seen such an endlessly long line, in his professional life. When we finally ran out of products, the line cried, the dogs sighed and the SPCA staff roared 'hallelujah'! Our time in Zambia had finally come to an end.

Our truck wove its way between the shanty homes, displacing frantic chickens as the dust evaporated in our wake, the locals waving us goodbye, each with a collar in hand.

The kids of Chipulukusu hadn't let the doggie treats slip through their fingers, but further south, the Nile crocodiles had let the juiciest doggie steak south of the equator escape their razor-blade teeth. The reptiles must have been fuming mad!

It was rare enough to witness a rather unlikely tourist handing out pet-related products in the middle of nowhere, but for Oscar to have also played the part of prospective organ donor in the Zambezi River was simply unimaginable!

8

Let sleeping dogs fly!

By the time we landed in Tanzania, we were seasoned jet-setters. We had relished the luxuries of a private aircraft for two weeks – getting used to it had been easier than swallowing a free-range chicken after a crash diet. Unfortunately, the higher you fly, the further you fall, and it was a very ruff landing indeed when the jet dropped us off in Zanzibar and our two top guns waved goodbye, flying our favourite toy back to South Africa.

It was one of the most depressing sights I'd ever seen and a big bugger, to say the least. For the first time since Cape Town, we were truly on our own. It was just me, Oz and cameraman Wally to corral our thin lips and seven battered suitcases! Losing our wings meant that we could no longer avoid checking in at airports. I'd be responsible for ensuring that our luggage followed us at all times, and for Oscar it meant trading the seat in the cabin for some space down under.

The hold is exactly what it says it is. It holds. The hold stores the luggage, any cargo and the 'live animals', although each animal has a separate section to itself within the same space. The hold looks and smells the same as the cabin above; it is just a bit noisier. There's no TV, no window and no pretty flight attendants to serve you bones and water if you're an animal in the hold, but there is cabin pressure, a pleasant temperature and, unless someone made a terrible mistake, no shrieking toddler to keep you awake!

After spending four days in Zanzibar, we checked in to fly from Dar es Salaam to Nairobi on Kenya Airways – one of the proud supporters of the tour. Oscar had never flown in the hold before, and, if my behaviour was anything to go by, you'd have sworn it was going to be my first night in a Turkish jail!

Before starting the tour, I had made my little treasure practise sitting in the plastic carrier box a few times, but there was no way to prepare him for the real deal. Having heard horror stories about dogs who had died in the hold, my nerves were spinning out of control just thinking about it. I had shared my concerns with Christelle on many occasions while planning the trip, and she had reassured me that unless Oscar was expecting a newspaper with a glass of sauvignon blanc en route, there was absolutely nothing to worry about!

She explained that the captain was always informed when an animal was on his aeroplane. Cabin pressure and the hold's temperature were always carefully controlled and monitored from the cockpit. She suggested that I keep calm, as a dog can sense when a human is stressed out, and recommended that I remind the pilot that a VIP was below whenever Oscar and I were on board a flight.

Other than walking or hitching, there was no way we could get to our destination. For a moment I seriously considered taking on the exercise, but with plenty of flights and scheduled events ahead of us, I knew it was only a matter of time before we'd have to give the hold the thumbs-up anyway.

Some airlines don't allow animals on board at all unless they form part of the meals that are served. However, the majority of airlines allow a 'live animal' to be checked in either as excess baggage or as cargo. Still others, like Kenya Airlines, allow an animal to fly only as cargo. To complicate matters further, certain countries do not allow dogs to enter as excess baggage, regardless of airline policies.

Flying a pet as excess baggage is first prize. It's a bit more expensive, but it allows your favourite piece of 'luggage' to stay with you right up until you have to go through the security checkpoints, and you find it in the arrivals hall in the same place and at the same time as your other luggage. Cargo items have to be checked in a few hours earlier, but either way, in both options pets ultimately still fly in the hold.

In addition, the design and construction of the container has to conform to the International Air Transport Association (IATA) 'live animals' regulations. You have to provide your pet with a correctly sized, well-ventilated and leak-proof box that has enough space for the animal to stand, sit, turn around and shake a leg in. In Oscar's case, he could rock 'n' roll and still barely touch sides! I had branded the crate to stand out so that everybody would humbly move out of its way or bow at the very sight of it. 'VIP: VERY Important Pooch' barked out in big, bold letters from all four sides. It sent a clear message to everyone assisting with its transportation to and from the aircraft that this wasn't a package to be transported lightly.

So now Oscar would be undertaking his maiden voyage as cargo. After checking him in, an airway bill was stuck on the roof of his 'cabin', along with other necessary documentation, including his import permit (kindly arranged by Simon Maitland of Crown Relocations). The paperwork ruined the otherwise perfect design, but we didn't want the box to land up in Timbuktu for lack of a bar code, so I didn't complain.

The flight took less than three hours, but it felt like the longest flight of my entire life! By the time we touched down, my nails were raw and half of my left eyebrow was plucked bare. The captain and crew were also exhausted. Every fifteen minutes I had asked them to confirm that the temperature in the hold was still at 21°C. The final response from the cockpit was a written note delivered right to my seat by one of the crew. It read: 'The temperature is a comfortable 21°C. Kindly confirm what music your dog likes, or would you prefer that I take him a PlayStation instead?'

Most of the cargo terminals are a distance away from the airport terminal and are a mission to reach. It also takes time for the cargo to be offloaded, cleared by customs and transported to the cargo terminal. Three hours after landing, my precious cargo was finally safely in my arms. Better yet, he looked to be in showroom condition, although a PlayStation was nowhere to be seen.

The next challenge was to remain calm during peak-hour traffic in Nairobi. Our accommodation was only twenty kilometres from the airport, but it took almost four hours for us to get there. Up until that moment, I was convinced that nothing could beat the traffic in Los Angeles. Now I knew why Obama didn't stick around in his father's native country!

Our driver reminded us that we would need to take the same route on only one further occasion – at three in the morning, to catch our flight to Cairo. Whatever – it was going be hell! We would spend the time between our two traffic jams visiting the Kenya SPCA, playing soccer with the children at the Nyumbani Orphanage and sneaking ourselves into the Masai Mara National Reserve.

The KSPCA is the only charitable animal welfare organisation in Kenya that deals with domestic animals. It was started some time after 1910, when some ladies took pity on the oxen bringing goods into Nairobi from the surrounding districts, and it evolved from there. Over the past twenty-five years it has been headed by the legendary Jean Gilchrist, and it was quite an honour to meet this incredible woman, whose tireless and dedicated efforts are geared towards working with the people of Kenya, educating, leading and encouraging them to treat animals with respect.

Her work is respected to such an extent that her name is mentioned in local school books. A month after our visit, she was to leave for London to receive an MBE (Member of the British Empire) from Prince 'Charming' at Buckingham Palace in recognition of all her tireless work in building the KSPCA up from a tiny operation consisting of three people to the great success that it is today.

Oscar and I were able to understand the significance of this sort of dedication during a trip we took down the road from the KSPCA with Jean behind the wheel. On more than one occasion, we suffered whiplash when Jean randomly braked, stopping the car in order to deal with whatever animal situation had caught her eye.

Oscar and I arrived at the Masai Mara ahead of schedule. Our necks certainly needed the recovery time! Free time was a luxury our schedule couldn't afford, but thanks to Oscar and some mud, an extra day was created by random default. We had been invited to stay at the Karen Blixen Cottages. Steeped in history and originally built as an old hunting lodge, the guest house was conveniently located a short skip from the Kenya SPCA, where we were to spend a day after our safari. But for boasting the whitest, brightest linen on the African continent, the place was perfect! The sheets looked like heaven, but their practicality was another matter entirely. It was the rainy season in Kenya, and the owners hadn't bargained on a guest with a fetish for torrential downpours to be enjoying their bedding.

We weren't exactly kicked out of Room 11. Let's just say that Oscar redesigned the bedding to make it resemble a muddy fusion of exotic paw prints. After paying to replace the most expensive threads on the planet, the manager strongly recommended that we get to the Masai Mara National Reserve as soon as possible, as there was so much wildlife eagerly waiting to meet us!

We didn't take the suggestion personally. After all, the Masai Mara is Kenya's premier game park, and with an extra day to spare we would certainly encounter the Big Five. The natural wonder that is the Masai Mara boasts a huge concentration of animals, but it was still crying out for 'migratory mutt' to be added to its impressive list of species. Wild dogs and disorientated hunting dogs belonging to the Masai tribesmen do wind up in the park, but spoilt domesticated dogs of the family 'Oscar canidae' were forbidden entry.

We wanted footage of Oscar in the park, and, besides, what damage could a cuddly little canine from South Africa really do in a park full of *wild* animals? He would wave to all the lovely wildlife and chase a few cats, gemsbok, springbok, impalas, wildebeest, warthogs and anything else that moved, from dawn till dusk – but other than that, he promised to behave.

Without losing even a buck in a bribe, our dented safari roadster drove through the checkpoint without any problems. Aside from a blanket covering the panting back seat, there was nothing suspicious about our arrival.

We set off to explore the fascinating landscape and found ourselves almost immediately surrounded by a multitude of wildlife. Game-watching on the great open plains of Kenya with their profusion of signature Balantine trees is a truly spectacular experience, and Oscar wasted no time in expressing his appreciation. He interrogated a few adolescent male elephants in order to check the acceleration capabilities of our old van in an emergency, and we managed to source an old femur from the hind leg of a dead giraffe before stumbling across the rest of the skeleton.

For Oscar, this was simply bone heaven.

We had longed to see a lion, but just weren't expecting to see one so soon and so damned close! There, lying right next to the side of the road, were *three* of them. Lazy by nature, they took no notice of our roadster as it came to a screeching halt within licking range. The scent of cats brought the back seat alive, and safari dog dashed to the open window to see what this new whiff in the wild was all about.

The sight of a furry tourist without a Canon fixed to its nose caught the lions' attention immediately. They seemed to know instantly that this wasn't one of their usual prey. And Oscar sensed that these weren't your average pussycats either.

Unfortunately for the lions, as far as Oscar was concerned, a cat was a cat and would be for evermore. And God had made them to entertain dogs, which is why they had been given nine lives in the first place; the make or model did not make an iota of difference. In that moment of realisation, the loudest and longest 'WOOF!' in the history of dogkind was unleashed from our exact location.

I leapt up to close the open window. We'd survived one episode of *Fear Factor* in Zambia – I didn't need another! Nor did I need an experience that would lead to us being immortalised in a Hollywood movie based on a real-life horror safari in Kenya. As the bark rang out, the lions bolted. They had never heard the roar of a city canine! Oblivious to the fact that this dog had more bark than bite, the lions scattered for their lives. Oscar had just become The Lions' King! (Take that, Andrew Lloyd Webber and Elton John.)

Now we were ready to face the biggest cat of all…

9

'Woof like an Egyptian'

To fly a dog as 'excess baggage' means paying for its weight and the sum of all the travelling parts. Whether you have no other luggage to check in or weigh half as much as any other passenger on the flight makes no difference. You have a dog, you have to pay the airline its penalty per extra kilo. I didn't understand the scale of the operation until we had to check in at the EgyptAir counter in Nairobi. It was three in the morning, and for a couple that was used to nine hours of sleep a night, it was not the best time for logic or reason. Oscar weighed in at nineteen kilos, and his bright-blue box muscled in at nine kilos. My excess was a whopping twenty-eight kilos. The bill? Five hundred and fifty dollars!

I promptly had one of my best tantrums to date in an airport terminal. Call me naive, but I had had no idea what excess baggage would cost. Worse yet, the amount was non-negotiable. The ground staff weren't even prepared to give me a discount because Oscar was so cute – nor were they prepared to charge me in the local currency. The airlines generally assume that anyone who is nuts enough to travel with her pet can obviously afford to pay for the excess luxury, especially on EgyptAir, whose managers would rather not deal with a dog.

I hadn't budgeted for Oscar's weight, let alone the box with frills, and there were still twenty-five flights ahead of us! The economic crisis would necessitate instituting a strict diet. Condensed milk and butterscotch interludes between room-service meals would be banned with immediate effect. I also now knew to remove the crate's decor before it was put on the scale.

Another requirement to import a dog into Egypt was excessive paperwork. If the Egyptians weren't fans of canine tourists, they were really rubbing it in. Every country we'd visited typically required a health certificate and an import permit upon arrival. This entailed a visit to a vet for a quick inspection and, assuming that all the documents were in order, a health certificate would be issued, which would then have to be taken to the state veterinarian, who would issue the import permit.

It wasn't a difficult procedure to arrange; it was just a major time-guzzler, and an improbability when we were scheduled to be in any one country for only a day or two. The Land of the Pyramids went one step further. They wanted Oscar's import permit to be endorsed by their embassy in Kenya prior to arriving in Cairo. Most embassies around the world take days to issue anything, and with a furry tourist, the Egyptian embassy would require weeks to process one simple piece of paperwork.

Animal Travel Services was affiliated with the Independent Pet and Animal Association (IPATA), and Christelle had lined up agents who were on standby to assist us in every country; in Kenya, it became critical. We had three days to organise the paperwork for Egypt, when it would normally have required a minimum of ten, and we were delighted to make it somebody else's problem! It was touch and go all the way, but thanks to SDV Transami Kenya Ltd, we managed to have the paperwork in hand just minutes before the final boarding gate closed.

I arrived in Cairo the proud bearer of all the correct documentation for my travelling companion. I was inspected, but the documents were not. I was mad. All that stress and expense to get the import permits in place and no one wanted to check them out? I insisted that they look at the file, and reluctantly they gave it the once-over. It was obvious that they didn't know what they were looking for, but after thinking about it later, it made perfect sense. How many dogs, I wondered, flew into Cairo airport? Oscar was probably the first!

In Muslim territory, the arrival of a dog is generally considered a breach of national security. The airport authorities were desperate to ensure that my 'luggage' remained in his 'cage'. Not a chance. I unleashed a wagging tail and, within seconds, I had a finger wagging in my face. The police had arrived at the 'crime' scene, and at last there was someone louder than me in an airport terminal! I pretended not to understand one word and promptly dropped to the terminal floor, where Oscar licked me all over my face. I knew this was an image that wouldn't fade quickly from their minds. I wanted to prove that Egypt would not collapse after a solid round of passionate licks from a travelling hound at Cairo International Airport.

The reason I was so keen to make a point was this: there was not *one* hotel in the country that would host our tour, let alone compromise their reputation for having a dog spend the night. (Having said that, there *was* one hotel that agreed to welcome us, quietly – for the princely sum of $700 a night. We graciously declined the offer, but I was intrigued to discover that, in some instances, money would prevail over religious principles.)

Instead, we were going to stay with the president of the organisation that we had arranged to visit in Cairo. Amina Abaza had started the Society for the Protection of Animal Rights in Egypt (SPARE) nine years earlier, motivated by the barbaric treatment to which animals were subjected in her country. It was common for dogs to be publicly shot or even poisoned in the streets – often for no reason at all. When Amina became increasingly distressed and depressed by the situation, her husband told her that actions speak louder than tears; if she wanted something to change, she had to stop sobbing and do something about it. The locals laughed when she built a shelter on some leased land on the outskirts of Cairo, but less than a decade later she had become a force they couldn't ignore.

We had met the impressive Jean Gilchrist, who had run the Kenya SPCA for the past twenty years, just a few days earlier. Amina seemed just as determined and decisive as Jean. It was a perception that was to be reinforced in the days that followed.

Swine-flu panic had gripped the country and the Egyptian government had ordered the destruction of every pig in Cairo. Pigs were being burnt alive and thrown into pits in scenes reminiscent of a Holocaust movie. The images were splashed across the covers of every newspaper in the country. Amina and a handful of protesters marched in the streets to take a stand against the cruelty; even my cameraman grabbed a sign in a language he couldn't read and started chanting after Amina.

I always knew that our visit to Egypt would be challenging. *Iwiws* (the ancient Egyptian word for 'dogs') may have played a significant role as hunters and guard dogs in ancient Egypt, but today they no longer enjoy the respect they might have had in the past. Although many Muslim nations consider dogs to be dirty creatures, in actual fact they are revered in the holy Quran.

The prophet Muhammad was very wise. He knew that dogs spread rabies and leishmaniasis – a disease then carried by dogs in the Mediterranean area who had been bitten by sandflies. Understanding that rabies was transmitted by a dog's saliva, the prophet advised his followers to wash themselves seven times after they had been in contact with a dog to prevent spreading the disease. He never prohibited Muslims from keeping dogs, and he certainly would never have approved of the shooting or poisoning of dogs.

In fact, the Quran specifically mentions several times that the prophet looked favourably on anyone who showed kindness towards dogs. In one specific incident, the prophet observes a prostitute offering a thirsty stray dog water in her shoe, and he comments to his followers that she will find a place in heaven for her good deed. The great prophet probably loved dogs, but as a result all the religious misinterpretation, Oscar was gaining a surprising amount of (negative) media attention.

It was a proud moment for dogs in Cairo when Egyptian television's most popular talk show, *Al Ashera Masa'an*, invited Oscar to appear as a guest. We may never have heard of Mona El Shazly in the West, but she's the Oprah of the Middle East. The *Al Ashera Masa'an* studio was certainly the real deal; from every corner, a camera lens was glued on us. An earpiece ensured that all the questions were interpreted into my right ear and, before I knew it, we were live.

Oscar, however, looked deader than alive. Cairo was scorching hot and the heat had clearly put a damper on his showmanship. We had spent almost three hours trying to gain permission to drag a hot dog into the pyramid complex, and another hour trying to photograph him looking excited about seeing the biggest cat on the planet – a rather sturdy character called 'the Sphinx'. The escapade had taken the last bit of hydration out of my dog, and he was pooped. Passed out in his seat, he was oblivious to the millions of sceptics who were about to view him on Egypt's most popular television show. Mona welcomed us and began, 'So, what did Oscar do this afternoon?'

'Well,' I explained, 'we visited the pyramids. Oscar isn't used to the heat and it was very hot at the pyramids. I decided he'd enjoy relaxing at our accommodation for the rest of the afternoon.' While it had taken us well over two hours to negotiate permission to take a dog to the pyramids, ironically, there are hundreds of stray dogs roaming the area. I even saw canine corpses scattered across the dirty landscape.

'Do you know that over 200 workers protested in the streets of Cairo this afternoon because they want more wages in order to feed their families?' Mona asked.

Ah, okay, so far the interview was not proceeding at all well; perhaps her next questions would be better, I thought.

'What do you feed Oscar?' Mona asked.

'Free-range chicken and rice ... and Pedigree if the former isn't available,' I replied – with the sweetest smile. Surely I would be congratulated for taking such enormously good care of my prized possession?

'Do you know that most Egyptians can't even afford a basic meal of *aysh*? Have you even considered that perhaps this was a country you should not have come to?'

Amina, who was also in the studio, jumped in to cover for me, but I knew where Mona was going with her line of questioning. How could I justify the expense and effort of taking a *mutt* on a world tour when human beings were suffering too? In fact, I felt passionately about the project because it wasn't so much about dogs as it was about alleviating *all* suffering, human and otherwise. Besides, why do we always have to compare humans with every-thing else? Suffering is suffering – all suffering disturbs me. I'm not the perfect Buddhist by any stretch of the imagination; I can't sit still for a second of meditation, for example, but I embrace many of the Buddhist teachings.

Gautama Buddha teaches compassion towards *all* sentient beings, whether they are poodles, AIDS orphans, cancer patients or ants stuck in a honey pot! Buddhists pray for all who have life to be delivered from suffering. It forms the very basis of Buddhism, and our mission was to try to make the world a better place for every living creature. If everyone played their part and focused more on what they could contribute than on what they could own, there wouldn't be a need for rebirth and the cycle of Samsara!

Mona's questions didn't improve, nor did Oscar's condition. He managed twenty minutes of quality siesta time while his mother was being interrogated and nailed to a cross-examination.

Our guest appearance on *Al Ashera Masa'an* sent the entire country into a flat spin. The newspapers ridiculed the show, and its ratings plummeted. Islam Khalil, one of Egypt's most renowned singers, released a song the following week calling for Mona to apologise to the people of Egypt.

'The dog is sitting on the chair and everybody is watching. Mona was almost going to give him a cigarette and a cup of tea! On this very same chair, important people have sat, including scientists, ministers and actors!' he sang. 'Oh how time passes with you, Mona. Certainly those are the important topics and programmes. People are glad and say, "Thank you, Mona." Everyone watched the show and wished they were an OSCAR!'

Mona had to get a bodyguard, Oscar's couch was thrown off the set and we decided to duck a little earlier than scheduled. Oscar swam a quick lap in the Nile and, before we knew it, we had taken off for Greece – on one-way tickets.

10
A Turkish bark

Departing Egypt meant departing Africa. One continent down, four to go. In just fifteen days we had visited seven countries; a record for most dogs, but just a warm-up for mine! What a difference a mere two-hour flight can make. After Cairo, Athens was cooler in climate and less dusty, which meant that we could last at least a week without a laundry visit. Just like the excess baggage, clean laundry was an unbudgeted luxury on tour and deemed necessary only if the armpits groaned.

The state of Athens's street dogs was also much better than I had expected. I'd never seen such fat, happy chaps loafing around a city centre. It certainly presented a case to cities around the world to emulate Athens and let their homeless dogs roam free in order to produce a surprisingly pleasant scenario. As part of the landscape, and acclimatised to the hustles and bustles of city life, the estimated 15000 feral dogs could even teach some kids a lesson or two on how to cross a road. A glance to the left, a glance to the right, and off they go. It was amazing to watch, especially for Oscar, who doesn't know the difference between slowing down a speeding bus or speeding up a lazy cat.

Stray dogs in Athens have quite a history. Up until the turn of the century, you'd have been hard-pressed to find a stray dog anywhere in the city. Dog catchers were paid to round up strays and take them to the local municipal pound, where they would be held for a maximum period of ninety days. Those that weren't claimed were put down. Then a local animal-rights group filmed one particular dog pound that kept its dogs in miserable and inhumane conditions. They showed the evidence to the local district attorney, who, in turn, arrested the mayor for the crime of 'maltreatment of animals'. The mayor was convicted and sentenced to several months in prison, along with getting a stiff cash fine.

As a result, almost every municipality in Greece closed its dog pound and fired its dog catchers. Of course the stray population exploded, but no one took much notice until Athens was awarded the 2004 Olympic Games. Naturally the municipality in Athens didn't want the world to see all the stray dogs in the city, nor did they want to have to award the dogs any gold medals either. (Some had already interfered with the Olympic trials, and one had even competed in the Athens Marathon!)

The plan the municipality came up with was simple. Just before the Games began, they would round up the dogs and take them to a farm or kennel somewhere outside the city. Once the Olympics had ended, they would bring the strays back and release them in the place where they had been found. It wouldn't solve the stray-dog issue, but at least it would temporarily save the city's image.

Between the hatching of the plot and the execution of the plan, 3000 dogs were poisoned in the autumn of 2003. Some people blamed the municipality, while others pointed at the Athens Olympic Committee, but no one was held responsible in the end. A decision was then made to sterilise more than 10 000 stray dogs ahead of the Games to curb the stray-dog population growth. It was a measure that set the standard for the future, and while poisoning is still prevalent in Greece today, no other municipality is as proactive in the humane control of a city's stray dogs as that of Athens.

Every dog in the city is sterilised, microchipped and vaccinated against diseases like rabies. The males wear blue collars and the females red ones, and the locals feed and care for them as if they were their own. We spent the day with the Greek Animal Welfare Fund president, Carol McBeth, and she pointed out that the Athenians really do care, which makes it possible for her organisation to focus on the rural and island areas, which are 'fifty years behind' when it comes to animal welfare.

Oscar and I had a full day in Athens to explore the city. We caught a taxi and headed straight for the Parthenon, which formed part of our itinerary to create entertaining footage for the documentary. Images of Oscar smiling in front of the Parthenon were imperative to illustrate his arrival in Greece. When planning the WWT, I hadn't once considered that a dog, accompanied by its owner, could be banned from posing in front of some of the world's greatest landmarks. I was, however, learning quickly that I was in for a challenge.

Ironically, stray dogs already lived in many of the places we were to visit, yet canines who were on a leash, with their owner, were strictly forbidden. And while Oscar could pass for many different characters, a stray dog was not one of them. He was far too groomed and refined!

Sneaking Oscar into the Masai Mara had been easy; smuggling him in to see the pyramids had been possible only after an almost three-hour negotiation with the authorities – but the pooch-at-the-Parthenon plan was going to the dogs, fast! I believe there is always a way to buck the system, which is not necessarily always a bad thing to do – most rules were made up in parliaments in order to control the masses. But Oscar was an exception, and the WWT was a mission that howled out for the rules to be ignored!

I scouted the three-hectare property to see if there was any way in which we could sneak Oscar in, but, alas, no gap presented itself. In a last-ditch effort, I headed to the Ministry of Culture below the Acropolis and begged for entry. I explained that my mutt wasn't looking for a slice of marble, nor did he want to deposit a swirl of digested breakfast on its doorstep. All we wanted was ten minutes at the Parthenon to take a quick snap for the family album.

The answer was an emphatic 'no!' – unless I followed the correct procedure: produce a written request to the ministry stating my objectives, along with a detailed thesis on our expedition. It would then take the department a minimum of two weeks to review the matter.

Forget it. This was one occasion when we would just have to bite the biscuit and accept defeat. A challenging 150-metre hike to the holy temple had been diverted, but how now to get a shot of Oscar posing in front of some classical columns in Athens – preferably of the genuine kind? Nikos, our trusty taxi driver, had just the answer. 'I take you to Olympieion. We take picture very good. Look like Parthenon, difference no one know.'

Within minutes we were in the city centre facing the mighty Temple of Zeus, which used to be the largest of the ancient temples in Athens. The ruin is now just a shadow of its former self, but we didn't care: between our parking spot and the bustling traffic soared sixteen big, fat Greek columns, poised perfectly against a blue sky. We were back in business. Our little group dodged the rather territorial stray dogs that guarded the entrance, and soon came face to face with the imposing columns.

The only obstacle between us and our goal was rope. *Lots* of rope! Getting up close and personal with the ruins was strictly prohibited for all creatures – except the strays, of course! And the Greek police were serious about enforcing the law. A policeman stood at every corner and CCTV cameras were positioned all over the property. We had this one chance to get a photograph – Plan C did not exist. We were scheduled to leave Athens the following day, and even if our 'crime' warranted a night in jail, we reckoned we would still be able to make it to the dock in time. And we would save on the hotel bill in the process!

Nikos went off to distract the policeman, who was keeping a close eye on us. With all coasts relatively clear, my cameraman grabbed Oscar, jumped the ropes and placed him neatly between two pillars. With barely enough time for him to hide behind one of the columns, the alarm rang out. So loud was the siren that even the stray dogs leapt up and ran for cover.

But my supermodel remained calmly posed between his props, and I kept on clicking. Moments later, I was surrounded by half a dozen policemen, who were in no mood to be told about dog adoption. The shoot was officially over. I was being yelled at in a language I couldn't understand, let alone hear with the noise of the sirens continuing unabated. Nikos explained to me in exasperation and panic that all the images on my camera had to be removed immediately, or we would be arrested. A heavily perspiring police-woman leant over my lens to make sure that I was deleting all the photos I had taken.

After a hairy twenty minutes, Zeus could be left in peace, my cameraman could come out of hiding and Oscar could stop harass-ing all sixteen columns he'd enjoyed sniffing while his mother was distracting his prospective captors. But ... all those images of Oscar posing in front of some ancient Greek columns – gone. Lost to the universe. It made me feel sick.

Nikos had been a fine campaigner for our cause, but when the time came for him to produce his bill, he blew it. He wanted €400 for the time he had devoted to us and for his exceptional service, but thanks to my malfunctioning credit card, he ended up with €200, cash.

According to schedule, the next day we waved goodbye to Athens and spent the night sailing across the Mediterranean. Oscar and I enjoyed the most marvellous sunset views from the confines of our private cabin. We had been on the road now for a solid two weeks, and this was the moment when I would usually start getting restless. I had a long history of beginning projects – relationships included – only to get bored after a while and to start wondering what the hell I was doing. I couldn't exactly quit the World Woof Tour, unless of course I wanted to waste my life's savings and the time I'd spent on planning it. Best of all, though, I didn't *want* to quit. For the first time in my life, I was absolutely thrilled to be on board.

I looked like hell and needed a good wash, yet I smelt roses all around me. I felt blessed to be travelling with my best friend, for a good cause, and I knew that as long as I was by his side, Oscar felt the same!

A brief visit to Friends of the Animals Kos was scheduled en route to Turkey. We would spend just half a day on Kos Island in order to meet with the founder of the organisation, the passionate, entertaining, politician-hating Mr Vangelis Trakossa. Vangelis's mouth didn't stop moving once, except to take a breath of fresh air; and that *he* certainly was. 'The Greek politicians!' he yelled, throwing his arms into the air in utter despair. 'They love money, and they are so lazy. It's easier to train a bear!' After hearing some of the tragic stories about the animal cruelty that was prevalent on the island, I could understand Vangelis's frustration. Politicians were the only ones who could enforce change, but they weren't interested.

Our visit was cut short when Vangelis had to dash off unexpectedly to strap himself to a bulldozer that was heading for a turtle-breeding beach. He was in mid-sentence as he hailed a car coming along the road. I somehow knew that the turtles would survive and live to hear the end of his story.

We arrived in Bodrum, Turkey, the following evening, where a private van was waiting to transport us to Istanbul overnight. Dogs were not allowed to travel on public buses, so we had little choice in the matter. This was our second night on the move and sleep deprivation was kicking in. When we arrived at the Yedikule Animal Shelter the next day, I thought I was hallucinating. This one shelter alone contained 2500 dogs! I had never been to a shelter that kept more than 200 dogs, but Turkey was going to rewrite the record books.

There are sixty-three registered shelters in Istanbul alone, and the Buyukcekmece Shelter claims to house a whopping 3000 dogs. Although far from perfect inside, it was a far better – and certainly safer – life for the dogs than a life on the streets of Turkey. Here, at least the dogs had food and water, and each day seven dogs were washed. At least every dog knew that it would look groovy once a year!

There were dogs everywhere: on top of the roof and inside the attic; outside the entrance to the building; in the office; and on your lap – if you were fortunate enough to find a place to sit down. Founder and full-time architect Meral Olcay had created the shelter back in 2000, when she couldn't find a place to take a distressed dog she had rescued at the roadside.

She and her twenty volunteers do not think of their jobs as a hobby; working there is a 'lifestyle', which probably explains why all of them know the name of every single dog in the 'house'. No dog is ever put down at this shelter – even the many dogs who have been hit by cars have their own enclosure, which boasts a massive red velvet sofa right in the centre.

The place moved me to tears. Each injured dog had a specially made harness strapped to some wheels that allowed it to be mobile. Each dog had a look in its eyes and a humble wag of the tail that reflected its undeniable gratitude for the attention and care it received. Meral had told me that she considered this work her ultimate destiny; I looked into the eyes of those dogs, and I knew why. What could be more rewarding than to know that the work you are doing is alleviating a tremendous amount of suffering?

Meral has many sad days working among all this heartache, but she draws strength from seeing the progress her team makes and knowing that, without their efforts, most of the dogs under her care would probably be dead. A few years back, I would never have been able to understand why anyone would want to invest their own time and money in a project without the promise of any financial gain, but now, being part of the WWT, I could finally relate to a heroine like Meral. Genuine purpose and ultimate happiness, I now understood, come from helping others – although I *was* rather missing a platinum credit card with which to buy myself a few new threads!

We couldn't depart Turkey without experiencing a *baño turco*, otherwise known as a Turkish bath. We took a chance and hauled our bodies off to the oldest *hammam* in Istanbul and, to our surprise, they let us in! The magnificent Sultan Süleyman had commissioned the famous 'architect Sina' to build the *hammam* back in the 1550s. It was a miracle we were allowed inside; after all, the baths do form part of the Süleymaniye Mosque.

I can't say that Oscar enjoyed wearing swimming trunks (a Speedo!) or the steam inside the baths, but we certainly needed the clean. Although the Bulut brothers and owners had welcomed a dog into the baths for the first time in Turkish history, what struck me more was our *tellak*. He was a tall, strong and utterly gorgeous male masseur with more hair on his chest than Oscar had on his entire body. If it hadn't been for a dog in the mists, I would still be soaking up the bubbles today.

It may have been Oscar's least enjoyable joint, but it was by far my favourite!

11

Lost and hound

Our route through Europe revolved around travelling by train. The system was safe and reliable, and dogs were allowed both on board and outside the confines of the luggage compartment. Our first leg would take us from Istanbul, Turkey, to Sofia, Bulgaria. It was the first time that Oscar would travel by train, and the first time I would have to share a bed the width of a pillow with anything other than myself. It was all very cosy, and we were looking forward to a good night's rest while we zipped across the Turkish landscape and into Sofia.

There were just a few pointers that the *Balkan Express* had forgotten to mention to prepare us for what lay ahead. Firstly, the train itself isn't exactly a new 'kid' on the track, so if we hadn't lost our hearing after being introduced to 2 500 dogs in Istanbul, we were guaranteed to lose it once the train started moving. Secondly, while they do inform you that there will be stops along the route, they fail to mention that the conductor will announce the approaching town every five minutes for at least one hour prior to pulling into the station.

And lastly, when you purchase your tickets, they certainly don't tell you that there is absolutely no point in paying more for a cabin with a bunk because, the fact is, you won't be getting any sleep anyway! Passport control between the borders is a nightmare and had me wishing I'd just deleted Eastern Europe from our programme altogether.

Our first experience of passport control came upon us just before midnight, when we crossed the Turkish border into Bulgaria. My cabin door was literally ripped open – knocking certainly wasn't a part of their on-board service – and two men sternly demanded: 'Passport!' Luckily I hadn't been picking my nose. I bent over to scratch around for my passport and, when I finally found it and returned to a vertical position, my eyeballs were staring straight into a torch. To make matters substantially worse, I had two South African passports, which, technically, was breaking the law. Obtaining all the visas I would require for the tour had not been a priority while planning the WWT; caffeine breaks had!

When I realised that I would need twenty-one visas without having nearly enough time to get them sorted out, panic struck! I had no choice but to be creative and arrange a second passport. It was a case of 'losing' the first and finding it minutes after the new one arrived. This took care of my visa issues, but explaining the case for two passports to border patrol in a foreign language proved to be impossible. The guards were convinced that I was up to no good, and spotting a mutt during the cabin inspection just added insult to injury.

We were delayed at every point, and some aggressive interrogation aimed within spitting range of my face at godforsaken hours of the night tested my patience to its limits. I swore that when I returned to South Africa I'd find a man with a British passport and do the deed before I travelled across Europe again.

Those were *my* issues; Oscar had his own that I had to deal with. For starters, he had never been on a train before, and the sound of the train on the tracks made him irritatingly restless, especially as he was sharing my bed. Then there was his paperwork. Christelle had arranged an EU certificate for Oscar, which was valid for three months after entry into Greece. Everything would have been simple but for one small error in my planning, which could only be attributed to a lack of experience. As long as we remained within the European community, we were cruising. The moment we crossed a different border, we were back to square one.

Greece was a part of the EU; Turkey was not. Bulgaria was a part of the EU; Romania was not. Croatia wasn't either, but, on the other side of the Adriatic, Italy was. Switzerland wasn't; France was. I couldn't have planned the route any worse if I'd tried! We were spending only a day or two in each European country, so without enough time to arrange new certificates on our own, we decided to risk it. I knew if it came to the crunch, Oscar was pretty good at playing dead and passing as the inside lining of my jacket.

No officials at our first two border crossings asked for any of Oscar's paperwork. Despite a few sniffer dogs on the border posts between Romania and Croatia, we managed to sail through Europe without any dogfights – or sleep! By the time we arrived in the town of Split along the coast of Croatia, we had travelled over 1 400 miles – equalling the number of stray cats Oscar had chased at each and every one of our border crossings! We had also visited the Bulgarian Society for Animal Protection and Preservation (BSAPP) in Sofia, the Romania Animal Rescue Foundation (RARF) in Bucharest, and Dr Tatjana and her staff at the Shelter for Abandoned Animals in Zagreb, Croatia.

As far as strays are concerned, these three countries are no different from any others in the region. There is a massive stray-dog problem in the whole of Eastern Europe, for which there are a number of reasons. Often dogs that were bought as puppies are discarded when their novelty wears off, and they are dumped on the street, forced to survive on their own and allowed to breed freely. Romania has one of the highest stray-dog populations in the world. The problem was exacerbated in the early 1980s, when the capital's civic centre was completely rebuilt by the communist dictator Nicolae Ceauşescu, who was, ironically, the owner of a few black Labradors, whom he fed veal.

As part of his scheme of systematisation, 40 000 families and 3 000 pet dogs were dispossessed with just one day's notice. These dogs became strays overnight and, by 2001, rapid breeding had led to a population of over 250 000. Then mayor and now president Traian Băsescu had initially planned to have many of these stray dogs put down, but because of an international outcry led by Brigitte Bardot, a spay-and-release programme was to be introduced instead. Traian, however, did end up killing over 400 000 stray dogs by having them shot and poisoned, and the spay-and-release programme was never properly enforced.

There are an estimated five million stray dogs in the country today, which is why organisations such as Bucharest's animal rescue group, the RARF, are so important. American Nancy Janes set up the organisation back in 2001, when she became aware of the barbaric treatment of stray dogs. Inspired by Nancy's undeniable dedication and commitment to improving the situation, her team focuses its time and resources on sterilisation, which is the only effective solution to reducing the dog population in Romania – and anywhere else, for that matter.

Livia Brenner of the RARF looked after us while we were in the country. Young, beautiful and nice enough to rekindle a romance with her ex-boyfriend just so we could have a handsome driver (and his nice car) for the weekend, we hit it off straight away. She took us to one of the only two registered private shelters in Bucharest, and 'probably the best shelter in Romania', the mere thought of which made my hair stand on end.

The shelter harboured at least 150 dogs, and it became obvious that the two women responsible for the place were hoarding the dogs off the street and into the overcrowded cages for a life sentence. Carmen and Roxanne had big ideas on what they wanted to build and create on the property, but at the same time they were too afraid to release any of their dogs 'in case they weren't given to good homes'.

Oscar took a liking to a ten-year-old dog in the pound by the name of Zara. (Sure, Oscar and I were inseparable, but there was only so far we could go!) We enquired about adopting the great white dame and moving her to Cape Town once the tour was over. The ladies said they'd have to look into the logistics of getting her to 'Africa'. I had just the gal who could help them out, but decided not to interfere.

It was heartbreaking to see the state of the dogs inside the shelter. For the first time, it really made me wonder if a dog wasn't better off on the streets than it was facing a life without parole at the hands of individuals who had probably started the facility with good intentions. Anywhere else in the world the answer would be a 'Yes', but in Romania, both options were equally heartbreaking.

The locals call a stray dog 'a skeleton clothed in skin', and according to *Mój Pies* magazine, 80 per cent of them have broken legs. I could quite easily understand how compassionate human beings can quickly become disillusioned after witnessing the situation in this poor country. Forget the overnight train and a restless pooch sleeping behind my back, the disturbing images and stories I saw and read in Romania were enough to warrant my getting a lifetime prescription for sleeping tablets. In the quietest moments of the tour, I contemplated the cruel nature of the race that I am embarrassed to call my own.

The grim weather didn't help improve our mood either. The sky was grey all the time, and the weight of decades of suppression still emanated from the demeanour of the people. It was as if the whole country was stuck in some sort of medieval time warp. Gypsies roam the countryside in a land where the horse and cart is still the primary means of transport. The only place worth lifting a leg on was Dracula's castle, and that was too far off our radar screen to visit. If it was atmosphere the count was looking for, he'd certainly picked the right country. It's disturbing, though, that nowadays it is no longer people who are cruelly tortured, but dogs.

The town of Split in Croatia would be our final train destination until we reached Switzerland. From Split, we were scheduled to take the overnight Blue Line ferry to Italy. We finally had a full day to savour the sights of this tourist destination and to shoot some footage of Oz and me playing hide-and-seek in the narrow cobbled roads of the old city centre.

I never kept Oscar on a lead while on the tour. After all, we were joined at the hip and in total sync with each other's movements. I kept an eye out for him; he kept his nose out for me. He knew what 'sit', 'stay' and 'hide' meant, and he trusted that my commands were always in his best interests.

During the course of the day, we landed up next to an ice-cream parlour. My cameraman and I agreed that it would be quite entertaining to get some footage of Oscar enjoying the 'flavour' of the city. It was also the perfect excuse for me to demolish the cone when Oscar had had enough. But I needed to find an ATM before diving into the dessert, and I told Oz to 'stay!' beside my cameraman. I returned with cash in hand, but *where was my dog*? We were standing in the middle of the second-largest city in Croatia, and my mutt was gone!

The cameraman had been shooting some historic gables looming over the street and had concentrated so hard that he hadn't even noticed that I had been gone for twenty minutes. My heartbeat kicked in and my forehead began to sweat. There weren't any crocodiles in Split, but there were thieves. Dog theft is a common practice throughout the world, and all I needed was one of Split's 200 000 inhabitants to turn into a dog thief upon laying eyes on the most exotic tourist in town.

I didn't know where to start looking. I didn't even have a friend to call or another lifeline I could use. But I would not leave Split until I found my dog; that I knew. The tour would certainly be over without its leader, but, more importantly, how would I find the strength to keep on living if I never knew what had happened to my right-hand hound? And how, if I couldn't find him, would I ever be at peace?

It had now been almost an hour since I had last seen my dog. Aside from our flying time in and out of Cairo, we hadn't been apart once during the tour.

Off I sprinted, back in the direction of the bank. Either no one had seen Oscar or they couldn't understand one word of my panic attack. I returned to the ice-cream booth ten minutes later, but still no dog. If only I'd used a lead, I thought. If only I had stayed a vegan, we would never have been outside this stupid dairy joint! A million 'if onlys' flashed through my mind; and then, just like that, they all came to a screeching halt.

There, in the distance, appeared a panting pooch. Suddenly the sun came out, a choir began to sing and the world was once again a place worth barking about. I always knew that Oscar's nose was of Olympic standards – he could sniff a squirrel from miles away and rescue a chicken bone from a garbage disposal in an area with a different postal code from his own. True to form, my champ had saved his greatest sniffs for when they really mattered. There he was, nose to the cobbles, tail between the legs, following my scent for all his worth, until he finally twitched to a halt between my hairy legs. In that moment, we knew we had both been saved.

They say you never know how good you have it until you lose it. I had always counted my blessings for having this creature in my life, so gratitude was never an issue. But because of finding Oscar, I would now have the peace of mind to keep counting them ...

We spent the latter part of the afternoon taking a swim in the Adriatic Sea before the famous Cathedral of St Domnius. Then we suddenly remembered that we had 200 kilograms of luggage to lug from our rented room to the ferry terminal, which was a conservative kilometre away.

Taxis weren't allowed in the area between the room and the ferry terminal, although I managed to wave down two tourists who helped my cameraman carry the case he was trying to balance on top of his head. We arrived at the terminal only one minute late, but we had missed the boat – literally! It would be forty-eight hours before another ferry would sail for Ancona. We had just blown our trip to Rome.

There was nothing for it but to sit sulking on the dock, our suitcases squashed below our butts. With nothing scheduled to happen for the next forty-seven hours and fifty-nine minutes, I had nothing to do but haul out the camera to take my first look at the images I'd captured in the preceding weeks.

Between a dejected cameraman on my left and a departing boat in the distance, I suddenly had plenty to celebrate. There, stuck between a pyramid and a Turkish bath, was a mutt ... beside a Greek column! My brain took a moment to piece it all together.

The Greek policewoman had failed to delete the last picture on the flashcard! My pooch had posed between the ancient pillars – and I had the photograph to prove it. Best of all, I had found my lost buddy, and he was right beside me as I spotted the image.

What priceless moment could be more photogenic than that?

12

Lap dog

Because of missing the ferry, my cameraman and I were forced to share an 'el cheapo' dingy room for two nights in Split. Sharing a compartment for five nights on a train across Eastern Europe had already tested a 'friendship' that was relatively new, but this was really the pits. On the train, we had teamed up against the powers of passport control, but on land it was the chain-smoker (Wally) versus a wannabe anti-smoking campaigner (me). *And* snorer versus sleepless!

The delay had seriously compromised our schedule for Western Europe, but we had sure learnt our lesson. Two days later, we were at the dock a full hour before the ferry smiled on the horizon. We were first in line and the first to place our smelly black toes on deck. There were a few other dogs on board, none of them nearly as well behaved or well travelled as mine, but they were all very polite towards each other, leaning over to sniff each other's behinds with the utmost respect. Across the Adriatic Sea we sailed, through calm waters and expensive junk-food dining, until we finally arrived at the Italian port of Ancona.

Packed and ready to go –
Oscar in his private jet

Oscar and me enjoying a run in the
wheat fields, Sossusvlei, Namibia

Exchanging wire collars and rope leads for Rogz collars
in Chipulukusu Township, Zambia

The long and the short of it – Oscar and a Masai warrior at the Masai Mara Reserve, Kenya

Oscar and some young fans at the Kenya SPCA

The columns that almost got us arrested in Athens, but the shot was worth it!

Another close shave in Rome – Oscar enjoying a dip in the Trevi Fountain

Oscar at the Coliseum, Rome

A striking likeness –
Oscar and the snowdog,
Zermatt, Switzerland

A pooch at Pisa

Paris by bus – joining up with the
Brigitte Bardot Foundation for a good cause

Oscar enjoying
the view over
Red Square,
Moscow

One hero pays tribute to another: Oscar at the statue of Malchik
the subway dog, Mendeleevskaya Station, Moscow

On top of the world – Khardung Pass, Himalayas, India

Oscar making friends
with Buddhist monks
at the Hemis Festival
in Ladakh

Mrs Sengupta
and the dogs of the
Sonadi Charitable
Trust, Delhi

Oscar at the
Taj Mahal

Agra Station –
a VIP and a cast
of thousands

VIP: Very Important Pooch!

A WOOF WANTS

Oscar at the Ganges – so <u>many</u> different smells!

The children of the Sunrise Angkor Orphanage in Cambodia with their Oscar drawings and the subject himself

John and Gill Dalley with their rescued dogs, Phuket

The kindly Mr Priyajana, our saviour and 'taxi' driver in Bangkok

Whether bleached or natural, being a blonde in Italy is like being an Oscar at the Academy Awards – you rock! The country is your red carpet and free pizza your prize. For the first time since Egypt, passport control was a breeze. Having lost time, we had to find some fast. This called for Schumie, and I was just the babe to accelerate our schedule from behind the wheel of a car. There wasn't an Indian guru who didn't know that I had been a Formula 1 racer in a previous life, and with 289 unpaid speeding fines to my name since 2007, no one needed further proof!

My cameraman waited with Oscar at the ferry terminal while I went in search of wheels to rent. This time, my dog was on a lead. I returned an hour later with a bright-green Fiat. It didn't have a turbo-prop engine, and it didn't look anything like a Ferrari, but it did have an accelerator – and a handbrake between the seats! It was a right-hand drive, the opposite of what I was used to back home, but thanks to crashing my car twice in the United States, I had learnt how to drive 'right' the hard way. It was only 100 kilometres from Ancona to the romantic town of Assisi in Umbria, where a priest had been patiently waiting since Saturday afternoon to bless my mutt.

Assisi is beautiful. The town is perched on a peak that overlooks a breathtaking landscape of wheat and wine. A long, straight road ascends to the Papal Basilica of St Francis of Assisi, and if there ever was a highway to heaven, this was certainly it. It was the birthplace of St Francis, the patron saint of animals, and Oscar had come to pay homage to the coolest saint in history. St Francis preached that it is the duty of humans to protect and enjoy nature as both the stewards of God's creation and as creatures ourselves.

It was customary for Catholics and other groups to hold ceremonies to bless their animals on St Francis's feast day, 4 October. According to Father Thomas's Calendar of Saints, we were still four months early! But the priest didn't mind. He met us outside the famous basilica, which was also St Francis's burial place and a structure worthy of its World Heritage status.

Before a group of curious and rather confused onlookers, I held Oscar in my arms and Father Thomas began: 'Blessed are you, Lord God, Maker of all living creatures. You called forth fish in the sea, birds in the air and animals on the land. You inspired St Francis to call all of them his brothers and sisters. We ask You to bless Oscar. By the power of Your love, enable him to live according to Your plan. May we always praise You for all Your beauty in creation. Blessed are You, Lord our God, in all Your creatures. Amen.'

Oscar wasn't religious, and his parents certainly hadn't been either, or else Oscar would not have been left on the streets. Oscar never prayed. Just as with our luggage, he was happy to leave those kinds of things to me. Domestic animals just seem to get on with living. They don't care much for religious ceremonies, marriage, divorce, internet connections or Hollywood celebrities. They aren't interested in killing or fighting each other, nor do they burn others at the stake. They just want to survive, preferably with a little love – and a round-the-world trip once in their lifetime!

Oscar received a splash of water on his forehead from Father Thomas and was happy to cool off, but he knew a bit of liquid wouldn't wash away his sins – not that he had any. According to Saint Francis, only humans suffered from sin, and who were Oscar and I to disagree with the boss of Assisi?

We spent the night close by and prepared for an early start. We had the option of taking a slow drive to Milan, stopping for pizza and arriving in Italy's fashion capital on schedule, or we could follow the route to Rome, as originally planned, cramping our lost days into one. I studied the road map and calculated the distances. We would need to drive 625 kilometres, which excluded eventualities like getting stuck behind old ladies in 1965 Fiats or being pulled over for speeding. We had been on the road for six weeks and had already visited fifteen countries! Thinking of the next forty-eight hours exhausted me even more, but the lure of my canine at the Coliseum and my pooch at Pisa was too tempting to ignore.

'Come on,' I quietly whispered to Oz. 'We gotta ride with the tide, my boy. We've got one life, one mission, one credit card and one more tank of petrol. What do you say?'

'Woof!'

Oscar had given the plan the paws-up, and the stopwatch was on! We eventually arrived in Rome slightly ahead of schedule, but in a traffic jam – though when in Rome do as the Romans do: park illegally. We found our perfect (illegal) parking spot on a red line in the shadow of the mighty Coliseum, grabbed our gear and proceeded to the entrance, where a long queue had formed. Having faced so much red tape already in trying to get my furry explorer into 'tourist' areas, I was feeling a little apprehensive about making it inside. My fears were realised before we'd even made it to the ticket booth.

A lady in uniform pulled us aside and told me that dogs were not allowed inside the Coliseum. Hey, but this was Italy! If I could just get my bleached-blonde mop and a nice big smile in front of one of the male guards to ask for an itsy-bitsy favour, I knew we would be home free. A mere fifteen minutes later, Oscar and I were on the third level of the Coliseum, overlooking modern Rome and waving to the camera below.

Although I had been to the Coliseum a few years before, I hadn't stuck around for long. I had signed up for a guided tour, but the Coliseum's horrific history had made my stomach turn. During the first hundred days after the opening of the newly built Coliseum back in AD 80, over 5000 wild animals were slain. Thousands of spectators cheered in absolute delight as barbaric and deadly fights ensued between man and man, man and beast, and beast and beast. Northern Africa's rich wildlife was dramatically depleted as lions, elephants and other 'exotic' animals were brought to Rome. These animals were kept underneath the stage in special enclosures and were deliberately starved for days before a 'fight'.

When the time came for an animal to die, special lifts would hoist it up to the stage and, as the trapdoor opened, it would run out into the arena, squinting against the daylight that it had not seen for a very long time.

One can only imagine the amount of noise the spectators made and the chaos that reigned in the stadium when the animals were in the arena. I couldn't begin to imagine the fear that these trauma-tised beasts must have felt as they were set against their worst enemy – man. After every slaughter the arena's wooden floor, splat-tered with the beasts' blood, would be covered with a fresh layer of sand in preparation for the next 'game'.

The Coliseum was centre stage for these atrocities for some 300 years, during which hundreds of thousands of men and beasts were slain in what were Rome's supposed 'glory days'. It is even written that when archaeologist Lanciani excavated the mass graves below the structure in the early nineteenth century, the stench of death was still prevalent – after seventeen centuries!

The Coliseum is one of the world's most visited historical monuments, and Oscar and I were just two more tourists on an ordinary day. As we walked through the ancient site, we wondered what it must have been like to witness the Romans' ancient blood-baths and how it had ever been possible for anyone to enjoy the butchery that was inflicted on man and beast. It occurred to me that not much has changed over the centuries.

I thought about bull fighting, canned hunting, dog fights and deer hunting and all the other sorts of unnecessary 'entertainment' that animals still suffer at the hands of man. I looked at my happy little dog and thought about what it would take to end the needless suffering that is inflicted on the helpless, and wondered if evil could ever be conquered. I recalled some wise words of Gandhi; I had made a point to remember them in times when I would be deeply saddened by something I saw: 'When I despair,' he said, 'I remember that all through history the way of truth and love has always won. There have been tyrants and murderers, and for a time they seem invincible, but in the end, they always fall – think of it, always.'

I was standing amid the proof. The Germanic chieftain Odoacer had eventually conquered Rome after a long decline in its fortunes, and Gandhi's passive resistance brought an end to British rule in India. The Allies had conquered the Nazis, and if winter could vanquish Napoleon, then global warming might be the nemesis of the human race!

Oscar and I needed a place where we could drown our sorrows and cool off, and we were in the right city. Rome has 280 fountains, but the Trevi Fountain is the largest of them all. It is famous, photogenic and infested with coins, not crocs! The stands that overlook the fountain were packed with people, but there was, of course, no one in the water: swimming in the fountain is strictly forbidden … but so was just about everything for a dog. I had decided to chicken out, but what could they do to a dog who didn't understand human law or reason? Besides, I was blonde; that was worth at least one 'get out of jail free' pass.

My cameraman set up above the crowd and Oz and I walked down to the fountain's edge. It was traditional to throw a coin into the Trevi, as legend has it that those who toss a coin into this fountain will always return to Rome; in fact, an estimated €3000 is thrown into the fountain each day. Heads aside, today it was the chance for 'tails' to get lucky!

In true Italian style, Oscar dived into the water and headed straight towards Oceanus, who wasn't in the least bit interested that a pooch was in his pond. This was Oscar's stage, and he loved every moment on it. The crowd laughed out loud as he swam his laps between Salubrity and Abundance.

Oscar may have been the first dog to dive into the Trevi, but he wasn't the first of its invaders to go bare. In fairly recent times, a thirty-eight-year-old woman called Roberta swam several lengths naked before police arrested her and covered her up for good! Oscar was breaking the law, but after three laps I was the one that got cuffed. The police were mad, and they weren't about to let me go free. I managed to retrieve Oscar from the fountain, and we were both hauled off to a spot behind the crowd.

Everyone was watching us – and the police knew that if they didn't make an example of us, they would have a thousand people and their poodles in the fountain before sunset. They were aggressive and unsympathetic – not even my blonde locks could save me this time. They wanted my passport, my address, my car keys and my dog's life. They even threatened to lock me up and 'bang bang' my dog!

It simply wasn't funny any more. I tried to explain that I hadn't known that dogs weren't allowed in the fountain, and that I had had a very thirsty and disobedient dog who had broken free from his lead to chase a pigeon heading towards the statue of Neptune. Oscar had tripped over the rim of the fountain and fallen right into the mouth of Signore Trevi. It was an accident.

The police didn't understand me, my cameraman was hiding away in the distance and Oscar was getting rather irritated having to drip-dry in a prone position.

After two long hours, the police finally warned me that if they ever saw either Oscar or me at the Fontana di Trevi again, we would be thrown in jail *immediately*! We counted our blessings and took a brisk walk back to the car. My cameraman had managed to film my 'lap' dog in the fountain, and we were ecstatic.

Next on the agenda? The Leaning Tower of Pisa … We arrived at the famous landmark after four hours of concentrated driving, which included eight toll gates and two squinting eyeballs. It was dusk, so we had basically blown the chance for my pooch to pose in front of the tower. I managed to take one shot of Oscar standing proudly to attention, and then it was back in the car and full throttle to Milan.

Driving through Milan is like speeding up a one-way street, but always in the wrong direction, over and over again. If the saying is true that an Italian who's missing two arms has a speech impediment, then surely it can be said that anyone driving in Milan is lost? As I zoomed passed Chanel for the seventh time, I realised that it was actually possible to go shopping but never to get to buy your favourite perfume!

We arrived at the Chedi Hotel at three past three in the morning. My cameraman wasn't speaking to me any more and Oscar was snorkelling in his sleep.

All I had to do now was to stay awake somehow and pretend to my Swiss lover, who awaited me, that my mojo was happy to see him!

13

Barc de Triomphe

I had been with only two men since the tour began: Oscar and my cameraman, Wally. Oscar may have been the wrong species, but he was otherwise absolutely perfect. Wally, though the right species, was the wrong specimen – not that I ever considered him a potential mate. Ours was a professional relationship, and Wally's glistening gold teeth, among other lacking credentials, created the perfect repulsion. Being a normal thirtysomething chick, I had arranged for a tune-up in Milan – a gorgeous golf pro I had met in South Africa at a golf shoot a few years earlier.

My golf pro couldn't break 89 on a mashie course, but he could crack 89 seconds indoors – *every single time.* He was the perfect lover for a worn-out woman on a world tour! Just outside of a minute it was all over bar the shouting, and within two, I was sound asleep.

The following day we took a scenic drive to Zermatt, Switzerland, home of the Matterhorn and fine purveyor of delicious chocolate. En route we paused to visit Foundation Barry, eponymously named after a great St Bernard (1800 to 1814). In his lifetime, Barry had saved the lives of forty lost hikers (although some say as many as 100) on the mountains. Foundation Barry serves as a breeding centre for the St Bernard breed, so I wasn't all that interested in the place. I deplore the fact that dogs are bred for profit when millions of dogs who already exist are being destroyed for lack of a decent home.

But the visit wasn't a total waste of time, as I learnt something that sank a childhood fantasy I'd harboured about this big breed. As a child I'd been presented with film images of St Bernards bounding through the snow, a cask slung around their necks, carrying brandy to lost mountain hikers. But it turns out that the dogs had actually carried mail more often than brandy, and thankfully so! The lady in the souvenir shop, which was doing a roaring trade in commercially produced kegs, informed me that the sudden infusion of alcohol would probably have killed a freezing person.

Zermatt is a greenie's dream spot. To make sure that pollution never obscures the town's view of the Matterhorn, the area was declared a car-free zone. Only vehicles that are battery driven and almost completely silent are allowed. In order to get to Zermatt, you have to catch a cog railway train from the nearby town of Täsch.

The Swiss live in a dream world that is all their own. Everything in their country is as perfect as their chocolate. The air is clean. The snow is pure. The mountains are beautiful. Even the cows 'moo' merrily! What was the best part of Switzerland for us? Simple: there weren't any stray dogs. Not one! Spot a non-pedigree pooch here and it's likely to have been adopted from Romania, Poland or Greece.

Idyllically happy with our environment, Oscar and I decided to channel Heidi and proceeded to prance through the yellow Alpine flowers that decorated the chalet-smitten mountainside, which turned it into a picture-perfect postcard. Next, I wanted to introduce my fair-weathered mutt to something he'd never experienced before – SNOW! Oscar was convinced that, with his superlative olfactory senses, he could find the elusive Abominable Snowman and prove his existence once and for all. The problem was, although we found some snow on the higher slopes, Oscar wasn't too enthusiastic about sticking his paws in it. He was far more interested in posing for the locals, who thought he was some sort of previously undiscovered giant mountain rabbit.

Oscar loved the cooler weather. If it was true that I had been a Formula 1 driver in a previous life, my dog had definitely been a snow leopard or a St Bernard in one of his. I built a snowdog to mark our visit, and Oz placed the finishing touch around its neck – an orange lead that we had brought along specifically for the occasion.

Oscar might not have been the first dog to play in the snow, but he was the first to help construct an abominable snowdog. And that was something to wag about!

The following morning Wally didn't pitch up for breakfast. In addition to a pack of fags a day, he had a huge appetite for breakfast, and his absence did not bode well. I went upstairs and found his suitcases waiting outside his room. I knocked on the door and walked inside. Wally was sitting on the bed, twitching his fingers and looking very uncomfortable.

'I quit!' he said.

Our contract stated that he had to give me two weeks' notice if he couldn't handle the pace. Obviously, he was suffering from amnesia – brought on by the high altitude, perhaps? Of course there was nothing I could do about it at that moment. Wally cried about the hectic schedule and moaned about the lack of sleep. He howled about his sore neck from carrying luggage that didn't belong to him and the flea that he had found on his toothbrush. Then, just like that, he left. Out the door and down the stairs he went, finally disappearing out of the entrance to the hotel.

I had just lost my cameraman, the only witness to my whereabouts if anything bad had to happen to me along the way. And, saddest of all, I'd lost my porter! I had also just lost all the time and money I'd spent on his visas and the non-refundable flights he had been booked on for the rest of the trip. But Wally didn't care. He was homesick. Some milk tart and a pair of clean underpants were all he wanted.

I was angry, upset and shocked all at once, but the show had to go on. There was no time to complain or cry, nor was he worth the lost energy. Oscar and I had been out and about on our own before. It was familiar territory for us and would make us even more focused. We had also known when planning the tour not to expect anyone to help us with anything. We all come into the world alone, and we all have to check out on our own too. Only you have the power to make your dreams come alive, and if you find a four-leaf clover along the way, consider yourself lucky.

I sprang into action and, much to the delight of my cellular network, managed to arrange another two cameramen for the next three venues after making a hundred phone calls. Things were looking up. I wouldn't have to buy Wally another McDonald's 'meal' ever again. Oscar and I would not have to breathe in any more second-hand smoke or have to look at those gold numbers in his mouth every time he had smoker's cough.

The golf pro dropped me off at the train station in Basel and kissed me good-bye. The last supper had been a little awkward.

The pro had never made any money on the links, but he had made plenty on property deals. Despite his wealth, however, his hand would clasp his pocket every time he had to pay for anything. A Lindt chocolate, a coffee break with extra froth, a train ticket – it was all an issue. Size or serving mattered not – only the pain of putting his hand into his back pocket at the cash register.

I had grown accustomed to splitting bills with him, but I was in no position to split hairs at this stage of the game. I'd heard that the transfer of my property had been delayed, and I was staring bankruptcy in the face. Besides, my pet peeve was anyone who hoarded money without giving just a teensy bit of it to a decent cause. It seemed to be a human condition that had spread far and wide. Everyone seemed driven to make more and covet more in order to be happy in their shallow existence. Greed – it made me sick to the bone. Giving up many material possessions for Oscar's cause had liberated me from my own selfish interests. And it had made me feel free and alive. It was certainly a lot more satisfying than sub-89 rounds in the bedroom! Nothing in my life had felt better than shedding my possessions to go and do something I believed in, and I thanked God that I had discovered the truth before rolling into a bunker with a stingy golfer.

For the first time since the tour began, Oscar and I were truly on our own. But it only made us more determined than ever to keep the faith – and, if possible, lose another suitcase! I actually had a reputation for misplacing things, especially if it was in need of a wash or I was responsible for lugging it around. Without a porter, we certainly could do with 'misplacing' a few more items, but as long as I kept an eye on my passport, driver's licence, credit card, tweezers and Oscar, we were good to keep going.

Oscar looked like a tick in a haystack of bags when the train pulled in. We had twelve minutes to load the luggage, which I managed to do with just three seconds to spare. The dogbox blocked the doorway, the two cases of Rogz leads cramped the passageway and my aching back prohibited any movement from my head to my hips. I was finished, and the day was only just beginning. It would be the longest and hardest day on tour yet.

After three hours of stretching out on the train, we rolled into Gare Saint-Lazare, Paris's most fascinating train station. Pulling our trolley of luggage through the terminal must have looked like a scene from *Saturday Night Live Does WrestleMania*: everyone knew we were up to something, but no one knew quite what. I must have looked like a homeless dropout with a dog and a trolley-full of what was probably a cache of stolen goods.

Our motley little group headed straight for the toilets, where I brushed my teeth, put in eye drops, sprayed my armpits and kissed another country good morning. I checked our luggage into the baggage-storage area, and by the time I joined the journalist who had arranged to meet me for an interview over a cup of coffee, I was looking fresher than an Alpine daisy in full bloom. From there, Paris went by at the speed of light. We had made up for one lost day in Italy; the other would have to be made up in France. So, having missed that ferry, we now, sadly, had only one day in the country's beautiful capital city.

Finding a taxi driver who could understand English, or one who could understand English AND would transport a dog to the state vet, evolved into an entire tour in itself. Once we had that sorted, we had to find *another* taxi driver – one who could understand English AND would transport a dog to the state vet AND could find the address our previous taxi driver couldn't find.

After being driven around the Eiffel Tower several times, to no avail, I had no choice but to ditch any further attempts at obtaining the export permit we required for Russia; we would just have to take our chances with the health certificate and a hundred bucks in cash.

We met our new cameraman two hours later than scheduled and spent the better half of the next two hours stuck in traffic and talking a whimsical mix of 'Frenchlish' within the narrow confines of a Citroën 2CV. Up the Champs-Élysées, past the Arc de Triomphe and across the Seine we crept.

Finally, we arrived at the Sauver Protéger Aimer (SPA) shelter located on the outskirts of Paris. We had only fifteen minutes in which to deliver Rogz collars and choose our 'Oscar' before hurling ourselves back into the traffic. We were scheduled to meet the members of the Brigitte Bardot Foundation and join their 'Adopt a Dog' awareness parade through Paris on a sightseeing bus.

The parade was followed by a news interview, followed by another attempt at trying to flag down an English-speaking taxi driver who would take a dog and its owner back to the station to re-trieve their luggage. From there, we had to hire another taxi to take us to a cheap hotel near the airport. We dropped into bed at one in the morning, and five hours later we were standing in line at the check-in counter at Charles de Gaulle Airport!

I knew before we started this project that it would be impossible to plot the perfect route. Mistakes were going to be made, and a big one we encountered was timing. As we prepared to leave Europe, I wished that we had had more time to spend in the region, especially Paris. I had been to Paris on a previous occasion and loved the place. Part of the problem was the visa issue. In order to get a Schengen visa, proof of accommodation as well as confirmed flights in and out of the EU were strictly required. And so we were victims of a tight schedule that had been planned months in advance, around events we'd attend during our stay. It was thus impossible to extend our time in one place at the expense of another, or amend our travel plans until we had exited Russia.

We had expedited our time in Paris, which meant that Oscar didn't have the opportunity to lift a leg on Eiffel's tower. But thanks to Chris Bellanger, *chef d'établissement* of the SPA shelter we visited, we had learnt a bit more about dog adoption in France. The French seem to love their dogs. On almost every corner you can spot a well-groomed dog doing his business on the pavement with the owner looking in the opposite direction. But, according to Chris, only one out of every eight dogs you see in France is adopted. The result? One hundred thousand cats and dogs are put down every year because there aren't any homes for them.

To make matters worse, dogs bought from breeders or pet stores are generally not sterilised, which has created a tremendous 'over-population' problem in the country.

'The challenge for Oscar and welfare groups like ours and those all over the world,' Chris said, 'is to try to change people's mentalities and their feelings towards adoption. Our dogs are not ill, aggressive, no-good looking! No, no, NO! They don't have behaviour problems. They were just bought one day and left months later for, in majority cases, no good reasons. They just leave on street, or bring in here.'

I couldn't imagine dumping Oscar on the street, let alone any-where else. How could any decent person do such a thing and still sleep at night? Even in the short time we spent at SPA, I couldn't help but notice what incredibly healthy, handsome dogs were in the cages. They were some of the best-looking we had seen. It was hard to believe they once had owners who had just thrown them away like so many old newspapers.

If only they could talk. If only they could tell us of the human they had once known who had done this to them. If only they could vote, perhaps the government would get more involved in educating the public about the causes of overpopulation and the wonderful dogs that are dying for a life at shelters like the SPA.

If only I had the time and resources to save them all, my God, I would ...

14

Ruff over Russia

Forty-two days on the trot, and I was learning a few truths along the road less travelled with a dog. Firstly, you will never have a bowl handy when your dog wants water. Secondly, you can teach a dog to 'sit!', but you can't teach it to 'carry luggage'. Lastly, blonde hair won't get you the stupendous service in Paris that it gets you in Italy.

I was also about to learn a significant tip when travelling with your dog: instead of considering only the cost of the human flight, *always* take into account the excess-baggage costs of an airline. I wished I had been aware of this before booking the flight between Paris and St Petersburg. There were a number of flights available between the two cities, but only two were direct flights. Naturally, with Oscar in the hold, I would only consider those, no matter what the cost. I had a choice between Air France and Rossiya Airlines, and it would all come down to the darling dollar. With such a limited option of airlines, I thought I had hit the jackpot with Air France: their ticket was half the price of Rossiya's.

I checked in ahead of schedule and tried not to look exhausted as I dragged my last suitcase onto the scale, but it was impossible to ignore their weight. Now it was up to the lovely lady behind the counter to decide on how to deal with it. I disguised my concern with the sweetest little smile south of the Mississippi and quietly prayed for my salvation. If ever there was a time in my life when I would need to suck up, this was it!

I was allowed two suitcases, free of charge, with a maximum weight limit of twenty-three kilos each. My carry-on bags alone weighed more than that, but I had hidden those at the far end of the line, out of everyone's sight but mine. As for the other two cases *and* Oscar, I was guilty as charged – there was no hiding all of that!

Up until that point I had been charming and reasonably well behaved whenever I'd heard the amount I would have to pay for being 'overweight'. This time, I decided that I had had enough. It was 'that time of the month' to defend my bags. After all, these were suitcases on a very charitable crusade. It wasn't as if my bags were bulging from a shopping spree at the Galeries Lafayette; they were heavy only because they were full of dog collars and leads that were on their way to the forgotten dogs of Russia. Was that a crime for which I was expected to pay?

UPS had sent 10 000 Rogz collars and leads to the societies ahead of our scheduled arrival, but the Russian society had asked us please not to send anything. They knew that it would be very expensive to get the collars and leads through customs once they were in their custody. I had therefore decided to transport them myself, which was not the wisest decision at the time. But having got them this far, I wasn't about to discard them in the terminal unless my life's savings depended on it.

The lady tagged my bags and sent them onto the conveyor belt. This was a very good sign. She hadn't mentioned anything about them being overweight. She then asked me to place my dog and the cage on the scale. This was normal procedure, and Oscar kindly obliged. By this stage, he knew the routine. The weight of the box remained nine kilos, but Oscar had added a kilo to his frame, compliments of his craving for croissants smothered in jam during the last two breakfast sessions. Up to that point everything had been going according to plan, and my smile was starting to feel like a genuine crush. Then she pulled out the calculator.

'Seven hundred and twenty euro. You pay over there.'

I knew I hadn't heard the number correctly. The accent was hard enough to understand, but the French were also known to get their English a little mixed up.

'Um, can you repeat that please?'

I heard the same number.

'You cannot be serious. There must be a mistake!' I reacted in a manner that would have made John McEnroe proud, insisting that she recalculate the amount and find it in her heart to discard the kilos, or at least to give me a 90 per cent discount. Christmas was only six months away and I needed the money to save Santa in the recession!

'*Please*,' I begged.

'I only charge you for dog. Your other bags very, *very* heavy, but I don't charge you for those.'

There was no way I could afford to pay what amounted to nearly a thousand dollars. I hadn't paid more than $500 to transport Oscar thus far and, even then, I had considered the tab outrageous. My smile cracked into pieces. I demanded to see the manager on duty. I tried to explain that I was on a world tour to promote dog adoption and that I was funding it myself. I offered her a collar and begged for monetary mercy under the charitable circumstances.

'Besides,' I added, 'I don't have any hand luggage!'

But she was on a mission to extract as much cash from this passenger as possible.

'Okay, I won't take the bag,' I snapped. 'Take a suitcase away. I can't pay for it.'

She told me that the bags had already gone and that they could not be retrieved. She also reminded me that the cost was not for the checked bags; it was for 'the dauwg'!

I couldn't tighten the collar I'd just given her around her neck, but I had one last paw to stand on. I asked the woman to cast an eye on the bodies waiting in the long queue behind me. Most of these people were going to be on the same flight as my 'dauwg', and each one looked as if he or she would weigh in at twice my and Oscar's weight combined!

'Their bags may weigh much less than my "dauwg", but their guts don't,' I said huffily. 'So why do I have to pay for my pooch and they don't have to fork out for their flab?'

Not exactly amused, she told me that Air France did not discriminate against its (bigger) passengers and that best I shut up and pay up, or I'd lose my ticket.

I knew I was losing my grip on the situation, and lo and behold, security was called to the scene. An hour later the cuffs were removed, my mouth and mutt were tagged, and my mom's credit card was charged. Her card was my back-up should mine have reached its credit crunch; that time had just arrived.

With difficulty, I managed to drag my hand luggage on board. Understandably, no one on the flight offered to help me. They had witnessed the soap opera at the check-in counter and wanted nothing to do with me. I was relieved when I finally found my window seat and had a chance to relax. I was about to close my eyes when I noticed Oscar's box on the tarmac below. I watched curiously as four ground staff peered into the cage.

At the same moment, one of the cabin crew tapped me on the shoulder and told me that the captain wanted a word with me. I went to the cockpit, where the captain informed me that the cage of my 'live animal' was not completely secured and would thus not be permitted on the plane.

I had really had enough of Air France, and now this? There was one lifeline in the mix: the pilot was Italian. I was back in business. Against the rules, he handed me an orange jacket. I had five minutes to fix the problem or I would have to catch the next flight ... only there wasn't one.

I knew that there was a small problem with one of the two metal rods that secured the top-right part of the cage, but no one had complained about it thus far, and the door was still securely closed. Air France was just being fussy – fussy with weight, and fussy with a wayward wire clip. I had a lock with which to fix the cage in my hand luggage and, moments later, I had secured it to the cage to the captain's satisfaction.

While I was down on the ground, I also had the chance to check the state Oscar was in just before he would go into the hold. My hound was a lean, mean, panting machine. Although Oscar panted all the time, at that moment, when I saw him, he seemed to be panting a lot more than usual. Admittedly, this was only the third time that he was flying in the hold. The engines were exceptionally loud and it was hot on the ground. But I still couldn't help but wonder – was Oscar a little scared?

I had considered sedating him on the flights, but my veterinarian had advised against it. Firstly, the effect of a sedative on an animal at high altitude is very unpredictable, and it's not as if there is any-one to monitor the situation if a problem were to arise. Sedatives are also known to affect a dog's equilibrium, as well as create respi-ratory or cardiovascular problems at high altitude. The only time an animal should be sedated is if it is overactive, nervous or prone to severe separation anxiety.

Aside from scratching himself and missing me when I was out buying his food, Oscar didn't have any of those issues. In fact, if he had, the World Woof Tour certainly would never have got off the ground ... with or without sedatives!

Some airlines insisted on sedation, but this was introduced more for the sanity of the passengers than the welfare of the dog. There had been a few incidences when a barking-mad dog had been heard from the main cabin, causing disruption between the captain's periodic announcements. Whenever those airlines had asked if I'd sedated Oscar, I just nodded my head. It had worked every time and nobody had ever asked for any proof.

Seeing Oscar in such a state bothered me intensely. I cried all the way from Paris to St Petersburg, occasionally pausing to bite what keratin was left on my fingernails. Oscar's comfort was of the utmost importance to me, and I couldn't handle the thought of my best buddy down in that dingy, dark hold, alone and afraid. I vowed that, from that moment on, I would find a way to liberate my hound from the dogbox and hail him back to bliss – even if it meant catching a tuk-tuk from Moscow to Delhi on the next haul. I would make a plan!

15

Cosmomutts

We finally touched down in *the* Russian Federation. I could hardly believe that we were here. I had studied the Soviet Union back at school, but never thought I would ever make it anywhere east of the Iron Curtain. With the possible exception of Mikhail Baryshnikov, the ballet dancer who wore his tights too tight, the Russians had been made out to be big, bad bears when I was at school. They believed in the evil practice of communism and were always threatening to fire nuclear missiles at the West and start the end of the world. I was too young to die, and I used to lock my bedroom door at night to prevent the KGB from spying on me and my dog.

St Petersburg was our gateway to country number 18 on the WWT. As I disembarked at Pulkovo International Airport, I was relieved to spot some movement behind the wire mesh of the cage when it was offloaded from the aircraft. I was even more relieved when, shortly afterwards, I realised that the airport authorities were not even interested in checking Oscar's incomplete paperwork, or the bursting case of collars and leads. We had both made the trip in one piece.

During the flight I had seen a familiar face on the aeroplane. I couldn't place the person at first, but then I suddenly caught on. Alice Cooper may have a rock career that has spanned more than four decades, but I had been a puppy through much of it. When I eventually grew old enough to understand stage antics that included props like guillotines, baby dolls, fake blood and big, long snakes, I decided that music by Neil Diamond and John Denver, with a tweak of Bruce Springsteen, was much safer for my inner harmony.

But fame knows no favourites, so I was still delighted to see Alice. I was also pleased to know that there was a person on the planet other than me who didn't brush their hair! I eyed Mr Cooper's long black locks as he waited for his luggage while he checked out Oscar, who was making his first turn on the conveyor belt in his bright-blue box. Next thing I knew, the rocker was standing right beside me.

Mr Cooper was intrigued by the 'very important pooch' and wanted to know the 'rap'. I told him a bit about the tour and, after a few minutes, I had him begging for Oscar's autograph. He kindly gave us free tickets to his show the following night.

I liked Alice Cooper, and to keep the conversation going I asked him about his golf game. I recalled him playing at the Pebble Beach Pro-Am in California on an occasion when I was caddying, and I seemed to remember him as a bit of a hacker. Thinking I'd score some points by being amusing, I asked him whether he'd managed yet to break 90 at Pebble Beach Links. In that instant, Mr Cooper's friendly face exited stage left and we went our separate ways. I Googled Alice Cooper later and learnt that he actually had a very competitive three handicap and had shot a 75 on the links the last time he had played there. Needless to say, Oz and I were unable to make the show!

If Mr Cooper made golf look good, Peter the Great had made St Petersburg look pretty. He had modelled the city on Amsterdam, and thus hundreds of canals wove their way through the 'Venice of the North', while over 300 bridges covered the canals. There are three animal shelters in the city. None of them has a fancy view over any of the canals, but I was privileged to visit the very first one to have been established, which Elena Valerianova Kurkholaine founded in the early 1990s.

Most of the shelters that we had visited prior to arriving in Russia had similar stories of how they had begun. Almost all of them had been started by women. None of these women had ever considered starting a shelter, but in one unexpected moment their fate had changed forever when they had been deeply moved by the plight of a distressed stray dog. There had been no one to call who could help and no facility to take it to. Each one of these women had then decided to do something to change the situation. They became pioneers in their field and angels in the eyes of stray dogs.

Elena's experience was no different.

She, along with three other volunteers, ran the St Petersburg SPCA. One of the volunteers was Mr Valeri, whose job was to cook food for the dogs in enormous old army barrels scattered around the rustic property. The presence of this old sailor moved me as much as the 120 dogs that were barking for a home all around us. Why Mr Valeri left such a lasting impression on me I am not quite sure, but there was something about his solemn, sad demeanour that captured my imagination.

In his worn-out clothes, he sat motionless on the edge of a wooden bench, a bottle of vodka waiting between his old peasant boots. He moved only to take slow puffs from his cigarette, his weathered face occasionally disappearing from view as he exhaled a cloud of smoke. Except for the food boiling in the barrel close by and his favourite dog, 'Spok', who barked in the cage behind him, he seemed to be unaware of anything that was happening in the world outside. Could he sense that I was watching him, or was he totally oblivious to my presence in the adjacent shed? Either way, did the old man even care?

His sunken eyes gazed expressionlessly into the distance. Was he reflecting on events in his past, or on the dramatic twists and turns of his country's tumultuous history? He would have been a young boy in the 1940s during the Siege of Leningrad. Did he perhaps recall the 872 days of unparalleled suffering, and were members of his family among the one and a half million people who had lost their lives in the famine when Nazi and Finnish forces had cut off their food supply? Maybe he had witnessed thousands of dogs lose their lives under those same conditions. Had this perhaps fractured his connection to the outside world? I would never know. I turned away and walked back into my own world, and that of Elena, who had been quietly waiting to show me the rest of the premises.

Moscow is 800 kilometres south of St Petersburg, and we had planned to take the train there. The good news was that there weren't any border crossings between the two cities, but the bad news was that we couldn't get any answers to any of our questions. No matter how hard we tried, we couldn't find out whether Oscar would be allowed on the train. Everyone I spoke to in St Petersburg told me that I needn't worry; making a little cash withdrawal from my wallet would ensure that even a cow could get on board.

I had hired a Russian travel agency to assist us with our passage through the country and, while they couldn't clarify the train story either, their help had already proved invaluable. Not one hotel in St Petersburg would accommodate a mongrel, but the lady at the agency with whom I had been liaising had organised for us to stay at her mother's flat. Five of us shared one small bathroom, but it worked out perfectly. After travelling for forty-eight days, my digestive system had stopped working anyway.

There were ten overnight trains between St Petersburg and Moscow, and all we had to do was pray that my ticket was matched to a coach that would transport a dog cheaply. We arrived at Moskovsky Station and approached Platform 3, Coach 6. I had a translator on my side and she knew the game plan. I waited in silence as a conversation ensued between her and the conductor. Whenever the Russians communicate with each other, it always seems as if they're fighting. They speak very directly and with great intensity. Whatever was happening now, I was certain that the conductor had refused the bribe and that I faced a jail sentence for attempting to corrupt a transport official!

But my assumptions proved wrong. Suddenly the stern conductor signalled for Oscar and me to get on board, and my translator instructed me to pay him $300 when the train started moving and 'when no one was watching'. Failure to do so would result in the immediate removal of the dog from the speeding train. I felt like I was caught between Mother Teresa and a drug deal.

As the train left the station, I decided to give the conductor only $150. I was taller than him and figured that he couldn't make a scene about the bribe once we were on board. My next challenge was to contend with the sleeping arrangements on the train. The compartments were very small, and each contained four bunks. I had tried to book an entire compartment for myself, but, like most things in Russia, this was 'impossible'. I was hoping to at least have an extra bunk-bed for Oscar.

After spending a few minutes on the train, I would have been happy just to see another female! There were men everywhere, and the smell of vodka permeated the dimly lit atmosphere. If only my friends could see me now, I thought. I took a deep breath and waited for James Bond to dive through the window to save me from what was beginning to resemble a scene from the Moscow Circus.

When I found my compartment, my eyes nearly popped out of their sockets. There stood three elderly Russian men: I would be spending the night in a compartment the size of my car with three men and their five bottles of vodka. Where were all the women? And why didn't my roomies seem more surprised at the sight of a horrified bleached blonde with too much luggage and a dog? One of the men offered to help me with my luggage, but gave up when he realised that most of it was still stuck at the back of the coach.

The compartment had obviously not undergone any changes since World War II. Faded satin curtains were drawn across the dirty window and green doilies with kitsch gold trimming covered the little table fixed firmly between the two lower bunks. Yuri was the oldest of my three 'roommates', and if we hadn't been so linguistically challenged, I bet we would have shared a few tots over warm conversations about golf and the Revolution!

After eight hours on the train with a whole lot of rowdy Russians, I was the most sleepless South African south of Siberia. We pulled into Leningradsky Station, where a driver was waiting to transfer us to our hotel. Upon our arrival at the hotel, we were told that Oscar could not go inside. When I had booked the hotel, however, the management had said he could stay. They had since changed their minds. Bribing the entire hotel staff was impossible. It took my travel agency the entire day to find a hotel that would accept us. It was probably the 'best' worst hotel I'd ever stayed in, and the most expensive worst one too. But Oz and I weren't complaining – at least we didn't have to share it with foreign men and alcohol fumes!

There are an estimated 100 000 stray dogs in Moscow. During the Soviet days, culling strays was a common practice, and many of these 'blanket' solutions still occur here – especially after a human gets a random dog bite. There is, however, public interest in building more shelters and restoring some sort of control over the stray population, but this is not a priority and, besides, only sterilisation can effectively reduce the number of strays.

There are currently fifteen government shelters in Moscow, and I was told that I wouldn't be allowed into any of them. Just like in the old spy movies, the Russians are generally quite a suspicious people, and if they knew I was a foreigner and unable to adopt one of their dogs, there was no way they would let me in. Brushing my hair wouldn't make any difference either.

The conditions in these municipal shelters are far from ideal, which basically means that Oscar wouldn't survive a day inside. There are also five private shelters in Moscow, all called BIM. They were started and are still supported by a remarkable woman called Darya Taraskina, who was inspired to build the shelters after reading the book *White Bim Black Ear*, which tells a heart-wrenching story about a homeless dog called Bim, who sets off on a journey to find his master. A movie based on the book was released in 1977 and was nominated for an Academy Award in the Best Foreign Language Film category.

We visited the first and biggest one of the lot, BIM Khoteichi Shelter. If it had been rush hour in downtown Los Angeles, it probably would have taken us an hour to get to the shelter. This being Moscow, it took us three! Eight hundred dogs, a camel, a few horses, the odd donkey and 300 cats make the four hectares of BIM Khoteichi their home. Oscar was once again in a state of bliss, and while he chased some of the free-ranging cats and pigs around the premises, I spent some quality time with the orphans from Maria's Children, who had come to meet Oscar.

Dogs are everywhere in Russia's capital. We saw them curled up near the Kremlin and lounging in parks and outside shops; it's even common to see them boarding the Metro or taking free rides on the trams! Muscovites tolerate the strays, and if you had been at Red Square on the day we were there, you would have seen a kind old Russian lady bending over to give a 'stray' called Oscar a scrap to eat with a passing pat!

Those who can't afford to keep dogs as pets continue to maintain strong feelings for dogs. This sentiment is no more visible than at Mendeleevskaya Station, one of the busiest of the Moscow subway stations. Down in the heart of this underground station is a bronze statue of Malchik, a stray dog that used to call the place home. The station employees fed him and the regulars who rode the trains all knew Malchik by his first name. One morning, a fashion model named Yuliana Romanova was walking her Staffordshire terrier when the pair came across Malchik. For no reason at all, Yuliana drew a kitchen knife from her bag and stabbed him. The locals tried to stop the bleeding, but they couldn't save Malchik.

The attack outraged the people of Moscow. Yuliana was forced to flee the country, but she was located, declared insane and committed to a mental hospital. Prominent artists and local residents got together and raised $15 000 for a statue of Malchik to be erected in the subway. It was unveiled in 2007, and simply called 'Compassion'. Oscar and I visited the bronze statue and observed a moment of silence for the stray dogs of Moscow.

Malchik's murder had not been the first act of cruelty visited on a dog, nor would it be the last. Among the bustle and chaos of the afternoon rush, I quietly thanked those who had cared enough to create this prominent symbol in protest against the inhumane treatment of stray dogs, and for making it a daily reminder to all who pass by that they should respect all living creatures.

Our main inspiration behind the trip to Russia had been to celebrate the contribution dogs have made to the development of space travel. I had spent months trying to get permission for Oscar to have a zero-gravity experience at the Space Centre in Moscow in commemoration of the pooch space pioneers. Everything in Russia takes light years to organise and, in the end, the visit was, unfortunately, 'impossible'.

I had always thought that monkeys made it into space first. While the monkey Albert II did make a sub-orbital flight in 1949, it was a dog called Laika that became the first living creature to go into orbit, on 3 November 1957.

Laika and Oscar had a lot in common. For starters, both had once been homeless. The Russian scientists preferred training stray dogs in Moscow for outer space as they were used to surviving extreme conditions, like cold and hunger. Both Oscar and Laika were 'rescued' at approximately three years of age, and both were products of a mysterious lineage that not even Nostradamus could have unravelled.

The only *major* difference between the two dogs is that Oscar lives, while Laika is dead. The Russians sent a total of thirteen dogs into orbit. Five of them never made it back alive, and Laika was one of them. The true cause of her death was not made public until forty-five years after the flight, when it was finally revealed that she had died from stress and heat exposure only a few hours after the launch. No amount of summers on the streets of Moscow could have prepared her for her ordeal. Her 'coffin' circled the earth 2570 times and travelled approximately 100 million kilometres before it burnt up in the earth's atmosphere on 14 April 1958.

In the original plan, Laika would have been euthanised with a serving of poisoned food after ten days in orbit, as *Sputnik 2* was not designed to be retrievable. Laika had thus been doomed to die right from the beginning. It was not until 1998, after the collapse of the Soviet regime, that Oleg Gazenko, one of the lead scientists responsible for sending Laika into space, expressed regret for having allowed her to die. He said, 'The more time that passes, the more I'm sorry. We shouldn't have done it. We did not learn enough from the mission to justify the death of the dog.'

Would Laika have agreed to the deadly 'experiment' had she known that she would be immortalised in human history? Would she have agreed to be sacrificed in the name of science in exchange for a monument and a plaque of herself outside the two main space centres in and around Moscow? Would she have wanted to trade the streets of Moscow for the confinement in progressively smaller cages for periods of up to twenty days in order to prepare her for the tiny cabin in *Sputnik 2*?

When we eventually left Russia and our aircraft – yes, aircraft: my plan to catch a tuk-tuk to India had been thwarted – took off into the night sky, heading in the direction of Delhi, I felt grateful that we would be cruising at 35 000 feet, and not a foot higher into space. I looked out at the zillions of stars from the safety of my seat behind the aeroplane window and wondered what it must be like to go into space. And then I thought of how insignificant we really are in the greater scheme of things, and whether anything except dog adoption really mattered to me. I thought about how fragile we are and how precious life is, whether it is the gift of life bestowed on a baby who is an orphan at Maria's Children or on a puppy that becomes a mangy mongrel in Moscow. Life knows no boundaries. It belongs to every living being, and every one of us is sacred. Life is fragile; it is so very precious, and it deserves to be treated with compassion, kindness and respect. Without life, there is nothing. Without life, we cannot know love. There is no life worth sacrificing, because there is no sacrifice greater than losing a life.

It must be incredible, I thought, to travel into space. But I knew that Oscar and I would never sacrifice our lives for such an experience. Would the scientists who were involved in Laika's project have been willing to sacrifice their own lives for their cosmic crusade? Somehow I doubted it.

And then I thought, if they had not been prepared to sacrifice themselves for the cause, why on earth had they expected a dog to do so?

Despite my promise to liberate Oscar from travel in the hold after our experience in Paris, he was once again in the dogbox. As it had turned out, there weren't any tuk-tuks in Moscow heading to Delhi. In fact, the only ways to get to India were either to fly or to walk. Footing the 4342-kilometre journey through exotic destinations like Kabul and Islamabad would be a bit risky, and Oz wasn't interested in becoming a sniffer dog either. The risks of dodging landmines and snipers far outweighed the paranoia of my pooch in a plane, so when the time came for us to leave Russia, we decided to fly 'one last time'. There was still an outside chance that I could get Oscar on the plane and that he could be in the cabin with me: in Russia, dogs bark and bribes talk!

When Oscar and I had visited BIM Khoteichi Shelter in Moscow, its founder, Darya Taraskina, had given us a tip. She suggested offering $200 at the airport check-in counter. She had got her dog into the cabin before using the same 'technique', and with degrees in both mathematics and physics, I figured she was smart enough to know how to operate the 'system'!

After our Russian jaunt, when we'd been dropped off at Sheremetyevo International Airport, we'd headed straight for the check-in counters for our flight. I'd eyed out one of the girls behind the counter. Innocence would be my prey; 'Miss Katjusha' would be my victim. Two hundred dollars could buy her a new make-up bag and a pretty little dress, and she wouldn't even have to sing or dance for the money.

I handed her my passport with the money tucked inside. My heart was pounding. I couldn't believe I was even attempting this. I was from a good family in Cape Town. Both my mum and my dad worked hard for their money. My brother and I had gone to church on Sundays, and even though we'd spent the time sticking gum under the pews, we were still believers – especially when a favour was needed. I knew God would understand that Oscar's welfare was more important than indulging in a little sin, and that my kind 'donation' to a poor young woman, who was having to sacrifice her Sunday mornings in order to check in heavy bags belonging to difficult, unethical customers, was an act of kindness under the circumstances.

Unfortunately, I had picked the only babe in Russia who wouldn't take a bribe. That, or, given her young age, she didn't yet know what a bribe was.

'What is thees?' she asked.

I didn't really know what to say. I fumbled over a few words, and before I could utter another, she handed the notes back to me. An hour later, Oscar was back in the hold, I was crying up above and we were well on our way to Delhi. Despite my bad intentions, I hadn't managed to get my dog into the cabin and, to make me freak out even more, the aircraft, which was apparently an Ilyushin Il-96-300, was old and worn out. The seats were torn and there were still smoking trays in the armrests. I looked out the window and could see that the two wings were still intact, and at least the crew seemed more experienced than the ground staff.

The best way to ensure that your dog is in good care 'downstairs' is to let *everybody* 'upstairs' know that he's there. The captain controls the temperature and the pressure, and the more you irritate him, the more he'll make sure he keeps his eye on the ball. The moment the seatbelt lights were switched off, I called for the cabin crew. I was a pain on any given day, but nothing could prepare the cabin staff for the new level of pain I was about to become. I explained the situation to 'Nikolay' and stated that I wanted to know what the temperature was in the hold *now*!

He returned a few minutes later and politely informed me that the captain knew about the dog, and that the temperature was set at a comfortable 21 °C. Five minutes later, I summoned another staff member. On this occasion, it was 'Yuriy' who heard the score, and I wanted to know what the temperature was in the hold again, as soon as possible. I continued to irritate the cabin crew until Nikolay approached me and said, 'Your dog is very much fine. If it makes you feel any better, maybe you want to see him now?'

What? Was he being serious? How could I see my dog *now*? Did the Russians have some sort of plan to push me out of the aircraft? My behaviour certainly warranted a push in the wrong direction.

'I would love to see him!' I said.

I followed the friendly Russian to the very back of the aeroplane. He knelt down and lifted up a latch situated in the middle of the cabin floor. As the 'door' opened, there, in full view down below, was a bright-blue box, and I could see Oscar inside!

Finally, I could see what the hold was like. The box wasn't stuck among a hundred suitcases or cargo boxes, as I had previously imagined, but was securely strapped to the floor, and there was plenty of space surrounding it. The noise from the engines was a little louder than I had expected, but the temperature was perfect and, best of all, Oscar seemed relaxed and content. I called out his name and he calmly lifted his head to acknowledge that he had heard me.

I wasn't allowed to go down to visit Oscar, but Nikolay was prepared to offer some canine cabin service.

'Is "Oskar" hungry?' he asked.

I didn't have time to answer. In a second, Nikolay had jumped to the floor below and handed my hound a tray of mash, carrots and chicken, perfectly complemented by a buttered roll and a bowl of clean water.

I could not believe what I was seeing. I rubbed my eyes to make sure I wasn't hallucinating. Here we were, cruising at 35 000 feet above sea level in what had to be the worst piece of commercial machinery flying the skies. Inside, I was witnessing the best darn service in the entire atmosphere. My fears that Oscar wasn't handling the hold flew out the window, and I didn't even have to fork out 200 bucks to see it!

When Oscar had licked the last bit of gravy off his plate, Nikolay returned to remove the tray. The canine cabin service was almost complete, but for one small formality.

With a few duty-free items in his right hand, Nikolay bent over and posed one last question to his unlikely but satisfied passenger: 'Vodka, Oskar?'

16

Slumdog

It's not a matter of *whether* you will get sick from consuming something in India; it's a matter of *when*. No matter how careful I had been on my previous three visits, something in the food always jumped ship and held my stomach hostage. This time, the mutiny would be no different. We arrived at Indira Gandhi International Airport at six in the morning. I was starving.

I decided to grab a cucumber sandwich from a kiosk. It was the healthiest-looking sarnie I'd ever seen on the subcontinent and, being so hungry, I was prepared to give Indian food a last chance. Just after sunrise, I was down on my hands and knees. Fortunately I had Imodium in my first-aid kit, and by sundown I was ready to eat again.

If my dad hadn't been born in Patna, I doubt whether I would ever have visited India before the WWT. But my dad's origins had always intrigued me, and although the country is a very different place now from what it was back in the 1930s and early 1940s, he must have had a childhood that only Hollywood could conceive of today.

Dad spoke of riding elephants through miles and miles of over-grown grasslands, and of sugar-cane fields in valleys that never seemed to end. His family's garden was bigger than the one at Buckingham Palace, and his 'toys' were pet partridges, pheasants and a little dachshund called Tiler. My dad's father managed the largest sweet factory in the country, and Pop was home-schooled by his mother. A half a dozen servants took care of everything else.

Then, in 1947, life as he knew it came to an end. India was about to win its independence from the British Raj, and the sons and daughters of the Empire had to flee, and fast. My father was sent to Calcutta, loaded onto a bath-tub-like boat and, along with several strangers, slowly sailed to South Africa, pulling in at every harbour along the way. The journey took over eight months. My father was just ten years old.

Understandably, my dad never took a liking to Mohandas Gandhi or anyone else who had been involved in 'destroying' his childhood utopia. Of course he had every right to pick a bone with India's past, but I certainly wasn't going to take sides and jeopardise an opportunity to stay at India's finest hotel – even one that had been built in order to mark India's independence.

Oz and I had had enough of roughing it; it was now time for luxury! All the who's who of the world had stayed at the Imperial Hotel in New Delhi. Gandhi and Lord Mountbatten had met there to discuss the partition of India and the creation of Pakistan, and the great presidents, actors, directors, musicians, kings, queens and queers had all followed. Now, for the first time in its seventy-five-year history, and thanks to a manager with a soft spot for demanding psycho-blondes with dark roots, a dog would have the chance to check in too!

We arrived at the imposing iron gates in the hotel's big black vintage Jaguar SS. Slowly we drove past the twenty-four king palms leading up to the grand entrance, gently waving in the breeze to welcome us to the historic premises. Although early, it was already 44 °C in the shade – we had picked the perfect spot to escape the temperature.

Oscar wasn't permitted in the dining areas, but he was allowed to order room service – and plenty of it, knowing as he did that he wouldn't have to pay for it himself! He demolished his main course while enjoying the fine view from the four-poster bed, occasionally rolling across the Porthault linen just to prove that he knew how to use the exclusive serviette service.

'I've got to hand it to you, Oscar,' I said, laughing. 'You've come a long way, and I'm not talking about all the mileage. You've come, in fact, all the way from death row, where you lived on a concrete slab, to an ultra-plush, pillow-top mattress made in heaven … Not too shabby, Oscar, not too shabby at all.'

We spent two nights at the Imperial, and I have to admit that barking goodbye to it was one of the greatest challenges we'd faced on the tour thus far. The time had come to trade climate control and a big-screen TV for a short flight north, into the heart of the Himalayas, where electricity was a luxury and Bollywood was as big a myth as Shangri-La. Languishing in the lap of luxury at the Imperial had us ill-prepared for the transition from grand to godforsaken. The only consolation was that we would be taking a two-week break in the region, and would at least have the simple pleasure of sleeping on the same mattress for longer than a night or two.

I had visited the town of Leh on three previous occasions, but it had captured my attention right from my very first visit. It was an experience that helped shape my future, so much so that I now considered the place my second home. I had discovered the town by pure chance when I was on a solitary photographic expedition in the Kingdom of Bhutan in 2006. Although the country transported me back in time, it was also a small step forward in educating myself about my newfound passion, photography.

I had developed a strong appetite for taking pictures of Buddhist monasteries, and any country that measured its gross domestic product in happiness just had to be Nirvana! During a visit to the Tiger's Nest, an awe-inspiring monastery that balances delicately on the side of a cliff by what must be the grace of Buddha, I met a group of spiritual travellers on a similar mission to mine. They told me all about a vast and very remote region in the Indian Himalayas called Ladakh and insisted that I go there, guaranteeing that the location would afford me and my Canon photographic 'ecstasy'.

I didn't know what they were smoking, nor did I care. I simply couldn't resist the lure of shooting better images. I also had an appetite for culture shocks and a weakness for rearranging my schedule at the last minute. I arrived in the small town of Leh a few days later, but it wasn't at all what I had expected.

The place was a desert, and tracking down the remote monasteries felt as if I was walking to a promised oasis (in the dust) only to find a small glass of water sans ice at the end. I wanted only to strangle the intoxicated informants from Bhutan and then go home. I was bored and disappointed, and then, for no specific reason, my attention turned to donkeys. Why donkeys God only knows, but there they were: thin, malnourished, used and abused during working hours, and then thrown out like garbage to scavenge for their own food before the next day's work started up again.

The donkeys mingled in the traffic, and every time I saw a mother with her foal I just closed my eyes and prayed that I wouldn't see a mangled corpse when I opened them again. I spent every minute feeding the starving animals, and by the time the week was done, there wasn't one carrot left in town!

I spoke to the owner of my hotel, Mr Stany Wangchuk, about the situation, and he explained that people weren't used to caring for donkeys. They simply didn't know any better. He told me about the winters and how the donkeys were left out in the cold in temperatures that dropped to below −30 °C. He described how he would see the donkeys huddle together at the entrances to the shops to catch a bit of warmth as they tried to survive the second-coldest place on earth!

The stray dogs weren't any better off, and it was common for them to attack the foals. I couldn't bear to hear the stories, and I simply had to do something about it.

'What about a sanctuary of sorts?' I asked Stany. 'A place where the donkeys could have the basics and hang out in peace?' Stany thought it could work ...

The town was small enough to make me feel as if I could make a real difference there, especially with the help of my blonde hair. Where Italians just want to sleep with blonde chicks, the Indians just want to listen to us! I knew I could make the locals jump; I just needed an honest local guy to take control and set it all up after I left.

Mr Stany Wangchuk was the man, and he agreed to help out, although I hardly knew him. We had had only a few brief chats at the hotel, but his aura had 'good guy' written all over it. I thought I might be able to turn him into a donkey-saving guru, and I decided to take a chance. I deposited $5000 into his personal bank account and crossed my fingers that I'd be able to find him and the fruits of my deposit the following year. When I returned, I cried like a monsoon.

Stany had done it! He had organised a ten-year lease on a hectare at the top of town. Three large stables that could each house twenty donkeys had been built out of large grey bricks, and close by there was a storeroom packed to the brim with hay. A river with

125

fresh mountain water ran through the property, and a gorgeous field of lucerne grew on the grounds of the 'Sanctuary for Old and Sick Donkeys'.

There were only two things missing: the actual donkeys, and someone to look after them when they arrived! Again, Stany had the answers. The local municipality agreed to lend us some of their employees, and a few days later we were at the dumpsite out in the desert, rounding up donkeys! The donkeys were living off plastic bottles and newspapers; there wasn't anything else on the menu.

We herded the donkeys all the way through town up to the sanctuary. The locals couldn't believe their eyes, and for the first time in the town's history, traffic came to an absolute standstill. Four hours later, sixty-one donkeys were in their new home, many of them tasting greens for the first time in their lives.

For the first time in *my* life, I really felt like I had done something purposeful. I felt like I was making a difference on the planet; nothing else I had done before had ever made me feel so alive. It might not have been as big an ego-boost as wearing a Springbok blazer and playing golf for my country, but it was much more exhilarating. This fitted. It had heart. This long shot had come from the right spot and it was going to last. I had come to the region to find photographs, but had uncovered the real reason I had been plonked on the planet! Purpose and passion weren't things I could buy, and there, surrounded by a herd of happy donkeys, I thanked God, Buddha, Allah and anyone else who wanted to be God, for the revelation.

For some reason I had got distracted on my life's path. I had travelled all over the world for a long time, but not in the direction of my true purpose. Leh had provided me with the tranquillity to listen, the space to create and the platform on which to believe that I could make a difference. In the greater scheme of things, it wasn't even an 'ee-awe' on the radar screen, but to those donkeys, it was nothing short of the Big Bang.

The biggest bang that one has to prepare for when arriving in Leh is the high altitude. At 3 505 metres above sea level, Leh is (in)famous for having the world's highest *everything*: the highest petrol station, the highest motorable pass, the highest golf course and the highest number of tourists that land up with altitude sickness. The air is so thin that flights can arrive and depart only very early in the morning, and failure of visitors to do anything other than *nothing* in the first forty-eight hours after their arrival will result in the coughing up of blood.

Dogs can get altitude sickness as well, and my vet suggested that Oscar take it easy too. Although we were both experienced missionaries by this stage, needing little or no sleep in order to function, Oscar rose to the occasion with plenty of snoring.

Even though Buddha had probably never intended for dogs and donkeys to be best buddies, sharing the sanctuary with Oscar was a dream come true for me. It took but a few visits for Oscar to learn to keep his head well away from the hind legs of a donkey.

Between visiting the donkeys and putting the finishing touches on the finer details of the rest of our journey through Asia, there was also plenty of exploring to do. Oscar and I chugged all the way up to the Khardung Pass and freewheeled down the other side. We passed rainbows of prayer flags that guided us safely around every twist and bend along the primitive gravel road. When we finally got to the bottom, we changed direction and headed towards Nubra Valley, where we landed ourselves right between the two humps of a Bactrian camel!

Balancing on top of a camel was challenging enough, but when the mode of transport also had plenty of gas, it proved to be a very scary and dangerous experience! Without making any excuses, the camel pooped after each and every step. The flies stuck to the results like glue, and my fellow passenger couldn't resist trying to catch every single one of them. Just managing to stay on board was a miracle, but making sure that we didn't accidentally wobble across the border into Pakistan during Oscar's hunting session was an entirely different matter.

Close camel encounters of the dangerous kind aside, Oscar and I also visited the Ladakh Street Dog Sterilisation Project. There are an estimated 7000 stray dogs in Ladakh, and the society sterilises approximately 900 of them over the summer months. Those that weren't under the knife were following us around as rumour spread that the most generous snack donors were in town!

As luck would have it, we were also around for the Hemis Festival – a much-anticipated event that is held every year at the Hemis Monastery, the largest and most beautiful monastery in the entire region. The Buddhists perform theatrical mask dances accompanied by drums, cymbals … and a barking dog from South Africa.

What made this year so special was that the Pad Yatra was taking place. This meant that over a thousand monks were on a 400-kilometre pilgrimage to encourage spiritual practice in daily life by assisting those in need – regardless of their religion, gender or racial group, or whether man, woman, child or animal – and would complete their journey at the festival. We arrived a day before the event, with all the right gear.

This would be Oscar's first go at camping, and my first experience of having three Indian assistants carry and pitch the tent, and also restore it after a claustrophobic outburst of mine in the middle of a pitch-black night – after which I cursed myself for ever having thought that I could handle a night in a tent. I was a girl, after all. Even as a tomboy I hadn't managed to make it through a cookout in the forest with the Boy Scouts. Girls need baths, feather beds and a dog to cuddle!

Oscar and I watched the monks marching into town the next day – an incredible sight. It was as if a long streak of maroon and yellow had been painted across the desert landscape. His Holiness the Gyalwang Drukpa conducted mantra sessions for most of the day and spoke of forgiveness, compassion and loyalty – all the good stuff dogs had invented in the region as long ago as 800 BC: one of the oldest recognised breeds in the world originated from this region, and it bore an uncanny resemblance to Oscar. The Lhasa Apso, as it was called, had been bred to live in the monasteries to warn the monks of any intruders.

His Holiness the Gyalwang Drukpa also talked about facing adversity, seeking detachment and the need to appreciate wonderful situations even in the 'frown of difficulties'. It was déjà vu – I had had just such an experience that very morning. Sleeping in the tent had been a nightmare. To make matters worse, we had pitched it right within hearing distance of a monastery packed with enthusiastic chanters bellowing out 'Om Mani Padme Hum' the entire night. When the sun had finally come up, the chanters had shut down, but it was too late. My head was spinning like a top, I smelt like a camel fart and I was in no mood to accept cold coffee with curdled yak milk!

I went to the bathroom behind a rock on the mountainside while Oscar dashed off into a courtyard below. By the time I'd caught up with my dog, he was well on his way to singlehandedly whipping a dozen young monks at football. As the game unfolded, laughing and giggling filled the dusty 'stadium'. I watched from an old stone wall that had become my seat for the match. How lucky was I? I thought. Here I am, halfway around the world, watching my best friend, Muttchester United, winning a game against an Arsenal of Buddhist children.

It was a priceless, random, spontaneous and precious moment that I could never have planned in a million years, and it was something I knew would warm my heart forever.

I was the luckiest person alive, even with no sleep, deodorant or double espresso!

17

The Taj Mahowl

By the time we left Leh, every yak had received a yap from my dog. With not one cat in sight to torment and donkeys more interested in kicking a canine than running away from one, Oscar had decided that yaks would be his source of entertainment, especially when approached from the inside of a safely locked car!

Back in Delhi there was no sign of a vintage Jag waiting outside the station terminal for us. Our days at the Imperial Hotel were well and truly over. It was time to get straight back on the campaign tail, and we had arranged to meet up with Mrs Vandana Sengupta, founder of the Sonadi Charitable Trust.

Mrs Sengupta had invited us to meet her at her home in New Delhi before we headed off to the shelter. For the previous twenty years, she had dedicated all her efforts towards rescuing and reha-bilitating sick, abandoned and injured dogs. It was an honour to meet her. Mrs Sengupta welcomed us and showed us around. Aside from noticing the old picture of the Mahatma hanging on the wall, it was impossible to miss all the dogs.

Every nook and cranny of her humble home was occupied, from

carpet to ceiling, by dogs! They were in the entrance hall, the passageway, under her bed in the bedroom; even the shower had been curtained off to contain new arrivals. I counted forty-one dogs, but officially there were sixty-seven! Mrs Sen, as she is fondly known, offered us some chai tea, which I accepted but used to water one of her indoor pot plants when she wasn't looking.

Mrs Sen was almost seventy, but didn't look a day older than sixty. She embodied the teachings of Gandhi, which were reflected in her gentle nature and peaceful spirit. She quietly sat on the edge of her grand old couch, while beside her on the floor sat 'M', her faithful, physically disabled dog who had been left with her after being struck by a car the year before.

Mrs Sen's life unfolded before me as she shared with me the highs and lows of her work. She rejoiced that, at her age, she had the challenging work, as it inspired her and gave her the strength to carry on. She strongly believed that it was our 'duty' as human beings to engage in social service, especially to help those less fortunate than ourselves, and those who cannot speak for or defend themselves. Her words reminded me of Gandhi's: 'The greatness of a nation and its moral progress can be judged by the way its animals are treated.' Given half a chance, Mrs Sen could have saved the world before lunch time. Without a doubt, she is the closest I shall ever come to meeting a real-life Mother Teresa.

After our chat, we headed over to the Sonadi Charitable Trust, one of eight shelters located in the country's capital. Established by Mrs Sen and a Dr Vijay Kumar Yadav seven years earlier, nothing could have prepared me for the depressing scenes I was about to witness. There, at the end of a quiet cul-de-sac, stood a three-storey building that looked like any other rundown apartment block in town.

Inside, a horror story unfolded before my eyes. The rooms were dark and dingy, and the constant barking of over 750 dogs echoed through the building. A heavy steel gate, each one bearing a large rusted lock, separated the floors, and each level housed countless dogs. On the first floor, dogs were being sterilised. Those recovering from the anaesthetic were also kept there.

The second floor held the 400-plus dogs that were waiting to be snipped. These dogs were a part of the shelter's trap, neuter and release (TNR) programme. The remaining 300 'live-in' dogs lived together on the third floor. These dogs were waiting to be adopted, but with an adoption rate of fewer than two a month, most would remain on the third floor for their entire lives. The aggressive dogs were chained to the filthy walls; others were cramped in small cages. The remaining dogs roamed 'freely' within the concrete 'garden'.

There were two small balconies on either side of the room that were the only areas where the dogs could experience the outdoors. A dozen large water dishes were scattered across the floor, and though some of them contained water, others had been knocked over in the chaos generated by the distressed animals. There was urine everywhere, and the smell of faeces conspired with the choking heat to create a stench that was almost unbearable.

Most of the dogs were thin, and many of them were sick. Some had mange. One young dog had rickets, a disease often caused by a lack of sunlight and bad diet. It was shaking uncontrollably – I saw it trying to walk, but it kept falling on its side. The dog's nails were so long that they had grown over the edges of his paws. It was one of the saddest scenes I'd ever seen.

But Mrs Sen wouldn't put any of the dogs to sleep, no matter how sick or traumatised they were. As a Hindu, she believes that euthanasia would cause the soul and body to separate at an unnatural moment, and that this would damage the dog's karma as it entered its next life. Furthermore, the very act of euthanasia breached the teaching of *ahimsa* (doing no harm), so no one at the shelter wanted to take on the responsibility him- or herself either.

I later learnt that there are definite exceptions to these religious 'rules', and that many Hindus and Buddhists actually believe that helping to end a painful life is performing a good deed and fulfilling a moral obligation. The whole issue was a sensitive matter, and I never discussed it with Mrs Sen. I didn't believe it was appropriate under the circumstances. She and her minimal staff of three were trying to do their best with very limited resources.

The term 'euthanasia' is derived from an ancient Greek word meaning 'good death'. In the situation I saw before me, I couldn't help but wonder whether a 'good death' was not perhaps better than a really bad life. If the salvation of these animals lay in my hands, what would I do? Would I act in accordance with the words of the Dalai Lama, who acknowledges that, while all life is precious, mercy killing should be permissible in certain exceptional circumstances? The third floor was an exceptional circumstance. If Oscar were one of the dogs circuiting on that slab of cement for the rest of his life, there is not a doubt in my mind that he would beg for deliverance – and as piercingly painful as it would be, I would provide him with it, even if it came from a syringe.

After spending two days with Mrs Sen, Oscar and I decided to lift our spirits in the magnificent ambience of the Taj Mahal. Besides, a visit to India just wouldn't be complete without lifting a leg on one of the most famous landmarks in the world. The three-hour journey from Delhi to Agra became a fascinating escape into Indian culture. There are over 2000 ethnic groups in the country, and the result is a rich concoction of diverse flavour, colour and religion, all under one massive 'roof'.

There was more than enough aromatic action to send Oscar's nose into overdrive. We occasionally had to pause when a holy cow was playing traffic cop in the middle of the road; a pit stop any other time was granted only when Oz needed to quench his thirst or satisfy a stomach grumble. For most of the trip, he had been eating a combination of Pedigree and free-range chicken. When neither was available, it was a matter of sniffing through the local menu, which wasn't always successful, given that Oscar had the world's fussiest palate!

Of course I'd been a bit concerned about what my dog would eat in India. I seriously doubted whether a main course of curry and rice and a *gulab jamun* for dessert would twist Oscar's paw, but, to my disbelief, it did. From the minute we landed in the Himalayas, it was *dal roti* for breakfast, *dal roti* for dinner and *dal roti* for dessert. Not even celebrity chef Sanjeev Kapoor could have enticed Oscar from his newfound craving with anything else!

I couldn't recall much of my previous visit to the Taj Mahal except for fertilising the Mughal gardens with a litre of regurgitated curry. This time, however, my focus would be on getting my dog into the world's most guarded landmark. I approached the dozen or so guards at the main (and only) entrance, where every visitor was screened and hand-searched, with no bags allowed inside. It was impossible to sneak Oscar into my pocket, hide him in a bag or, unless I wanted to kill my canine, throw him over the imposing walls that surrounded the white marble masterpiece.

After a solid round of begging the guards to *please* let us in, all to no avail, we admitted defeat. There was, however, Plan B. The Mughal Empire must have envisioned that a dog would one day want to visit the mausoleum and that he would face enormous discrimination, because the architects had designed the masterpiece to look identical from both ends. We drove to the other side and launched the definitive (photographic) attack from the banks of the dried-up Yamuna River. As I put my arms around Oscar, we watched as the architectural jewel turned from a hazy shade of white to a vibrant gold in the setting sun.

The Mughal emperor Shah Jahan built the Taj Mahal as testimony of his love for his third and favourite wife, Mumtaz Mahal, after she died giving birth to the emperor's fourteenth child. Theirs is an enduring love story (and a lesson in population control for all the ages) that hadn't been experienced again by anyone until I adopted Oscar.

'Don't worry, Oscar,' I whispered quietly. 'I can promise you that if I had been as rich as Shah Jahan, I would have built a Taj "Mahowl" as a symbol of my love for you.'

If the Taj inspires a million photographs, India's train stations do not. We had to catch an overnight train from Agra to Varanasi. There are 63 000 kilometres of railway tracks in India, and we thanked Shiva that we needed to ride only 577 of them! This wasn't exactly the midnight train to Georgia or the *Royal Orient Express*. It wasn't Russian rail on vodka either. This was the choo-choo chugging to the Ganges River, and it was quite unlike anything we could have imagined on two tracks.

It's true – India does have some of the most spectacular and unforgettable rail journeys in the world. Spectacular because, when the conductor shouts 'all aboard', the entire Indian population comes running; and unforgettable because you'll need to remember what you wish you could forget so that you'll never make the same mistake again!

First class was sold out, but we had second-class tickets in our paws. We weren't complaining, as at least we didn't have to sit on top of the train – or take a bus, for that matter. And at 1 000 rupees a ticket, they were a bargain. The tickets guaranteed us our own seat that we wouldn't have to share with anyone *and* that transformed into a bunk-bed when the time came to lie down. They also gave us unlimited access to the on-board entertainment, which included a mixed bag of vendors who passed by selling anything from quiz books to bananas to personalised shoe-polishing services.

And we had unlimited access to the toilet, which any tourist would attempt only as a last resort if their window wouldn't open. Each berth was curtained off for privacy, which allowed me to keep Oscar hidden all the way to Varanasi.

The stations were just as exciting as the on-board bazaars: complete and utter pandemonium, with plenty of curry in between. By this stage, I had managed to track down a cameraman from a Delhi TV station. Inaam had never travelled beyond his birthplace and was absolutely thrilled to be part of the expedition through Asia. I liked him. He was humble and professional, not to mention wise enough to expand his CV to include professional luggage-locator and transporter at my simple request.

In fact, everyone in India claims to be a qualified porter, even when faced with the impossible task of balancing a box twice their size on top of their head! Aside from the usual load, we had two new additions to our luggage – a pair of boxes, each one the size of a single mattress, stuffed with Rogz collars and leads that had been flown from South Africa courtesy of UPS. These would be our tidings of joy for the underdogs we would be hooking up with through Asia.

As for whether or not a dog qualified as a piece of luggage, not even the authorities at the station knew the answer to that question! The only information they could give me was that caged chickens were permitted in the separate luggage section. I decided not to panic. For starters, I was bigger than most of the Indians I'd come across, so I'd probably be able to take out a difficult conductor in a physical confrontation. Secondly, we were travelling in Gandhi's territory; he was the 'Father of India' and everyone's hero and had, in his day, been thrown off numerous trains for being a different colour from white South Africans. These experiences had awakened him to the social injustices of his time and influenced his successful, non-violent campaign to uplift his people.

Just like Gandhi, Oscar wasn't looking for trouble on a train. He just wanted a little peace and harmony in which to move around, regardless of the colour of his hair or the size of his ears. We had all the historic ammunition if we needed it; all we had to do was to climb on board before the whistle blew!

With twenty minutes to spare before the train departed, I ran ahead with Oscar, leaving Inaam with a few hundred rupees to oversee six happy porters loading the luggage onto the train. But as the train started to move, I couldn't find Inaam or the luggage anywhere. I looked out the window and there he was, desperately trying to load the last of the two 'mattresses'. I lost sight of him as the train moved forward, and figured I had lost both my cameraman and the box. I could find another cameraman, but the Rogz gear? That was irreplaceable.

I'd seen only one dog lead in India thus far: it had been hanging on the wall at a dog-grooming parlour when I'd taken Oscar for a haircut a few days earlier. We had just arrived in Delhi from Leh and had had the morning off before our meeting with Mrs Sen. The heat was getting to Oscar, and his constant panting was driving us both crazy. I'd tracked down the only dog-grooming facility in Delhi, where we'd waited for over an hour for the chief groomer to arrive. That's when I'd noticed the lead on the wall.

When the 'barber' finally arrived, I covered Oscar's coat with my hands. The barber's shears were so large, they made Edward Scissor-hands's fingers look like nail clippers.

'Madam, please don't worry. Don't worry, madam, I been grooming dogs for forty years. Yes, forty years!' I wasn't sure whether that was a good or a bad thing in India. I hadn't yet seen a dog with a collar, so how many dogs had ever seen a groomer? Not many, I imagined, but we had no choice in the matter. Oscar had too much hair in too much heat; it was time to surrender to the blunt blades!

Three hours later, my dog had undergone a fine-tuning in hair removal, and even though his coat looked like a lawn that had been cut by a drunk mower, there was nothing I could do but pay up: it would take a lot more than a bad haircut to ruin my dog's image. Without a question, he was the champion in attracting attention on the streets of India, and the only pooch that owned a lead! With all his fancy fashion statements he was a doggie in style like no other they had ever seen. For many Indians, it was probably the first time in their lives that they had seen a dog lead, and collars were as rare as a dog catching a ride in a Jaguar SS.

Oscar didn't like leads, and I never had to have him on one unless we were in India or in an airport terminal where the security guards were in a panic because a pooch was on the loose. Oscar always stood by me, followed me and obeyed my traffic signals. I hadn't trained him to be the perfect pedestrian, but we had spent a lot of time together on our travels and he had figured out the right road-side manner himself. When we arrived in India, safety precautions became incredibly important. I didn't want Oscar to wind up being the most travelled *dead* dog in history.

Back to the train. My cameraman did make it on board, but the 'mattress' didn't. I could hardly fire Inaam after only one day of looking after the luggage; after all, I hadn't lifted a finger to help move anything except my dog. We took a friendly bet on what would happen to the box. We agreed that the 'lost' collars wouldn't be going to the dogs in Agra.

But if not to the dogs, where? We both started to giggle, and by the time we had concluded our bet we were both rolling around on the floor in fits of laughter. Chances were that the porters of the Agra Cantonment Railway Station were about to get a free make-over, courtesy of the World Woof Tour and Rogz, manufacturers of the coolest 'necklaces' on the planet!

18

The howling Ganges

There are roughly twenty-five million stray dogs in India, and every single one of them wanted a bite of Oscar. They instinctively knew that he wasn't one of them, but rather a rare breed of the 'spoilt-rotten' kind passing through their domain. I reckon they were just jealous. Why should this furry foreigner be so lucky when they were forced to scavenge for food and then check it for poison when they finally found some? Whatever the reason, we had to be careful that my hound's chops didn't become a steak. Out of the thousands of dogs we passed in India, only one got 'lucky'.

Our infamous train from Agra spat us out in the ancient city of Varanasi, and after checking into the hotel, we caught a rickshaw to the banks of the Ganges River. For just a split second between getting off the bike and admiring the famous view, a stray dog ran up and nipped Oz on his back leg. It was more of a love bite than a hunger strike, but it still upset him. Oscar wasn't a pugilist; he was a freedom fighter for dog adoption.

Oscar's tail retreated to underneath his belly for the rest of the day – after a full day of it, it was almost touching his nose on the other side! I wasn't safe from the canine combatants either – or so I was warned. According to the World Health Organization, about 35 000 people die of rabies in India each year. That accounts for about 81 per cent of the global total. A single bite from a dog can ignite a cull of hundreds of thousands of stray dogs by the municipality and, while the government does provide rabies clinics as well as sterilisation initiatives to reduce the problem, shooting or poisoning the strays is still 'cheaper'.

My doctor in South Africa had suggested taking along an anti-rabies vaccine, but I had declined the offer. Needles weren't my favourite things; dogs were. Getting my finger pricked for a choles-terol test was enough to set off a tantrum of enormous proportions. Needle phobia was also one of the reasons I'd lasted only two weeks in vet school at Texas A&M University. That, and being allergic to studying, I guess.

Luck favours the stubborn, so I'd decided to take my chances. It was a good decision: I never once felt threatened by a stray dog while I was in India. They were smart animals, and, if they occa-sionally bit someone, they were probably just trying to defend themselves against an aggressive human.

From the moment we arrived at the 'River of India', we knew we were in for a cultural treat. This was a landmark of religious and cultural proportions like no other in the country, and we immersed ourselves in it, soaking in the smiles of the local women dressed in their bright saris, the colours of which would have made Joseph green with envy. Over six kilometres of terraced bathing *ghats* leading down to the water stretched out before us and, despite having to hold our breath due to the rather pungent aromas wafting through the atmosphere, it was a visual delight to behold.

The Ganges is a sacred place of pilgrimage for Hindus; bodies are brought here from all over to be cremated in 'Mother Ganges' or the deceased's ashes are scattered on the water. The Hindus believe that by being cremated in this holy river, their soul's journey, or *moksha*, will be accelerated through all the life cycles. Some 50 000 cremations a year take place here.

It was impossible not to notice the commotion at Manikarnika *ghat*, one of the oldest and most sacred of the *ghats*. When it came to cremation, this was the 'it' place. We watched in awe as the bodies of the dead, swathed in cloth, were carried from the old city on bamboo stretchers. Each corpse was then doused in Ganges 'juice' and lifted on top of a huge pile of firewood stacked along the top of the *ghat*. The logs were each carefully weighed on giant scales so that the price of cremation could be calculated. Even when it came to reducing yourself to nothing, it sure didn't come at a clearance price! Oscar and I watched, agog, as the human form disintegrated into a smouldering heap of ash.

The Ganges may be a holy river to the Hindus, but to others she's a holy mess. For a South African chick with a touring dog, it was like being on location for the final episode of *Survivor*. Dodging the dead was one issue; running from the rickshaws, tuk-tuks and stray dogs was another matter entirely. Getting through both was a miracle. And the thought of cooling off in the brown stew of dirty socks, homeless underpants and stray boats, stirred with a freelance porta-potty for added flavour, was unthinkable, unbearable and undesirable – unless you were dead, a local … or Oscar!

Having escaped speeding feluccas on the Nile, crocs in the Zambezi River and police at the Trevi Fountain, Oscar figured that a drowned cow or any other missiles of mass flotation could do little to him. He dived into the Ganges clean and jumped out dirty, drenched from head to paw in gourmet gunk, enriched with E. coli 'preservatives' that would no doubt keep him polluted for the rest of the day. He smelt like a rotten samoosa. He was untouchable. There wasn't one dog groomer in town who could clean up the mess, nor was there a veterinarian to pick up the pieces if his tail should fall off.

To get rid of Oscar's odour, we decided to charter a boat from an old Hindu man, whom we fondly named Bubba. Bubba had been trying to convince us to hire a boat from him since we'd landed on his shoreline. So off we went to explore the sewerage tank that is the river. Cruising along the Ganges isn't quite like sailing the Seven Seas on the *Queen Mary*. This is adventure without an inch of luxury; similar to riding a reckless roller coaster in a chlorine-free water park.

We sailed out dry, soaked in the view, drank in the atmosphere and eventually docked on dry land smelling like *two* rotten samoosas. The locals were amused by our ordeal and welcomed us back to shore as if we'd just won the Volvo Ocean Race. Throughout the tour, the locals in almost every country had referred to Oscar as 'Nice dog, nice dog'. In India, he was 'Great dog, great dog, *Jai ho!*' – even when he looked like a drowned rat!

When Oscar and I arrived back at the hotel, we dived straight into a hot shower, followed by an extended soak in the bath. Two whole bars of soap and a lot of scrubbing and brushing in crevices never before explored later, we were once again smelling like savoury, seasoned travellers. Before turning off the bedroom lights, I made a final full-body inspection of both of us. Everything still seemed to be in the right department: we had survived the gruesome Ganges. It was time to give my nose a rest and call it a night.

To save Oscar another flight 'underground', we had decided to travel from India to Nepal overland. Leaving the Ganges behind us, we headed due east towards Kathmandu. The 350-kilometre journey would take almost a day to traverse in our private vehicle, and we had included a few interesting stops along the way to keep Oscar's curiosity piqued. Crossing the Nepalese border was a piece of cake for my canine. We had all the correct paperwork, should we have been asked for it, but the authorities were interested only in making sure they were paid 'commission' when I exchanged my Indian rupees and US dollars for Nepalese rupees.

We spent the night in Lumbini, and, after paying our respects to Buddha's birthplace the following morning, we headed for a protected area of the subtropical Inner Terai lowlands of south-central Nepal, otherwise known as Chitwan National Park. Puru Timalsena, a good friend of mine from a previous visit and the owner of Nepal Guide Trek, had arranged our itinerary in the land of 'Mutt' Everest gratis.

More impressive was that Puru's is the only trekking company that donates its time and gives money back to the community on a regular basis. Being such a humanitarian, Puru was delighted to branch out and support a canine's mission. And he was keen to see if Oscar could handle a safari atop an elephant!

Dogs were apparently not permitted inside the national park, but Puru was convinced that the elephants wouldn't blow our cover – as long as we gave them an extra bunch of bananas after the trek. Our 5 000-kilogram means of transport arrived to collect us from a boarding tower a few metres from the entrance to the park. The elephant was a lot bigger than I had imagined it would be.

The Asian elephant is the largest living land animal in Asia, and only slightly smaller than its African relatives. We had tried to get permission to ride an elephant in Kenya, but our request had been declined. African elephants are known to be both aggressive and unpredictable, especially when exposed to acts of random craziness, and no one wanted to be in the way when a panting pooch landed on *Elephantus maximus* for the very first time!

Our tracker in India introduced himself as Bishnu, and he gently nudged our elephant to the platform. Oscar and I got into the basket secured just behind the elephant's earlobe, and soon dog, woman, guide and Jumbo were cruising through the local village in the direction of the park. Bishnu was sure he could get permission for Oscar to enter the park, but we weren't going to risk a rejection. We had changed our tactics since our defeat at the Parthenon, and our new approach had worked perfectly ever since. It was simple: Don't ask, just do.

If we found ourselves staring down the barrel of a gun, the strategy was for me to act like a real blonde, and preferably to do so as quickly as possible! True to fine form, we snuck the panting basket past the game wardens without a glitch. At this stage of the escapade, canine and elephantus were still trying to figure out who was what and what was who. It didn't take long before we were viewing wildlife in the heart of Nepal's very first national park.

My canine might have been the king of Kenya, but I knew it would be impossible for him to depose the king of *this* jungle. Shy and cautious, the Bengal tiger would never be found napping in our path when an elephant with a yapping hat was headed in its direction.

We were content to settle for a throne's-eye view, especially when we spotted one of the most unusual-looking animals on the planet: within ten minutes of entering the park, we were thrilled to see a Great One-horned Rhinoceros wading in a small watering hole inside the dense forest. Observing this prehistoric-looking creature was a very rare privilege indeed. Oscar thought it was Christmas. The Big Five had been a treat in Africa, but this was Jurassic Park – back to the future!

Better yet, Oscar's elephant was beginning to realise that one of the objects on his back wasn't 'barking' like a regular passenger. Suddenly, Jumbo sounded his horn and every organism in the park assumed the brace position. As long as the basket stayed stuck on Jumbo's back, so would we, but we were being stomped round and round like a rodeo moving in slow motion, destroying every tree and plant in our wake.

By the time the game wardens finally arrived, the garden service was complete. We were herded back to the entrance, where we dismounted and were charged with illegal deforestation and traumatising an elephant. Of course that was the last thing we'd wished to bestow on such a graceful fellow, so we paid our dues with a dozen bananas and, by the time we arrived in Kathmandu later that same day, peace, wildlife and regular tourists had returned to the park.

When I woke up the following morning, I found that there was something very wrong with Oscar's tummy, which was covered in a red rash. My poor dog was scratching it uncontrollably. Despite late nights, flights, flea mites, H1N1 scares, tick-bite fever fears and rabies on the loose everywhere, neither Oscar nor I had been sick once since the beginning of the tour. But, I wondered, could one dog's resistance withstand the contents of one of the world's most polluted rivers?

Looking at the rash, I was convinced that Oscar had picked up a bug in the Ganges. Now, at least, we were in the proximity of a veterinarian, and it was good timing too. We had to see him anyway for the import certificate to Thailand, so we just moved the appointment forward. The vet took one look at my dog and immediately asked me if we'd been to Chitwan National Park. He knew his stuff – what a relief. I nodded.

Oscar had picked up a common strain of parasitic mite endemic to the region, called Demodex. The condition is treatable with medicated cream, and as long as we promised to steer clear of any more Jumbos in the national park, Oscar would be in good shape after a few days.

While I was planning the tour, I had received unwavering support from each one of the hundred organisations I'd contacted, except two. Both of these were shelters in Kathmandu. They had, in no uncertain terms, expressed their disgust in my wanting to 'drag an innocent dog on an exhausting world tour' where he would have to 'endure travel in the hold of an aircraft'. They called for everyone to boycott the project and asked that Miss Lefson be locked up for life!

I didn't waste too much time with the tissues. I knew these organisations didn't fully comprehend the methodology of the tour. But the proof was in the pudding: Nepal was our twentieth country in eighty days, and in that time Oscar had been in the hold on only four commercial flights for an average of three hours per flight. That meant that for every hour he'd spent in the hold, he had been right by my side for 160!

Most homed dogs on the planet typically find themselves home alone each and every day for at least twelve hours – the total time of Oscar's holding space – waiting for their owner to return home from making a living. I bet that there isn't one dog in the whole universe who wouldn't have dug to be Oscar!

The only organisation that would receive us in Nepal's capital was the Kathmandu Animal Treatment Centre (KAT), and they did so with paws wide open. Jan Salter and her dog Mango greeted us with a roar of excitement and contagious enthusiasm. Despite being born and raised in Britain, Jan has done more for dogs in Nepal than prayer flags have done for peace.

Jan founded the society back in 1994, when she decided to do something about the estimated 55 000 stray dogs in the Kathmandu region. These dogs were in shocking condition: they were starving, weak and afflicted with every skin problem and disease imaginable. Today Jan and her thirteen staff at KAT work in conjunction with the same governmental authorities that used to poison street dogs in the city, and they have implemented one of the most effective spay-and-neuter campaigns in history.

For Oscar it was a treat to meet Mango, KAT's mascot, who had some very good looks of his own. Mango had been picked up by Jan when she was in the process of building her centre. She had been waiting for a bus when an almost unrecognisable creature had stumbled past the queue. But for a few strands of hair, it was bald, scrawny and covered in the most revolting, oozing sores.

Much to the horror of everyone watching, Jan had bent over, picked up the creature and taken it back to the centre with her. The staff had discussed euthanasia for the poor animal, but they had decided to give the dog a chance to see if it would make it.

Mango, as the dog was then named, never looked back. The ugly duckling grew up to become a raging beauty and the big boss in the office. He's the heart of what Jan and her society stand for, and, as we had witnessed in many of the shelters we'd already visited, he is living proof of what can be achieved with compassion and determination.

Oscar wanted to visit the Monkey Temple before leaving for Thailand the next morning, and, after a short taxi ride from KAT, we arrived at this ancient landmark, Swayambhunath. We climbed up the 365 stairs and ended up right in front of the religious shrine. Oz headed off to chase every single monkey in the complex, in the process spinning prayer wheels and dispersing prayer flags, prayer candles, stray dogs, pigeons and anything else that got in his way. I went to sit below the impressive *stupa* with its two giant painted Buddha eyes and lollipop nose.

I thought about Mango and the other dogs I had met at KAT: Lucy, Gaida, Beauty, Sherab and Taxi. And I gave deep thanks for 'top dogs' like Jan Salter. While the Buddhists' symbol of wisdom and compassion kept a static eye on the valley below, Jan was right in the heart of their philosophy, reaching out to the thousands of dogs that were trying to survive within its sight.

19

Raiders of the Lost Bark

While Oscar was busy monkeying around at Swayambhunath, I had decided at the last minute to send our taxi driver to take the vet's certificate to the state veterinarian so that he could issue the official import permit into Thailand. This was a process that every country required and one we had followed – for the *most* part – since our departure. No one had inspected our paperwork since leaving Europe, however, and I was seriously considering whether all the effort was worth it. Gambling isn't my game, but eternal optimism is. As long as I had Oscar's vaccination records in hand, I was convinced that I could talk my way around anything.

But when we arrived in Bangkok, I thanked Pluto for Oscar's great obsession with monkeys. The animal quarantine section in Suvarnabhumi Airport was top-notch – the best we'd yet seen – and they meant business! Even the porters knew where the 'live animal' had to be cleared before we could leave the arrivals hall. It took over an hour and 1 000 baht to do that, but I considered it a bargain. If the taxi driver back in Kathmandu hadn't located the state vet, we would have been on the next flight back to the Monkey Temple.

Bangkok is a cultural phenomenon, a shopping heaven and a tourist treasure. But for my mutt it was a nightmare; a cosmopolitan and contrasting metropolis that hadn't considered any of its 120000 stray dogs when it was designed. Bangkok was a steamy, pulsating concrete jungle without any real jungle where one could sit down and read the paper or have a good, healthy dump!

Of course there were a few parks in the city, but even though we managed to find a small one tucked away a few blocks from our hotel in Sukhumvit, staff informed us that dogs weren't allowed in it. We were desperate; Bangkok was to be our base for the next few days, and I couldn't keep Oz indoors all that time. Picking up sloshed poop on concrete is like trying to retrieve spilt ice cream on a hot afternoon – impossible!

Contravening the law, Oscar and I ventured into the tiny park, hoping that no one would notice us. Like clumsy burglars on a quiet night, however, we were soon spotted, and the subsequent scolding roused the entire neighbourhood. When the police arrived at the canine scene a few minutes later, I had had enough.

'Just fine me!' I demanded. 'We're *not* moving, unless you can come up with a better solution!'

To our disbelief, they left us alone. Oscar carried on watering the plants for the rest of the morning, and we weren't fined or growled at again.

Our time in Bangkok would consist of visiting the organisation SCAD. At SCAD, we would be in the company of Miss Universe 2005, Natalie Glebova, at a dog-adoption event. Oscar wasn't afraid of the competition when it came to good looks, but I had for some time believed my pooch to be gay: he never took any notice of the girls, and he didn't take much notice of Natalie either, despite her beauty. He had only ever tried to hump one dog, the male mutt Diego at the Windhoek SPCA, as well as a few pot plants outside my front door. To lend further credence to my suspicions, Oscar wasn't the least bit interested in sticking his nose into any of the neon-lit strip bars or risqué sex shows in Bangkok later that evening.

Patpong is one of the world's most famous red-light districts, but all Oscar wanted was room service, *Scooby-Doo* on the telly and a souvenir ping-pong ball in case I decided to go out. To most men, Patpong means 'adult shows', but for a woman with no wardrobe to speak of and an empty suitcase, it means a cheap date with Ed Hardy and Louis Vuitton. I arrived back at the hotel a transformed (fake) fashion plate for the first time since leaving the African continent.

With the Thai capital as our base, we could travel to Phuket, Koh Samui, Cambodia and Malaysia. First on our itinerary was Siem Reap, the magnificent ancient capital of the Khmer empire. The thought of going to Cambodia was an exciting prospect. I had watched my fair share of Indiana Jones movies, and my ego prided itself on being a gung-ho adventurer and explorer.

Of course I was really just a wimpy pumpkin in disguise. But as long as I didn't come face to face with any snakes, worms, spiders or ants, I was ready to raid every tomb to unleash and instil hope in the hearts of the homeless in Cambodia.

That being my mission, I had certainly landed in the right place. The country of Cambodia is synonymous with war and genocide. It has one of the highest occurrences of death by landmines in the world, and diseases such as HIV/AIDS run rampant in this impoverished nation. Half of the population is under the age of eighteen, and an estimated 100 000 of these children are orphans.

Not surprisingly, there isn't one animal welfare organisation in Cambodia, but there are nineteen listed orphanages. We had arranged to visit two: PACDOC Orphanage and Sunrise Angkor

Village. I had never been to an orphanage before, but Oscar and I were well prepared. We had already visited twenty-six shelters as part of our World Woof Tour, and there wasn't much difference between one and the other. Both animal shelters and orphanages housed beings that were crying out for a quality of life above and beyond that which destiny had thus far provided them.

The Sunrise Angkor orphanage was situated right next to Tonle Sap Lake and directly below the monsoon. We arrived on schedule and were met by a security guard, who was expecting us. Child trafficking is a serious problem in this country, and every visitor is screened before being allowed to visit the children. Mr Robert Madsen, the man in charge, showed us around the facility, which was set up by the famous Australian Geraldine Cox.

A large grassed courtyard spread out before the old but charac-ter-filled buildings, dating back to the days when the country was still a protectorate of France. Sixty children call Sunrise Angkor their home, and everyone we met was friendly, gracious and ador-able. I could see their curious, smiling faces peeking around doors, watching us closely. Perhaps they were wondering whether the blonde girl with the funny dog had brought one of them a ticket to ride to the other side …

As we walked past a window, Madsen pointed to one of the small boys in the room, who couldn't have been more than ten years old. 'Phirun was brought to us by his desperately poor mother six years ago – along with two older brothers, who were deaf,' he said. 'Their mother's only means of support was to do construction work whenever she could, where she earned as little as sixty cents a day. It was very difficult to explain to Phirun's mother that it was not possible for Sunrise to take in the older brothers, as we have no facilities or trained staff to care for deaf children. Cambodia is a harsh country for those with disabilities. Phirun settled in after a few very difficult nights, when he would yell the place down at bedtime, but now he is well and truly part of the family.'

We walked to the next window, and Madsen pointed out another boy, who was sitting at one of the wooden tables at the far end of the room. 'That boy and his brother were abandoned on a rubbish dump in Takhmao town by their father, who had become very ill and was unable to cope after his wife left him. The look on their faces when they saw the amount of food that was on the table at their first meal was a sight to see!'

The hardest part of Mr Madsen's job is to verify these heart-breaking stories and to try to fathom how parents can do such unimaginable things in the first place. But, as he pointed out, these are everyday occurrences in Cambodia, and at least Sunrise was a new beginning for each child in its care.

If Sunrise was their new day, Oscar and I were going to be their playground. Today, *Cambodia's Got Talent* had come to town, and it was time to paint Oscar red! These kids would have the chance to immortalise the travelling woof-berry from Cape Town, South Africa, on a piece of white paper with brand-spanking-new crayons. As they got stuck in to their works of art with the most colourful enthusiasm, I began to tell them all about Oscar's journey from down and out to up and running. This wasn't your typical adoption story, nor was it going to be an art class that anyone would have to pass. It would be a simple tale about an unlikely character called Oscar – and one that wasn't much different from their own stories.

As I spoke, Madsen translated my words. I told the children that Oscar had never known his parents. Through no fault of his own, he was abandoned, left helpless, hungry and disillusioned, and many times he wished that he had never been born at all. Then, just when he thought he could not carry on any more, a stroke of good luck carried him into a new world. Call him a dog of destiny, but it took just that one perfect moment in the universe for Oscar's dismal life to change for the better.

As I told Oscar's story, the children started to realise that they had more in common with the bushy-eyed mutt from Africa than just the scribbles in front of them. As the rain continued to pour down and the children's crayons wore thin, I continued: 'It doesn't matter who your parents were or whether you even knew them at all. It doesn't matter what the colour of your hair, the length of your tail, the size of your paws, or the name of your God is. It doesn't matter if you're goofy, nutty, loopy, dopey or the next 'Mutt-isse'; it doesn't even matter what species you belong to.

'Right now, all that matters is that you're here, and you're alive. And that you believe that you are a miracle just waiting to happen. With a neat twist of fate, you, too, could wind up making a wish in the Trevi Fountain. You, too, could launch yourself into space like Laika and be the first to pitch a tent on top of Pluto. Or you could climb the seven summits and sail the Seven Seas, or choose never to once roam away from your home, Angkor Woof.'

The children giggled. 'You could become the King of Cambodia and pave the way for peace in your wonderful country, or perhaps start a school for disadvantaged children. Better still, you could just adopt a street dog right here in Siem Reap and live happily ever after.'

A rainbow of joy lit up every corner of the room as the children giggled in glee. There was just one last penny in the pot of gold to deliver before Oscar and I would have to continue on the road less travelled. 'If a previously disadvantaged dog like mine can make lions retreat, Italians weep and snow on the Himalayas melt, my goodness gracious me, just imagine what "fairy tails" await each and every one of you!'

A crowd of hands waved us goodbye, and as our mechanically

challenged tuk-tuk pulled away from the kerb, an explosion of mud and dirt erupted in all directions. Everyone was immediately drenched, but nothing could have spoilt what had otherwise been a perfect afternoon. I was again overwhelmed by the quality and depth of my experiences at both the Sunrise Angkor and PACDOC orphanages. I felt alive and invigorated; it was the kind of uplifting feeling that you can't buy in a hundred visits to Patpong, and that you can't manufacture or perfect in a hundred visits to a plastic surgeon.

Oscar and I didn't need a winning lotto ticket or Brad Pitt's hand in marriage to feel like we did. All we needed was the presence of a hundred orphans in a small Cambodian town to feel as if we'd seen five loaves and two fishes transform into a lifetime's supply of food for the soul. A miracle can be so simple, I thought. It can arrive in the smallest smile of a homeless child, if we just take the time to notice it. *Every* life is precious, and we should value, nurture and appreciate each one. We should create opportunities that inspire others to emulate us.

I wrote my thoughts on my heart and vowed to reflect on their significance every day.

During the course of playing 'jungle gym' the following day through the Angkor ruins and jumping over the infamous Angkor Thom tree, whose python-like roots suffocate every corner and crevice of the grandest temple, the children I had met in the orphanages continued to occupy my mind. Although I had adopted numerous dogs in my time, I had never considered adopting a child. If I were to consider such a scenario seriously, I didn't think it would take long before Oscar would wind up with a human brother or sister.

Certainly, if I took into account the state of my sex life, I'd have more chance of having puppies with my pooch than conceiving a child with a Swiss golf pro. But seriously, I thought, if Oscar's story was so similar to the children's, why would the case for human adoption be any different? I knew that breeding more dogs on this planet was ridiculous when there were such fantastic shelter dogs desperate for a home. And with an estimated 143 million orphaned children on earth, it seemed only logical to conclude that they were in a similar predicament to the unwanted dogs.

Then my mind ran wild. The human population stood at 6.818 billion, a number that was placing enormous pressure on the earth's resources. Was the case for sterilisation or some other sort of population control perhaps not worthy of debate in the United Nations? Of course this is a controversial issue, but aren't we all affected by a world population spiralling out of control? Don't we have a responsibility to look after the living, now, and ensure that we have the resources to do so? Introducing more and more people into a finite space with dwindling resources surely decreases our ability to look after everyone already on the planet.

Whenever winter arrived in Cape Town and a storm would wash through the city, I always lay awake in the early hours of the morning thinking about all those dogs at the shelter, living on cold cement. I would wonder what kind of life the three homeless men who slept in De Waal Park, down the road from my home, led. My heart ached every time I saw anyone who was hungry, helpless or hurting, simply because no one wanted them. How many of them wished that they had never been born at all?

But Oscar wasn't in the mood for a new brother or sister; he had no immediate interest in anyone who would invade his sniffing space. Now that we were almost halfway through our journey, however, and with an added suitcase that contained my (fake) designer gear, an extra hand could really have helped. But I took Oscar's advice and decided to give up on the idea of adopting a child for now.

Angelina took a Cambodian orphan home with her, but Oscar and I still had quite a few more stops before we could settle down again. Besides, we were expected at a fundraiser in Phuket the very next day.

20

'One Mutt in Bangkok'

Getting from Siem Reap to the Andaman Sea was not going to be easy. Oscar would be entering the most efficient and sophisticated animal quarantine department in the business, and he was about to do so as an illegal alien. It had simply been impossible to organise his import permit into Thailand, as only the state veterinarian in Cambodia could issue such a document, and he was inconveniently located in Phnom Penh – a mere 314 kilometres away from Siem Reap. But in this part of the world, such a relatively minor detour could potentially turn into a major expedition.

So, unless we wanted to dodge mudslides, landmines, road closures and, inevitably, succumb to extreme road rage, we had no choice but to re-enter Bangkok without any paperwork and pray that the authorities remembered Oscar and winked him through with a customary *sawasdee*.

A few friends in high places didn't hurt either. In addition to Animal Travel Services at home base, we had the best animal importer in Asia, Mr Chinda Siri-Aree from Dynamic Air Cargo, on our side. He was situated only minutes from Swayambhunath

Airport, and we were confident that if the dog hit the fan, he would come to our rescue.

With the A-team on standby and Oscar looking like a famous frequent flyer in his blue box, now stickered with flags, everything ran like clockwork. We weren't deported, nor did we have to worry about missing the Soi Dog Foundation fundraiser that was being held at the Phuket Yacht Club later that afternoon. It had been a while since I had felt a bit glamorous, but I was all set with my Ed Hardy purchases.

It was an honour to meet John and Gill Dalley, the founders of Soi Dog. We hit it off right from the first handshake, probably because we all considered ourselves partly insane. John was also a golf fanatic, and he couldn't believe that, given some time to tee up, I would have whipped his tartans on the golf course. The British couple had fallen in love with Phuket when they had come to the island to get married a decade earlier. The island's beauty wowed them, and they, in turn, vowed to retire on its golden shores one day. The plan was to stretch out on Patong Beach and soak up a bronzed tan, and to keep their handicaps down at Blue Canyon Golf Course in between beach sessions. In their spare time, they would put something back into their new community; perhaps spend a day or two helping out at a special-needs school or at an orphanage. Saving homeless dogs was never a bleep on their radar screen.

True to fine planning, the Dalleys found that they could make their dream come true a lot earlier than expected. And it wasn't long before Gill had a tan and John was all golfed out. After looking for a charitable project that they could support, they realised that plenty of people and organisations were already involved in wonderful causes.

But it was impossible not to notice the vast number of *soi* (street) dogs roaming the streets in pitiful condition, and, after a little bit of investigation, it was apparent to the Dalleys that no one seemed to be doing anything about the situation. Worse still, street and stray dogs in Thailand had no protection under the law and usually fell victim to the most barbaric and malicious abuse. Thailand is predominantly Buddhist, so euthanasia was not an option. But if a dog 'chose' to eat some poisoned meat, it was its own doing and was simply 'meant to be'. Strychnine poisoning was the only method that the locals were using to tackle the growing population, which involved a slow and terribly painful death.

At around the same time that John and Gill moved to the island, they met an elderly woman by the name of Margot Park, who was looking for volunteers to help her bring dogs from Laem Sing Beach to have them sterilised. She owned a beat-up pick-up truck decorated with dog stickers – just the kind you'd have seen in California in the 1960s, with a flower dangling from the rearview mirror. Margot was funding the operation herself, and John thought she was just a loony trying to fight a forest fire with a cup of water.

But he soon realised that Margot's sterilisation project was the only viable way to reduce the suffering on the island, and the Dalleys dived right in. When Margot eventually returned to Australia, they picked up where she and her pick-up had left off, and it was from these humble beginnings that John and Gill created the Soi Dog Foundation.

It was a roller-coaster ride right from the bark 'Go!', and their dedicated efforts would come at a cost far greater than they could have imagined.

On a day that Gill recalls was like any other, she headed out to dart some dogs that had to be brought in for sterilisation. She came across a dog sleeping on the side of the road, but, as she darted it, it ran off into a flooded buffalo field. Knowing that the dog would drown when the anaesthetic kicked in and it collapsed, she chased after it, caught it and took it in to be sterilised. A few days later, Gill started to feel as if she were getting the flu. But the symptoms got worse and worse and she landed up in hospital with excruciating pain in both her legs. Shortly afterwards, her legs were amputated; her arms were saved just in time. Gill had contracted an infection from a very rare bacterium in the water of the flooded buffalo field. It was a freak occurrence, a random stroke of bad luck that couldn't have come at a worse time.

Gill was dismissed from hospital on Christmas Eve. Two days later, the tsunami struck. It wiped out everything in its wake; it also took the life of Gill's best friend. Gill had lost her father on Boxing Day exactly one year before, and losing her best friend one year later, within a week of losing her legs, was almost more than she could bear. But surrounded as she was by the dead and the dying, Gill had no time to dwell on her own problems. In the overcrowded hospitals, with relief efforts still on their way, she found strength in comforting those who had lost loved ones.

I couldn't help but wonder what had kept the Dalleys going after they had faced such adversity. Not surprisingly, it was the one answer I'd heard consistently on our World Woof Tour: they had a purpose. In the Dalleys' case, they were constantly motivated by the obvious and considerable difference that Soi Dog was making in the lives of animals on the island.

Since 2003, John's golf had gone to hell and Jill didn't have as many body parts to bronze, but their relationship was stronger than ever. By the time Oscar and I arrived on the scene, Soi Dog had already desexed over 26 000 animals and rehabilitated and rehomed thousands.

The fashion show that we were attending was just another good excuse to raise funds for their work. Oscar had donated one of his toys, which would be auctioned off for the occasion by a soon-to-be contestant on *The Biggest Loser Asia*. He was the perfect person to threaten the audience with exposing his cherries and wafers if they didn't pay his personal reserve of $5 000 for 'Oscar'.

The final bid of $5 250 fortunately came mere seconds before his rods were to be dropped. Unfortunately, though, we were forced to cast our eyes on his fleshy buttercups when, in celebration, he made a noticeable splash in the nearby yacht basin before the curtains were drawn.

I was amazed at what John and Gill had achieved after just six years of hard work, and this despite their hardships. It was also amazing to me that nothing had been done about the stray situation – aside from the work of Margot Park – before the Dalleys had arrived in Phuket. For starters, the local population was predominantly Buddhist. Didn't their religious beliefs translate into a sense of compassion towards the suffering that they saw every single day?

And what about the three to four million tourists who visited each year? Almost every one of them would have seen a pathetic, hairless creature walking past. Not all of them would necessarily have cared much for a mangy dog, but the vast majority would have been horrified by what they saw. Maybe a few had taken one or two dogs home with them; perhaps others had handed out a scrap of food out of pity. But the majority would have turned a blind eye and relaxed, conscience-free, on the white sand, sipping a perfect piña colada!

I was all too familiar with that attitude. I had seen hundreds of stray and starving dogs in Mexico. My then husband and I used to take a short drive from San Diego to Tijuana every other Saturday for an overdose of guacamole and margaritas. There are a great many dogs in Mexico and in other South American countries, mainly because of a common belief among locals that sterilising a male dog makes it 'gay'. Electrocution is one of the most common methods

used to try to control the massive stray population. Companions to
none, these dogs were everywhere: beat-up, pavement-like garbage
waiting to drift off in the breeze to another corner.

I dreaded the moment of visual impact every single time. It
would break my heart. I would turn against the world, enraged, in
the confines of my passenger seat, and my husband would tell me
that this was just the way it was; I couldn't save the world. But I
would feel so despondent and so very sad. I prayed for some kind of
salvation for these animals. How could it be so easy to ignore such
suffering, and why did people find it so hard to extend just an ounce
of kindness to those who cannot cry out loud?

The scenery around me would always wreck my day – until I was
safely ensconced inside a restaurant on the Tijuana strip, where
piñatas dangled in every direction, margaritas were on tap and some
fine mariachi players were singing 'AY YA YAY YA!'

These distractions were the perfect painkillers, and they worked
every single time. By the time hubby and wife had driven back
across the border, it was siesta time in San Diego and my inebriated
consciousness would be convinced that 'someone else' was doing
something about the dogs in Tijuana. I could free my mind and,
instead, focus it on all the important things I had to take care of
before the world collapsed. I had to buy groceries, brush my teeth,
feed the cat, clean the dishes, fill up with gas, moan about the
politicians and catch up with Oprah, all before the evening news. I
had my aerobics class, my yoga class, my Pilates class. And before
I knew it, it was time for another glass of tequila in Tijuana! It was
the same story every time.

The more I saw in Mexico, the more I convinced myself that
there were even more 'someone elses' doing something about the
situation in some parallel universe to my own. In reality, someone
was. Tijuana's animal control consisted of rounding up the dogs and

taking them to the city pound every day. There, these dogs would receive no nutrition or medical attention and, if not claimed – as they never were – were electrocuted within seventy-two hours.

After our engagement in Phuket, Oscar and I found ourselves at a fork in the road, and we didn't know quite which way to go. The original plan had been to head into Malaysia to celebrate World Day for Homeless Animals with the Penang SPCA, but Malaysia had a 180-day quarantine period and we hadn't yet received confirmation from Christelle, who had been on their case for months, that they would waive it for Oscar.

We had to make a decision on whether to risk it by crossing the border or to backtrack to paradise and spend a few extra days burning more freckles. After some strategic discussions, Oscar and I decided that I had enough sunspots to last me a lifetime. We would smuggle him across the Thailand–Malaysia border at 06h00 Greenwich Mean Time.

Our little group settled down for the night in a small town just half an hour from the border, making sure that we were well rested for the top-secret mission that lay ahead. We had hired a large 'tank' with tinted windows, three rows of seats and plenty of trunk space for the ammunition. The seating arrangements would be vital to the success of the mission: I would sit in the middle row, with Oscar carefully positioned beside my right foot, covered by a brown suede jacket; Inaam would sit in the front seat and thus undergo the first wave of inspections.

Our driver was a Thai student who didn't speak or understand a word of English. He had been briefed by the 'infantry' at the hotel and ordered to race us to freedom when the border had been cleared. He had also been given a few thousand baht to hand over to the enemy in case our vehicle was held back. As we drove closer to the battle lines, I became increasingly nervous and apprehensive about the clandestine operation about to unfold. Malaysia was Muslim territory, and an undeclared, albeit cute, canine would likely be considered an enemy of the state. He would be a spy, a terrorist, a hound hostage that they would probably want to make an example of in order to deter others who were planning to challenge Malaysian quarantine laws.

I started to panic. Only guacamole and a margarita could save me now, and I wasn't about to find either at this duty-free post! I feared the worst. If we were caught, would they let blondie retreat back to the Allies with the contents of her brown suede jacket, or would we be stripped of all command and thrown into a dungeon, never to be seen again? I recalled all the horrific torture scenes I'd watched on the History Channel. If I couldn't even handle a needle-prick during a cholesterol test, how the hell would I tolerate the pain when my fingers went missing, one by one?

'RETREAT!' I cried. 'RETREEEEEEAT!'

My bold deliverance roared through the vehicle and ricocheted off every piece of its contents. Every hair in the tank stood to immediate attention. Unfortunately, it was too late. We had just arrived at the first of three checkpoints. A man in uniform approached our driver, and a few unintelligible words were exchanged. The uniform circled our vehicle once, then opened the trunk. Fortunately we managed to curtail any inspection of the inside of the tank itself with a withdrawal from our mobile ATM.

Although we were officially still on the Thai side, I knew, as we drove towards passport control on the Malaysian side, that there was no turning back. Sounding the alarm now would signal surrender and almost certain defeat. Our vehicle passed through an X-ray machine and then a Malaysian immigration officer boarded it. His name tag read: 'Rudy'. A double dose of distraction was in order.

'How are you, Rudy? Rudy's a wonderful name. Many of my friends are called Rudy in Afrique du Sud. Have you ever been to South Africa? If you need a place to stay, you're always welcome in my home. Do you know my mate Nelson Mandela?' As I jabbered away, I realised that I was starting to flounder. Even my unassuming cameraman was giving me looks that suggested I was completely losing the plot. My heart and nerves were under siege. May Day, May Day!

Oscar, however, was remaining as calm as a cucumber, proud to be serving his canine community. Not even a sigh escaped his camouflage during the inspection.

Rudy disembarked seconds after my mouth stopped firing blanks, and for a brief moment it seemed as if D-Day was almost over. Our vehicle was directed to the parking lot, and all I had to do now was clear passport control, situated in an adjacent building. That, surely, would be a piece of steak. South Africans didn't even need a visa to get into Malaysia. My passport was duly stamped and I exited the building at a brisk pace. Zipping the van door shut, I ordered the driver to step on the pedal. Dame and dogkind were about to be liberated, and that with every finger intact!

But I didn't hear the engine starting. Again, I ordered the driver to move it. But he pointed at the front seat and said, 'Inaam.' Of course! I had forgotten to count the cavalry and, indeed, we were one man down. Where was Inaam? My heart sank. I realised immediately that he was stuck in passport control. And if our experience at Nepal's Tribhuvan International Airport had been anything to go by, we could be delayed at the border post for hours.

Inaam had indeed experienced a problem entering each new country. He may have been a small, polite and extremely well-mannered Tibetan whose only vice was swallowing curry and rice for breakfast, lunch and dinner, but his passport set off a red flare everywhere. Inaam was an Indian Muslim from the notoriously unstable state of Jammu and Kashmir. He might as well have had the words 'terrorist in transit' stuck to his forehead. I felt really sorry for him. He had been taken off the aircraft between Kathmandu and Delhi, detained in Bangkok, harassed in Cambodia, and now he was being held in Malaysia.

Inaam's situation was a potential time bomb waiting to explode, and I thus had no choice but to barge back inside and behave atrociously. When forced to perform, I hate to admit that Joanne Lefson is the world's greatest living brat. No one must rock my boat when I'm on the verge of having a nervous breakdown, especially on the Malaysian border! I had Inaam out of the interrogation room within seconds. He couldn't believe it. If he'd had suspicions of me being a witch before, these were now confirmed. Where Inaam came from, women didn't talk much and did not own a dog, let alone blow their dowry on a world tour *with* a dog.

We pulled away from immigration and cruised towards the highway that would lead us into Kuala Lumpur. There was just one more – unexpected – hurdle we would have to clear. Out of the blue, an officer appeared in the middle of the road and pointed to a checkpoint. We couldn't believe our eyes. From the look of the set-up, this was a random checkpoint on its very first day of operation.

Just our luck.

We had been ambushed and there was no escape. The side door opened and an officer nodded at us sternly. He then tilted his head to the side so that he could look under the seats. I looked up at the ceiling, closed my eyes and imagined I was in a happier place – at the dentist, having every single tooth pulled from my mouth without anaesthetic would do! How could we possibly make it through this ordeal? Oscar was a sitting duck; surely he was in full view from floor level, and by this stage the inspector had his head so far under the front seats that his buttocks were nearly in the back seats.

Then, in what felt like a lifetime, it all came to a satisfactory end. Our driver and the official exchanged a few words. Expecting the worst, I placed both my hands in front of me and assumed the position. I had the right to remain freaked out … but the handcuffs never arrived. We were free to go.

As we drove away, I wiped the sweat from my brow and shoved my head under the front seat to see where Oscar was. He was in fine fettle, and his tail began to wave. Only by some miracle had our top-secret agent not been uncovered. Maybe good karma from Cambodia was on our side? Perhaps we had a guardian dog watching over us from above? Either way, we were safe. I returned to the back seat and sighed with relief. The highway was unfolding before us, and we were right on schedule.

We were hound and dry.

21

In the dogbox

Making it into Malaysia was one challenge; being able to do anything with a dog inside the country was another completely.
The plan was to stay in Penang for one night and celebrate World
Day for Homeless Animals with the Penang SPCA the following
day. Thereafter, we would catch a ferry to Langkawi Island and
meet up with the LASSie Foundation (Langkawi Animal Shelter
and Sanctuary Foundation).

By the time we made it to Penang, our driver was livid. He had
been ordered to drive a dog, a madam and a cameraman from
Betong to Penang. Subjecting his health and livelihood to a highly-
strung blonde and her hairy dog was not a part of the contract.
Needless to say, he was in no mood to taxi us around Penang in
search of a hotel that would take in his passengers. No, his job
was to dump us at a two-star joint downtown, and that's exactly
what he did.

The hotel was a little run-down, but it had character. It might
not have been the Imperial, but it did remind me of the colonial-
style structures I'd seen in India. Our driver pulled up outside the

hotel, threw our bags out of the boot and left in a huff. Good grief, I had just provided him with the most exciting morning of his life and *this* was how he showed his appreciation? Ungrateful sod. I would spend his tip on a cold beer once we had checked in.

We dragged our bags into the hotel lobby, only to find that that was as far as they would get. The staff were *disgusted* that a dog had arrived at the hotel. The manager rushed in and ordered that the beast be removed *immediately*. I was a fighter, but I had lost this one before I had even had the opportunity to step into the ring. So, as all good losers should, I decided to have some fun in the face of defeat.

'But, sir, this is a very special animal!' I now had his full attention. 'Oscar is the only creature known to have swine flu and fleas that survive in the same micro-ecosystem. We're in Penang to calculate whether the same strain of swine flu can be suppressed when the fleas experience a volumetric humidity of 30 °C saturated, which is the critical climactic point of transmission through physical contact. *Comprador, señor?*'

Our bodies, along with our bags, landed on the pavement three seconds later. The porters didn't stick around for their tip, either. The joke was on us.

Finding a taxi in Malaysia that was prepared to transport a pooch turned into a nightmare. We hadn't even been in the country for a day and we had already faced two of our greatest challenges. I was beginning to wish that Oscar had gone barking mad on the Thai side of the Malaysian border so that we could have stayed there. Although I understood that Muslims, in general, do not consider dogs to be their best friends, the reaction to Oscar in Malaysia thus far had been insanely negative.

It took three hours and seventeen minutes before an old brown Toyota Cressida pulled up beside us. This was the kind of car you'd never get into unless you fancied a leading role in a mysterious abduction, but we were desperate. Besides, a disappearing act, given the current circumstances, was exactly what the vet would have ordered. We jumped right in. The man behind the wheel introduced himself as Mr Khane. His mother hailed from West Africa and his father was Malaysian. Mr Khane considered himself an international Muslim with a little bit of Hindu mixed in.

This basically meant that he liked my dog. Mr Khane spent the next four hours driving to every single hotel in town, but not one of them wanted to be the very first fabulous establishment to accommodate a canine. The Malaysians aren't into breaking new ground, or records for that matter, and the answer was a resounding 'NO!' every time.

I was starting to feel as if I were conducting a canine crusade on the back of a donkey in Bethlehem. Fortunately, Mr Khane knew of one more place we could try – a Chinese hotel at the bad end of town. Although not the Ritz, this would be our last shot. It was getting late, and if we were turned away at yet another inn, we'd have to accept Mr Khane's offer to share his stable with his virgin mother and seven sisters!

An old Chinese lady was seated at the front desk of the hotel, her eyes buried in a stack of ringgit bills, which she clenched tightly in her hands. A dusty old cigarette machine stood behind her, and a public phone hung on the stained cream wall in the far corner, an 'Out of Order' sticker plastered on its front. Two couches, which had also seen better days, were positioned just inside the entrance to the hotel.

A cloud of stale smoke hovered above a few Chinese men huddled together in the foyer, transfixed by a tiny TV and what sounded like a cheap Chinese talk show. At least they had satellite, I thought; how bad can the place be?

'Hello, can you help me please?' The lady seemed oblivious to my presence. I could tell from the slight movement of her tight-set lips that she was still counting the most prized commodity in her world.

'Dog? You take dog?'

'Dog? You have *DOG*?' Suddenly I had her full attention.

'Yes, I bring good dog. No pee-pee. No bark. No *problem*. Okay?'

The old lady took hold of her chair and climbed on top of it. Ever so slowly, she leant over the desk to see if she had misunderstood my English or if she had indeed heard me correctly. Oscar looked up at her and smiled.

'You pay $10 more, okay? And any bark, you go, dog go. No money back. Okay?'

She handed me the room key and pointed to the very first door in the hall. I walked over, opened the door, and immediately caught my breath. The room was dark and dingy and stank of urine. Something had stayed here before that hadn't been hotel trained. If it wasn't a dog, I'd hate to imagine what it could have been! A faded red lantern hung by a thread from the centre of the ceiling. It didn't work, but the traffic lights outside were bright enough to illuminate the room so that I could find what I needed and leave the rest well enough alone. Ignorance was bliss anyway, and, in this case, it was the intelligent choice. There was a toilet and a mattress in the room, and both appeared to be in working order. I shook the old girl's hand. We had a deal.

The next morning, without having experienced bed bugs or any other dreaded night-time visitors, Mr Khane made sure that we arrived at the Penang SPCA on time. Afterwards, he took the initiative and escorted us to the offices where we could sort out Oscar's export papers, which we needed in order to return to Thailand. When it was time to leave the mainland for Langkawi

Island, Mr Khane even drove us the long way through town to the ferry port so that Oscar could bark his lungs out at the locals in a gesture of comradeship and tolerance towards all.

This was also an opportunity for Oscar to enjoy one of his favourite pastimes. He calls it the 'freak-out-motor-man manoeuvre', a modified version of something he had seen while watching Animal Planet. Whenever we pulled up at a traffic light, he would sit quietly behind his open window and, just like a cheetah on the African plains, wait patiently for a humanoid to pull up on a scooter. He would then stalk his prey and, only when the light had turned green and he sensed that his prey was taking off, would he explode his body halfway out the vehicle and unleash a massive 'WOOOOOOOOF!'

It was a roar of such magnitude that even grown men wet their pants. For anyone watching from our side, it was wonderful entertainment. But for the person on the receiving end of Oscar's vocal chords, it was both humiliating and embarrassing. Penang was the perfect location to let Oscar have a party, but it nearly cost the Cressida its life.

Being a bit out of practice, my hunter fired a premature bark from the back seat while the light was still red. The prey fell off his scooter and, if the lights hadn't turned green a second later, Mr Khane's car would have been stoned to death with a bag of bad apples. Oscar and I were called every name under the sun, names that I wouldn't even have wished on an ex-boyfriend! (Although I did take notes just in case I ever change my mind!)

By the time we reached the ferry terminal, we were in good spirits and ready to face the captain of the ferry. We knew that the dog was going to be a humungous issue, and sucking up to someone for a 'favour' had never been one of my talents. When I was young, I got what I wanted. If I didn't, I would throw a tantrum and then get what I wanted. End result: I always got what I wanted. However, standing before the man in charge of our only means of transportation to our next port of call forced me to consider an alternative tactic.

I had speed on my side. Unlike a taxi driver, the boat's captain couldn't just say 'No' to me and drive off. If the moment called for action, we could jump from shore to ship at the last second. I also had my canister of mace in my right pocket just in case we needed to start a mutiny on the bounty!

Inaam stood guard beside the dog and the luggage while I approached the ticket collector. I could tell that he, along with every other one of the devout Muslim men and their wives that were adorned in black *hijabs*, had already seen the dog. Not amused, he told me to stand aside and wait. When all the passengers had boarded and the engines started, I figured it was time to stand up and be counted. I ordered Inaam to throw the luggage onto the back of the boat and to leave Oscar with me. As I tried to board, a scuffle ensued between the ticket collector and me.

Thanks to having had a crush on Bruce Lee back in junior school, I had my brown belt in karate, and I knew exactly where to land a knock-out blow between the bananas. I was ready to rock 'n' roll, even though I hated conflict. At heart I was a cherry swan, but we had to get on this ferry; there was simply no alternative: Mr Khane's Cressida didn't float – we had asked him – and it was too far to swim.

With the luggage and Inaam on the boat, I made my last move and managed to get on board just as the ferry was pulling away from the quay. The ticket collector started shouting and pointing at me, and a staff member on board grabbed me. I was ordered to remain at the stern of the boat, right beside the exhaust pipe, which was already farting out litres of black smoke. It was a *pleasure*. We were on our way!

The most exciting part of our time on Langkawi, aside from meeting the stylish Narelle McMurtrie, ex-pat Aussie and founder of the LASSie Foundation, was our accommodation on the island. The Datai, one of Asia's finest hotels, had kindly offered to sponsor our stay. Unfortunately, we had arrived a day earlier than expected, so we had to make our own arrangements for one night.

Fear not, I told Oscar, we are now experts at manoeuvring you sight unseen into sensitive territory. So we hired a car and drove down to the main drag, where a few dozen hotels were located. I sent Inaam off to find the most easily accessible premises for dog-sneaking, and he and I checked in after nightfall. It was easier getting into a beach bungalow than it was dodging *vrot* apples at a traffic light; staying inside, however, was not.

The bungalow was arguably the worst 'accommodation' I had ever occupied. Granted, there was a bed, and even something that looked like a toilet, but I had never stayed in a place that didn't have a basin! I decided to chalk it down to experience and went to lie down on the bed. As I closed my eyes, I tried desperately to convince myself that the twitching inside my sheets was a figment of my wild imagination and not a hairy spider on a collision course with my unshaven leg!

I beat the sun to breakfast. I also had to feed Oscar a can of Pedigree, but I had misplaced the tin opener. I walked to the nearest restaurant on the strip, but the chef wouldn't subject any one of his kitchen tools to opening a can of *dog* food. Once I had removed the label, I had better luck next door.

Having been deprived of sleep for three days, I was now officially fed up. Blame it on the devil inside, but I couldn't check out of the dump we were staying in without leaving a lasting impression … something that would alert *everyone* to the fact that a dog smuggler and her illegal hound had stayed at Cenang Beach.

This was the stuff that makes headlines in the local newspaper. I wiped clean a small area of the floor in my room and then pounded the dog food out of the tin, making sure that a little bit remained stuck in the bottom. I then gave Oscar permission to enjoy his feast with a creative touch. He could lick up the mince, but he had to attack it from as many different angles as possible; something resembling a malfunctioning bulldozer on heat. By the time Oscar had finished, it looked as if a mop with a crush on Pedigree had been on a publicity stunt. All that was left to do was to stick the label back on the tin and leave it hanging from the vacant light bulb above the bed.

If the bungalow on Cenang Beach had been hell, the Datai was paradise. However, getting inside this hotel wouldn't be without its fair share of drama too. At check-in, we found out that the Scottish-born manageress had mistakenly assumed Oscar to be my husband, not my rather hairy best friend. Fortunately she was amused at her mistake and still agreed to accommodate us, as long as we kept a low profile. We were in!

And it was sheer bliss. I had four basins in my suite and I made sure I used every single one. After all, I didn't know when I would see another basin again. Oscar's entertainment took the form of the macaque monkeys jumping around in the ten-million-year-old rainforest within which the hotel was situated. Oscar finally had some time to reintroduce himself as the boss of all creatures, great and small. Doing nothing at the Datai also provided the perfect practice for what would turn out to be an enforced two-week break in Koh Samui, our next stop.

22

Hound and out

Koh Samui is just like Phuket. It's heaven on earth – unless you're a dog! Coconuts don't fall far from the same tree in Thailand either. The Dalleys in Phuket are virtual carbon copies of Brigitte and Werner Gomm in Koh Samui. The German couple holidayed on the island in 1997 and vowed to return to help the street dogs. The rest, as they say, is history. Before the Gomms arrived on the scene, there weren't any sterilisation programmes in place on Koh Samui. Government author-ities were carrying out mass poisonings to try to reduce the stray population because the tourists were finding the situation 'disturbing'.

Through the efforts of the Gomms and their Dog Rescue Centre Samui, there are now eighteen full-time staff members who oversee a clinic and the shelter, which houses up to 250 dogs at any given time. Other dogs, as we soon found out, become in-laws at the Gomms' place. On the day of our visit, sixty very vocal dogs were running blissfully free throughout the house. It was commitment and chaos beyond even my wild imagination! I could only marvel at how far some people will go – even sacrificing their personal comfort – for a cause greater than themselves.

On the other side of the island, we managed to track down Linda Kirk and Janine Hafliger, two volunteers who give all their time to the society. It is extremely common for Thai people to dump puppies at the temples, as they assume that the monks will look after them. Linda and Janine visit nineteen temples three times a week to provide basic medical care and 500 kilograms of dog food to the forty dogs that are in the monks' care.

After our visit to Dog Rescue, our schedule was supposed to be simple. Only an adoption event with Animal Refuge Kansai in Osaka, Japan, was on our to-do list, and that would happen in exactly one week's time. In the meantime, Inaam would return to Delhi in order to sort out his visa for Japan, and I would have to endure as many cheap massages as humanly possible. And we were waiting for written confirmation that Japan would waive their quarantine requirements for Oscar.

In principle, Japan had already agreed to do so, but we still needed the proof in writing. One thing was certain: there would be no more contestants on the *Who Wants to Have a Nightmare Border Crossing?* show, although Japan might turn out to be a challenge. If we didn't receive a chop-chop tick from Japan by high noon the following day, we would boycott the bullet train and, instead, wave hello from the Great Wall of China.

Oscar and I checked in to a rustic resort at the far end of Chaweng Beach, which I had managed to find the previous morning. It was the only place that would accept a woman and her dog.

The Seaside Cottages Resort belonged to a Chinese couple. On condition that I paid for the room in advance, they were more than delighted to have us. I was beginning to believe that the Maneki Neko, the cat that symbolises luck for the Chinese, was my four-leaf clover in Asia! The accommodation was cheap and nasty, but for $9 a night we had a genuine, handmade wood bungalow with all

Oscar on the Great Wall of China,
where he would leave an indelible mark

On the road again – Oscar being weighed at Beijing airport

In the land of the
free - Oscar at the
Golden Gate Bridge,
San Francisco

Our lady of liberty -
Oscar in the Big Apple

A star is born - Oscar on the Hollywood Walk of Fame

Mr and Mrs
Oscar Lefson
and their
wedding officer
– Las Vegas

Monument
Valley,
Arizona

An upgrade to business class is always welcome

My guide dog and I pay a visit to the cockpit

Our friends (clockwise Valerie, Alexandra and Patricia from the Costa Rican Animal Sanctuary El Arca de Noé

A gyrocopter ride over the Arenal Volcano, San José, Costa Rica

Zipping over 135 different species of snakes in Turu Ba Ri Tropical Park, Costa Rica

Oscar in the Amazon

Playing ball, Amazon-style, in the
Pacaya-Samiria National Reserve

Sightseeing on the greatest river in the world

Oscar the
soccer star,
Pacaya-Samiria
National Reserve

The little girl who
didn't know how to
smile, Iquitos, Peru

The reason for the World Woof Tour –
a stray dog on a dumpsite in Cusco, Peru

Oscar gets friendly
with the llamas at
Macchu Pichu

The statue of
Christ the Redeemer,
Rio de Janeiro. And then,
homeward bound ...

the amenities that a single girl and her dog could ever need. We had a mattress elevated on a cardboard frame, a shower, a toilet, a basin and, as long as the wind didn't come up, a crooked roof over our heads! The loo paper cost extra, but with all the different time zones and my poor diet, my system didn't need a roll anyway!

I attributed the missing planks in the floor to being part of a ventilation system made in China; at least it would give Oscar something to pant into when the fan packed up. Best of all, our spot boasted the best darn location on the entire beach – it was just fifteen metres from the emerald-blue waters of the Gulf of Thailand. And smack-bang between room and ocean, two Thai hunks were hanging out, obviously just waiting for a well-travelled South African girl.

There was also a resident dog at the resort, called Nam. Oz had been very wary of the overtly territorial dogs roaming around Asia, but Nam and Oscar took an instant liking to each other. Play and exercise were exactly what we both needed. Earlier in the week, a lady sitting next to us on the *songthaew* had fondly pointed at Oscar and said 'fat dog', and I was also starting to feel a roll of flab gathering around my waist. It was time to get some cash, start on a health kick and get the bellies rolling.

I hadn't kept any record of what I had been spending on the road, as I knew I would never do or buy anything beyond the call of duty. What, then, would be the point of taking stock? I had to spend what I was spending to get the job done, and when the tank dried up, well … I would just dial 911.

When the ATM swallowed my card later that afternoon without spitting out any cash, my mum was the first to receive the call. Erica is smart, articulate and a very successful businesswoman and, by virtue of being my biological mother, she was obliged to bail me out of my credit crunch. (Her credit card had already come to my rescue in Paris, when I was charged to fly my 'dauwg'.) Unfortunately, though, she couldn't make money grow on coconut trees halfway around the world, overnight, so I would have to find a charity closer to my temporary home. And, by the way, why wasn't I married with 2.2 kids instead of treating my life like a circus in the first place?

The funds from the transfer of my property were scheduled to clear into my account in another eight days; in the meantime, I would have to survive on the single $100 note that I had in my pocket. Either that, or I would have to start gyrating my booty around a pole in the centre of town after I had put Oscar to bed. (He would never approve of such behaviour.)

I calmed down to a panic and made some calculations while I could still think like a kept woman. A hundred bucks would buy me six nights at the run-down Ritz, twelve cans of Pedigree to keep Oscar alive, two one-way tickets for the bus, ferry and train rides back to Bangkok when the long wait was over, and a box of Kleenex for mopping up the disappointment I felt for the back massage I now knew I would never have.

For the first time in my life, I was officially broke. One consolation was that Japan had not responded to Christelle's dozen emails, so the country was removed from our itinerary. I now had a week to finalise the arrangements that were only tentatively in place for China, and to pray that the money transfer would go through before we took off for Beijing.

The days went sailing past. I tried to sleep in, but I woke up early. Oscar and I swam, and sat, and swam, and cried, and swam again. I even tasted dog food for the first time, and realised that, when you're hungry, everything starts to taste like home cooking! By the time Day 6 broke through the morning mist, the piggy bank was stone dead. We still had to endure one more night before we were to head back to Bangkok, but we didn't have $9 to cover the cost of the room.

Not even a tantrum could save us now. I would, for the first time ever, have to join the estimated 475 million homeless dogs on the planet and sleep under a starry, starry night. There wasn't any time to feel sorry for ourselves, as we needed to stake out the *best* free accommodation in the neighbourhood. Oscar looked left and I headed right. We both ended up at the same place.

Just to the right of where we had been staying, a tented massage shack was erected on the beach. It was definitely our best bet. The tent would keep us sheltered from the romantics who walked the beach until late at night, and there was also a mattress inside. Although the mattress was at least ten years old, covered in oil stains and probably the main breeding ground for every bug around, it was still better than nothing. Or so I hoped.

The hotel agreed to store our luggage while we were on our fantasy 'full-moon party'. When Oscar and I finally lay down for what I knew would be the longest night of the tour up till then, something in my subconscious insisted that I look at the date on my watch. Over the past few days I had completely lost track of time. As one of the final two contestants in another of my own episodes of *Survivor*, it simply didn't seem to matter.

When I eventually had to get up for a potty break, I used the light of the moon to look at the date on my watch. It was 5 September 2009; my mother's sixtieth birthday! I walked away from my puddle, sat on the cool sand and made the call. Thailand was five hours ahead of South Africa, but I managed to wish my mom a happy birthday just as she was making her grand entrance into the biggest bash of our family's history.

I had looked into flights home a few weeks earlier, but the expense involved in flying back home for a day was ludicrous.

Besides, what would I have done with Oscar? I sat wrapped up in my own silence and gazed out over the sea, which sparkled serenely in the moonlight. It was all *so* beautiful, just like my mother. I was suddenly overcome with emotion and could no longer hold back the tears. I felt so grateful for everything my mom had given me.

When I was younger, my mother and I hadn't always seen eye to eye. There had even been times when I hated her. When a seven-year custody battle had ensued between my parents, I had taken my father's side. And when my mom had got married for the second time, I'd hoped that I would never have to see her again. But over time I grew up and she and I grew closer – and not only because she became a director at a favourite retail outlet of mine, which afforded me a 40 per cent discount on all the latest fashions!

In fact, it was only once the clothes had gone out of fashion and I was old enough to finally appreciate the enormous sacrifices that every parent makes for his or her children that Mom and I became best friends.

As I sat looking at the tranquil ocean, I thought back on some special times I had shared with my mother. After a while, a few SMSes trickled in from friends and family who were attending the party. Each one said that they wished I could be there, and I wished the same back; and no more so than when I read the final message, which beeped through just moments before the battery on my phone died: 'I couldn't tell you before Joey, but I just got married. Love you. Chat tomorrow, Mom'.

What? I looked at the SMS a dozen times before the reality sank in. Was I dreaming this up, or was I really on an island off the southern coast of Thailand playing the part of 'Hobo Jo' while the single most important woman in my life was turning sixty and had exchanged wedding vows with a man who had been a part of my life since I was seven years old?

'You *can't* be serious!' I thought, aghast. I sat and watched the tide roll in until the moonlight surrendered to the sun's seductive rays. They say that home is where the heart is, and up till this point mine had felt cosy and warm in every location on the tour. I hadn't looked back once, until tonight. Indeed, this moment was the exception, and for the first time since I'd left South Africa, I was homesick. Terribly homesick. At that moment, I would have given anything to be home, raising a glass of bubbly to the most wonderful woman ever to grace the planet.

On the upside, Oscar and I were ready to head back to Bangkok. Although the money had not yet cleared in my account, I knew I could buy one day off the hotel manager in Bangkok, whom I'd charmed on my previous visit. Assuming everything went according to plan, I had all expenses covered bar the taxi ride to the hotel. Fortunately I had set aside eighty-five baht for that very reason.

A minivan was scheduled to take us to a bus, in which we would board the ferry. The ferry, in turn, would transport the bus to the mainland, whereafter it would drop us at the train station. We would arrive in Bangkok a day later. When the minivan arrived, I immediately sensed trouble.

Yes, the agency from which I had purchased the ticket had not informed the driver of the van that a dog would be one of his passengers. And this man hated dogs. From the expression on his face, he was more of an inflexible atheist than a compassionate Buddhist – a lean, mean tattooed machine. But he was shorter than me, which gave me the psychological edge I needed to handle the situation. With the exception of my dog and Muslim hotel managers, *no* male with a lesser height had ever won a battle against me.

That's just the way things have been ever since a short-arsed serial rapist tried to attack me on a remote beach in Cape Town back in 2002 and I knocked him senseless.

I got into the van with Oscar and locked the passenger door. We were not going to get out until we were within sight of the bus at the ferry terminal. But the mean old driver threw down his keys in disgust and refused to drive anywhere until we got out. He had apparently just cleaned the van, and proceeded to lecture us on how dog hair would completely destroy the air-conditioning unit, which would then cause the engine to overheat and, ultimately, the vehicle to explode.

Yeah, right.

I knew he had a few more passengers to collect on his route and that he would thus have to give in eventually. By the time he did, he was virtually foaming at the mouth. He vowed that I would pay him an extra 500 baht at the ferry terminal so that he could cover any additional cleaning costs. I *assured* him that I didn't have the money, but he just laughed. He'd heard that bulldust before.

When we finally pulled into the ferry terminal, the driver demanded that I pay him the 500 baht, but I ignored him and started walking towards the bus. But he wouldn't disappear. Instead, he started behaving like an aggressive drug addict possessed by the devil. And there was no Mr Khane or Bruce Lee around to defend me! Oscar, of course, wasn't exactly a pit-bull either.

The minivan driver ran ahead and frantically instructed the bus driver not to let me board until I had paid him the money I 'owed' him. When I got to the door, it was slammed right in my face. These two were brothers in arms, and my valid bus tickets were now null and void. I was shaking from head to toe. The scene had become very scary, and I still didn't know how we were going to get on the ferry.

There was no time to waste, though. I left the idiots behind and started running towards the ferry. Seconds before it signalled its imminent departure, I approached one of the ticket collectors and managed to convince him that I had briefly disembarked so that my dog could relieve its bowels, and that we now needed to board again. It did the trick. We were on the ferry!

Of course, my next challenge would be to figure out how we would get to the Surat Thani train station once the ferry had docked at the pier. The station was just over an hour's drive from the ferry terminal and, having completed seven marathons when I was still in my prime, I could probably have run there if my life depended on it. But with a dog in tow, it was one 'walkies' too far.

Oscar and I sat down on the open deck. I felt a fresh breeze wash across my face and took a deep breath. What would our next step be? Fortunately, a very handy survival mechanism kicks in to gear when you find your arse up against a brick wall. Every single inhibition you ever thought you had evaporates almost immediately.

I went down to the basement, where the cars and buses were parked, and spotted our bus in the distance. I headed in the opposite direction. I knew there had to be *someone* on board who was bound for the train station; a person who wouldn't demand any money in exchange for a huge favour. It was time to knuckle down. Swallowing my pride, I started knocking on car and bus windows.

Here I was, barely a day after my mom's birthday, when I should have been hung-over and eating cake for brunch, in the basement of a ferry droning across the gulf of Thailand, begging for a ride and carrying a handbag that resembled a dog. It must have looked like a set-up, but an unsuspecting driver in a silver Nissan Frontier didn't have enough time to think about it. He couldn't exactly reverse either! We had found our lift.

Oscar and I jumped into the back of the truck, and when the

iron gates of the ferry opened, I heard the sweet sound of the truck's engine as it started to purr. Mr Priyajana went out of his way to drop Oscar and me right outside the train station. I thanked him profusely and promised him that his photograph would wind up in a book one day. After Mr Priyajana drove off, I had one more task to complete before we could board the train.

I walked outside, stood at the side of the road and waited patiently. Eventually the moment came when I could raise my hands and give a humungous welcoming wave to the bus just pulling in.

We hadn't just edged in before the bus; we'd beaten the bastard by thirty-six minutes! The expression on the driver's face made the entire ordeal worth it.

23

The Great Woof of China

'Be the change you wish to see in the world.'
                                    – Gandhi

We were supposed to be climbing Mount Fuji with the Tokyo ARK foundation, but instead we were on a collision course with a country infamous for its cruelty to dogs and everything else that moved on four (or more) legs! China had not been part of our menu, but Oscar's welfare had been my top priority. We could have taken a direct flight from Bangkok to Los Angeles, but putting Oscar in the hold for sixteen hours was not an option. We needed another stop to bridge the gap, and with Japan in the dogbox, the Middle Kingdom was our one-shop stop.

Organising a trip to that country with a hound, however, was a giant jigsaw puzzle that could only have been made in China. I had hired the best pet-travel business in the country to help us through every second of our passage, as we couldn't afford to take any chances. In China, there is no legislation in place that protects animals except for the Wild Animal Conservation Law, which was promulgated in

1988 to protect cuddly panda bears. I certainly wasn't paranoid, but if anything went wrong and my Oscar fell into the wrong hands, he might reappear as a fur coat or resurface in a hot pot.

Beijing and Shanghai both have quarantine laws, but there are legal ways to get around the system. The appointed agency had worked out a 'safe' route for us: we would fly into Hong Kong and catch a train to Guangzhou, otherwise known as the dog- and cat-eating capital of Asia. From there, we would fly to Beijing and visit the Beijing Human & Animal Environmental Education Centre (BHAEEC), and then continue to Shanghai.

A few factors made me feel rather uncomfortable about flying Oscar on a Chinese airline. For starters, an additional rabies jab was mandatory for every pet travelling on a domestic flight in China. Secondly, there was no rescue package if the cargo staff mistook him for a prime cut of meat. Our only travel alternative was to drive from Guangzhou to Beijing, but we really didn't fancy subjecting ourselves to over two days of solid driving.

Seoul and Manila started looking like more suitable alternatives, but then news came from the agency that, for a 'nominal' fee, Oscar could do 'home quarantine'. I wasn't sure what that meant exactly, but, at the last minute, the agency assured me that we could fly directly to Beijing and that Oscar could be cleared immediately, without any problems, guaranteed! This agency had been in the international pet-travel business for many years, and what they said at least *sounded* legitimate. The only minor detail that they conveniently forgot to tell me was that it would cost me $1500, and that I shouldn't expect a receipt after the transaction.

It was too late to argue. I was a Westerner in a communist state and would do as I was told.

The other problem we faced was accommodation. It was potentially dangerous for a dog to stay in the centre of Beijing. If in

Malaysia we had to duck and dive to avoid religious and cultural phobias, in China it became a matter of life and death. Dogs are prohibited from public places such as markets, parks and sightseeing areas during the day and, by will of strict Beijing law, any dog bigger than 35.5 centimetres who is found on the streets is picked up and put down by the authorities.

Size wasn't everything, either. Failure to have your dog licensed (at an annual fee of around $150) was a crime that exacted the same penalty. According to the locals, the laws hark back to the late communist leader Mao Zedong, who condemned dog ownership as a bourgeois affectation and anyone who kept them as time wasters. As a result, canines were hunted as pests.

Be that as it may, no one had ever come up trumps protesting against the Chinese government, and Oscar, clocking in at a handsome 43.9 centimetres, towered over the local Chihuahuas and Pekinese. It was best that we stayed on the outskirts of the city; it was, in fact, non-negotiable. To push the boundaries in this country would simply be too risky.

Oblivious to the risks that lurked beyond Beijing's very first eco-tourism resort, Oscar was in sheer sniffing heaven at the Red Capital Ranch, where we stayed. Set on over fifty Chinese acres, I never had to worry when my little explorer set off in the footsteps of Genghis Khan. Furthermore, the Taihang and Yanshan mountain ranges protected us from the dog-eating countries in the north and west, and, with a 360-degree view of the Great Wall that surrounded us from up high, we were safe from any Mao Zedong hogwash.

When Oscar and I eventually ventured out from the divine confines of our safe harbour, it was to visit BHAEEC. Established in 1997

by animal lover Madame Zhang Luping, this had been the first and only private animal shelter and protection entity in Mainland China at the time. Some of its aims were to educate the public about animal protection and to nurse sick animals.

It was unlike anything Oscar and I had seen at a shelter thus far on the tour. Most shelters that we had visited were similar to the ones in South Africa, where it was like walking into a sweet shop and finding a huge variety of delectables inside that would not give you tooth decay or make you fat! Walking around this centre was like entering a sweet shop, but one that served only white Pekinese pralines! Of course there were a few liquorice allsorts walking around too, but for the most part the grounds were saturated with 600 adorable, cuddly white cotton balls.

Its small size makes the Pekinese the ideal pet to have in Beijing. When the one-dog-per-household policy was introduced in 2006, many pet owners were forced to hand over their surplus dogs to the Public Security Bureau for a certain dead end. Intrusive laws are the norm in China, and the locals were already used to going to enormous and rather creative lengths to circumvent the one-child rule. With this experience in hand, many smuggled their canine companions to the countryside, or registered them as belonging to friends and neighbours while keeping them at home and out of sight. The few who knew where BHAEEC was located simply abandoned their dogs outside its gates. Not surprisingly, most of them were Pekinese.

The Chinese government introduced the one-dog rule to combat the spread of rabies. Only 3 per cent of dogs in China are vaccinated against rabies and more than 2000 people die of the disease each year. Just one case of rabies will usually spark off a mass culling of dogs, despite the fact that, since the middle of the last century, the World Health Organization has stated repeatedly that indiscriminate dog culling is not an effective method of controlling the disease.

Just four months before our arrival, 40000 dogs had been culled in the most brutal fashion when twelve people had been infected with rabies in the Shaanxi Province. The international media covered another such crackdown that took place in 2006 in Yunnan Province. On that occasion, over 50000 dogs were destroyed. Dog owners were offered five yuan (sixty-three US cents) to kill their own dogs, or they could wait for the government's assassins to do it for them.

The workers at BHAEEC were quick to tell me that the one-dog rule is not as bad as it sounds. Dog adoption is very low in China. BHAEEC itself has just one or two adoptions, on average, each month. Most Chinese who want a dog will almost always buy one from one of the many pet stores and markets in and around town.

I had the chance to visit one such market, and it was a very sad experience. The puppies at the markets usually originate from puppy mills, which are essentially dog-farming operations in which the dogs are kept in tiny cages and forced to have multiple litters. Most of the puppies are sold as pets to China's growing middle class, but many are also bred for fur or meat. The puppies that I saw were confined in cages so small that they could barely turn around. Most didn't have any water and many had skin or ear infections, which in most cases are covered up by administering antibiotics while the animal is in the shop.

Puppies are considered a fashion and status symbol in China, and many people buy dogs only to abandon them months later, when the pet grows too big or the person doesn't feel like taking on the responsibility any more. At least the one-dog rule stops many potential second-time buyers from purchasing another dog that would have been bred in the most horrific conditions.

Beijing is connected to Shanghai by a highway, and this was the laborious but single route we had to follow in order to meet our obligations in Shanghai. It is a painful, long, insanely straight highway occupied by an unimaginable number of trucks transporting Chinese junk from one economic centre to another with drivers who are clueless about how to use an indicator or adhere to any rules of the road.

To make matters worse, Oscar was a hopeless passenger. Anywhere else he could sit still for hours, but in a moving vehicle he was always on the prowl for unsuspecting motorcyclists. The window had to be wide open at all times, and if I closed it for a minute to give my hair and hearing a break, he would revert to a howl, which he knew would always result in his desires being met.

Whenever we had an excuse to get out of the car, we did. We stopped at every petrol station, where we would visit the restaurant and shop and explore the parking lot, which was usually twice the size of Red Square. All of the petrol stations looked exactly the same. They reminded me of the bland, grey cement factories back home, and most of the snacks inside tasted much the same.

Exactly 1 237.32 kilometres and fourteen frustrating hours later, we arrived on the doorstep of Lee-Anne Armstrong, the animal operations and foster care director of Second Chance Animal Aid (SCAA). Unfortunately, Lee-Anne had been unable to find us any accommodation that would accept dogs; dead dogs, of course, were permitted in the city's kitchens. She had therefore kindly invited us to stay in her miniature apartment, on condition that Oscar was cool with kitty cats. She had recently rescued seven that had been abandoned at the side of the road. I assured her that Oscar was a lover, not a hater, but when two kittens landed on top of the curtain rail and another in the laundry box within the first five seconds of our arrival, she knew we had lied.

I spent the duration of the weekend apologising on Oscar's behalf. Between the guilt trips, we attended two functions for the SCAA. One was an adoption event during which Oscar and I consumed far too much pizza, and the other was an event in an Irish pub, where we consumed far too much beer!

We had a tentative plan to visit the underground dog-meat market. Although this visit would have nothing to do with dog adoption, I felt it was important to include it in our tour. Whenever I had mentioned to *anyone* that Oscar and I were going to China, the reaction had been exactly the same on every single occasion: 'You had better watch out that they don't eat Oscar over there,' and they would laugh. Although everyone thought it hilarious, they actually had a point. Many of the dogs that wind up as hot dogs were once owned, had been stolen and were then sold to be sliced up.

Oscar didn't leave my sight for one second in China, except when we were inside Red Capital Ranch. I wanted to visit the meat market to see first hand what was really going on. I knew that there was plenty of stuff about these places on the internet that would make you lose your appetite forever, but perhaps seeing it for myself and filming the scenes would make for a more powerful documentary.

Lee-Anne, however, said that I should take a few issues into consideration before I decided to go to an underground market. The dog-meat traders are very wary of undercover agents or foreigners who look like they are there to expose the operation to the world, and they tend to take matters into their own bloody hands.

Would my blonde hair, blue eyes and the rolling camera in my right hand classify me as a local restaurateur looking to stock up my kitchen, I wondered. Lee-Anne and I didn't think so, and Oscar wasn't keen to be orphaned in China. I thought about it carefully. I could perhaps handle a confrontation, but, to be honest, I was much more afraid of what effect the images would have on my psyche. If I couldn't even watch Nemo being caught without crying my heart out, how did I think I was going to react when confronted with yelping dogs being skinned alive in front of my eyes?

The year before there had been a news article about a Chinese girl who had committed suicide after investigating the cruelty associated with factory farming in her country. Would I want to live after witnessing the terrible scenes, which would inevitably haunt me long after I had left China? I wasn't ready to quit the planet yet; I still had a tour to complete and a dog to lead. No matter what I did in that hellhole, no matter what I saw down there, I knew I wouldn't be able to stop the unheeded cries.

Over dinner off a busy street in Shanghai, Lee-Anne and I discussed the matter in more detail. I finally gave in and agreed to give the engagement a miss. As Lee-Anne stuck her fork into a succulent sirloin steak that had just been brought to the table, she recalled the time that she and some other activists had managed to stop a transportation of cats intended for the meat market.

She also described in detail all the horrendous conditions in which the cats and dogs were bred, transported and eventually killed in order to satisfy the Chinese consumer. The Chinese like dog meat because it keeps the body warm in winter. There are also those who believe that eating dog meat will boost their virility.

What was it about Chinese men, I wondered? With a bit of well-placed propaganda I could have them begging for Oscar's poop if I told them it would give them erections! The horrendous part is that, in order for the meat to have any medicinal 'value', it must contain adrenalin, and the slaughters are executed accordingly.

The methods are basic, crude and barbaric. Dogs are severely beaten, strangled or blow-torched. Pouring boiling water over a live animal is just one of a few ways adrenalin is stimulated just before death. Other methods include cutting off the dogs' paws so that they bleed to death, or handlers breaking the dogs' legs the night before slaughter only to return the following day to skin them alive.

The skins satisfy the demand for furry toys and coats, while the meat satisfies the tummies and penises of the masses.

Lee-Anne took another bite of her steak and continued. 'The market is expanding at such a rate that New Zealand and European breeders are now being approached to supply large breeding dogs, like the Saint Bernard and the German Shepherd, to China and the other Asian countries that also consume dog meat.'

Lee-Anne knew her subject. I liked her. She was honest, responsible and kind, and she was passionate about helping dogs and, specifically, cats, in Shanghai. She was like so many of my friends around the world who just *loved* animals. They loved their pets. They volunteered at their local pound. They gave generously to animal charities and despised the Chinese for being barbaric consumers of helpless dogs and cats.

But how could anyone with a fully functioning brain fail to make the direct connection between consuming a dog in China and eating a cow, pig, goat, sheep, whale, dolphin or chicken anywhere else in the world? Aside from a bit of cultural conditioning and brainwashing, what was the difference?

My friends would never consider themselves murderers, and neither did I, until I was sixteen. I was spending most of my time at high school trying to raise money for the SPCA, wanting to save as many dogs as I could because I loved animals. One day, while my best friend Evelyn and I were having a casual chat over lunch, she asked me why I spent all my time trying to save a few dogs when I would sit down to a meal and consume a different dead animal every day without even really thinking about it.

What was she talking about? I didn't eat animals. I ate ham and bacon sandwiches with a bit of mayonnaise and a slice of tomato. But Evelyn just looked at me and, after a few seconds, I glanced down at my sandwich. For the first time in my life, I made the connection between my lunch and an animal. My lunch box didn't contain a wholesome ham sandwich any more. It was a piece of dead pig disguised as something completely removed from its former self and stuck between two slices of bread. It bore no hint of suffering, pain or death. By the time that sucker was put on my sandwich, it no longer cried. It had been magically transformed into something that would satisfy the desires of my palate.

After our chat, I did some investigating on my own. I couldn't believe what was going on behind the scenes. Western society is showered with images of happy animals living on farms where the cows graze in lush green fields, pigs play in mud, and chickens chirp and chase the farm dog. It was all a lie to cover up the real story. If everyone knew what was really going on, no one would eat an animal ever again. The vast majority of animals that are raised for food live miserable lives in intensive confinement and in dark, overcrowded facilities politely called 'factory farms'.

Just that brief conversation with Evelyn more than twenty-two years ago ended my obsession with dead meat. That ham sandwich was the last time I ever contributed towards the greatest, most intense, widespread, expanding, systematic and socially sanctioned mass destruction of life forms in the planet's history.

Just how many animals are killed by people every year for food is not recorded exactly, but we're talking trillions of animals since World War II. Even if I had thought when I was sixteen that it was normal and morally acceptable to consume animals, it is the absolute disregard for their welfare before they are killed that was so disturbing. Every bite that I was taking was sending out a vote of approval for the industry.

I just didn't understand how 'animal lovers' such as Lee-Anne and others like her, who 'couldn't *possibly* eat' a dog or a cat, were able to condemn those who did just before swallowing another piece of cow! Pigs, for example, are smart and loveable creatures, and they also make wonderful pets. 'Pigcasso' had been able to catch a Frisbee!

Just like the dogs in China, broiler chickens, pigs and 'regular' lambs are slaughtered between six and twelve months of age. Only a calf is lucky enough to be murdered within a few days of being born. Just like the dogs in China, most ham, veal and drumsticks spend their short lives in filthy, cramped conditions in which it is often impossible for them to even turn around.

The true facts behind animals' living conditions and their quality of life may be a rather inconvenient truth, as we *love* our braais and biltong. But all meat is simply a dead animal that suffered a horrific fate to make it to your mouth; it doesn't matter what the species is. Cultural indoctrination and consumers' selective compassion are the only factors that make one kind of meat taste great and another taste bad.

I never raised the issue with Lee-Anne, but I had plenty of time to dwell on the subject during our long drive back to Beijing. I had never been a Bible-thumper on the issue, although I sometimes wished I had the courage for it. On our way to Beijing, we passed an open truck transporting pigs to an abattoir, where they would be made into neat little packages that would go on sale on supermarket shelves. The pigs had been thrown into the truck like shovels of sand. I noticed one pig that had obviously been one of the first to be tossed into the back of the vehicle. It was stuck under the others, which had been thrown on top of it, and its face and body were bleeding.

I knew that it was just one of the twelve million pigs that were being killed every week in China, so who really cared except me? The total disregard and disrespect for animals' welfare really got to me at that moment. Who was the man who had loaded all those animals? Who are these monsters who feel nothing for an animal's distress? Who are we to think that we have the right to treat animals the way we do?

I cried and cried and cried. In fact, I cried all the way back to Red Capital Ranch. Sensing that not all was kosher, even my dog left me alone. I cried enough tears in the back of that van to create a pond. And I wished with every ounce of my being that the pond would become a river that could turn into an ocean, which would rise up and wash away all the sorrows of the helpless, the weak and the defenceless who were at the mercy of the cold and callous animals known as human beings.

By the time we arrived at the ranch, my seat was sopping wet and the driver's right ear had been given a roasting, having had to listen to my rapidly expanding anti-Chinese sentiments. I have to admit that I did feel bad for subjecting the poor guy to my verbal outrage when he had no means of escape, but I don't think he understood much anyway. Although, in retrospect, I wouldn't be surprised if he did in fact quit his day job, never again to be seen transporting foreign blondes with dogs.

I had once again been reminded to be more conscious of everything I was doing in my life, whether it was what I wore, ate, bought or thought. It was proof of what I knew to be true: that every single person alive is making an impact on the world and the state of its existence every single day. Every decision we make has an impact, whether great or small, good or bad. It could even change the entire world. Would apartheid have prevailed in South Africa if Nelson Mandela and others of his ilk had not chosen to take a stand against it? Would the Chinese economy still prosper without the influx of capital from Joanne Lefson?

Unfortunately it probably would, but *I* was finished with supporting it. The 'Oscar' toys had been made in some factory in

Shanghai, but I wouldn't be placing another order. We had already spent far too much of our own money here. The cost of our stay in China had far exceeded the entire budget we'd had for Europe, and Oscar hadn't even lifted a leg on a famous landmark in a whole nine days! All things considered, there was one last piece of business to take care of before we would pack our bags.

If dogs over 35.5 centimetres aren't allowed in the heart of Beijing, how the heck was I going to get my super-sized mutt up the Great Wall of China? There are four main sections of the wall that have been restored and where everybody goes to take their snap. We needed only one of these sections to let us in, and we tackled the closest first – Mutianyu Great Wall. My interpreter, Kevin, was from the agency, and he knew the drill. Kevin would tell the guards at the main gate that Oscar was my brunch, which wouldn't sound nearly as ridiculous to them as hearing that the dog was my companion on a world tour to promote dog adoption!

If we got arrested, I had to insist that the dog remain with me no matter what. Separation would likely be permanent. We approached three guards, who looked a little confused when they saw us. Stunned is perhaps a better word. I didn't have to be a genius to realise that Oscar was the very first canine tourist wanting a date with *the* Great Wall! I also knew that dogs were forbidden on the wall, but I wasn't saying a word.

The stern-looking guards, dressed in uniform, stopped us at the gates, their black eyeballs piercing mine. I knew they didn't understand *what* I was doing there with my *dog*. Kevin started talking to them, and soon another two guards joined them. An animated debate in Mandarin ensued, but Oscar and I weren't sticking around to hear any more, as it would almost certainly be a 'no go' from the guards!

Instead, we slipped through the entrance, boarded the cableway and, within a few minutes, were walking upon one of the greatest landmarks of all time. The wall itself is over 5 500 miles long, but we weren't interested in getting any exercise, given the humid conditions. All we wanted was one good sniff, and it didn't take us long to find it.

It is said that if one has not climbed the Great Wall, one has not been to China. Well, Oscar and I have officially been there, done that! This wonder of the world, which has captured the imaginations of people throughout its long and distinguished history, that day captured something unfamiliar and enduring. Not even an army of cheap labour would be able to remove Oscar's scent from the bricks. Being the good dog that he is, he had held himself in the whole morning, and it was at least a litre of the finest, most potent golden juice I'd ever seen erupt from my little champion that perfumed the Great Wall of China.

This the Chinese could not eat nor lick up. They couldn't skin it, sizzle it or sell it. Indeed, on behalf of every dog in the People's Republic of China, Oscar had vanquished their triumphant symbol and national treasure with one final salute.

24

The Hollywoof Walk of Fame

Arriving in San Francisco felt like the start of a brand-new day. I knew California like the back of my dog, and I loved the place. Here, I didn't have to worry about Oscar's safety as I had in China.

I had first been introduced to San Francisco when I was eleven years old. My aunt and uncle were living in the Bay area at the time, and they invited my family over for the American summer. I loved every second of it. I loved the people, the food, the zillion TV channels and the weather, and my young eyes were delighted to see that famous rock, Alcatraz, for real. Heck, I even doted on the fog.

America was the place to be, and I vowed to return the moment I bunked school. And I did return, many times. Whenever I did, I would head straight for the Golden Gate Bridge. There weren't many man-made structures that really turned me on, but the orange vermillion bridge did it every time. I would take my time to walk the length of it from start to finish, gazing down on the ocean below from the safety of my safety net. The wild tides beneath me would invigorate my senses.

This was what I wanted Oscar to experience first as we touched down in our twenty-fifth country! As we walked along the Presidio, everyone stopped to fuss over my dog. The Chinese had been very scared of him; the mere sight of my teddy bear on paws had sent them and their rice cakes scurrying in all directions. But now, a day after leaving China, it was back to the good times. Everyone thought Oscar was the best thing they'd seen since pecan pie, and they felt obliged to remind me that my dog was 'Oh my gawd, so damn *cute!*' I didn't need to be told that, but boy, was Oscar happy to regain the top spot.

I may have lost my green card a few years back, but I still considered America to be my home away from home. Now it would be my pooch's playground too. We would be in the States for six weeks, and here I knew all the rules. I knew how to stretch the speed limit and when to act blonde. I knew when to use my accent to win favours and that I always had the democratic right to remain silent or sue anyone who didn't agree with me. More importantly, with the fake fashion I'd bought falling to pieces already, I knew the exact location of the best mall in town!

I figured Oscar wouldn't be allowed inside the shopping mall, so I left him in the car in the undercover parking lot with the windows slightly open. I couldn't have been in a better mood. I knew my credit card had fuel, I knew where my favourite jeans shop was located on the third floor, and I knew where my neck could get a free spray of its favourite fragrance in the department store on the ground floor.

Little did I know that I was going to purchase more advice than clothing that afternoon, and that it would forever change the way Oscar and I manoeuvred our way around the planet.

Upon walking inside the mall and stepping onto the escalator, a moving object in the corner of my left eye caught my swift attention. It wasn't a bird and it sure wasn't a plane. It wasn't for sale or part of a display fixture in a window either. It was someone's *dog*! I couldn't believe my eyes. Were dogs allowed to come shopping in the mall too, I wondered?

I turned around and charged down the up-escalator. I needed to get to the bottom of this story. I ran up to the woman, whom I assumed to be the owner of the dog. She looked as if she had just spent the entire day at every single make-up counter in the mall without washing her face once.

'Are dogs really allowed inside the mall?' I asked her.

'Don't be silly, honey, of course not,' she said.

My next question was an obvious one. Although I was hoping she would give me the answer without my having to beg for the obvious, my curiosity quickly got the better of me.

'So how *did* your dog get permission to come inside then?' I waited patiently for her answer, holding thumbs that it wasn't some secret from Tutankhamun's tomb.

As I listened to her story about her 'service dog' and the American Disabilities Act (ADA), I realised that there was indeed a reason why God had blessed America. She told me everything that I would ever need to know about being mentally suspect for a good cause.

Upon further investigation, I learnt that the ADA affords handicapped persons the right to be accompanied by a service animal in public places. An animal is considered to be a service animal if it has been individually trained to perform tasks for the benefit of a person with a disability. Most notably, disabilities and handicaps do not mean only physical impairments, but can also include having a mental disability.

Now we were talking. This was the Declaration of Independence for my dog, and one I'd only ever dreamt about. I had never peeped through such a big loophole in all my years as a self-confessed rebel, but I wasn't even going to need to tell a white lie to wrap this one up. I already had a few handy psychologists in Cape Town who would be able to verify in a court of law that their patient was a diagnosed nutcase for taking her dog on a world tour! But only one of them would be required to state that, when accompanied by her dog, 'Oscar the Great', she is a little less nuts.

In other words, with Oscar by my side, I was more capable of normal behaviour and less scary to the general populace. A faxed and dated copy of the psychologist's statement with his signature would seal the deal. I sent an email straight to my favourite head doctor, explaining what was required.

I had met Dr B the year before, when the Swiss golf pro had suggested we chat to an expert about our crumbling relationship. Unfortunately, when I'd brought up the subject of our 'el pronto' sex life, he had run away before any Viagra could be dispensed.

I had the letter from Dr B in my paws within a day, and, along with Oscar's medical record and a letter from his vet stating that he was a perfectly trained graduate, I sent the documentation off to a registration company in Washington.

Three days later I received a certificate and a wallet-sized card that officially confirmed my little star as a registered 'service dog'. I had spent four long years copying everyone else's hard work at university in order to get my degree, but in less than three days, Oscar had received his!

From a legal perspective, I didn't even *have* to get the paperwork. By law, Oscar didn't have to be registered and I was not obliged to show any written proof of my disability to anyone. But having the document, I was told, would just save a lot of hassle and questioning barks, especially when I didn't show any symptoms of ever having been an inmate at a nutty farm at an airport check-in counter.

Who would have thought that one small step in the mall would turn out to be one gigantic leap for muttkind? It was the kind of stuff that could start a revolution, and it did – certainly from the perspective of our travel arrangements. America was now our oyster. I was the shell, Oscar the pearl and America the sea of opportunity. Wherever I roamed, Oscar could follow, and at no extra charge. According to the Constitution of the United States of America, no one could stop us.

For the first time in Oscar's life, he was in the land of the free. He could come shopping with me and tell me which pair of jeans made me look thinner; he could stay with me in any hotel I checked in to, regardless of their pet policy; and he could join me for a gin and tonic in the lobby bar after a workout – together – at the gym. He could even fly with me in the aircraft cabin, and sit on the seat right next to me if it wasn't taken. Quite simply, it made our travel options so much more flexible; it turned our schedule upside down and all around the continental United States.

We had arranged to visit a dozen adoption agencies and shelters located in seven states, but now that Oscar had wings, we could do so much more. Oscar and I were so excited, we could barely contain ourselves, nor did we need to. Was travelling together in the cabin really going to be this simple? We were both a little sceptical and somewhat apprehensive, but decided to put the system to the test before truly celebrating our good fortune.

Our first flight would be from San Francisco to San Diego. After a visit to San Francisco Animal Care and Control, Oscar and I set off for the airport. We had been scheduled to drive to San Diego, but with a front-row seat at 35 000 feet, who needed to wend their way through the traffic? I had informed the airline at the time of my booking that I would be bringing along a service dog; all that was left to do was to make it to the airport on time.

Checking in with Oscar was a summer breeze. The staff smelt a rat, but they saw a dog. Then they asked for some sort of proof or identification, and the certificate did the trick. Although we were stopped a number of times by airport security before finally boarding the aircraft, it was all good experience for me. By the time we reached the plane, I knew that the system *worked*. I now had the confidence to growl my way past anyone who might just hint that I wasn't nuts enough to have my pooch by my side – even agents in the strictest security at JFK International!

After all the emotional drama and expense of having Oscar in the hold, boarding the aircraft *together* was truly a moment to behold. I don't recall the colour of the carpet, but it felt red – very rich, royal red, with a silver lining. By the time I sat down in my seat, my grin was so wide it touched both armrests. And I just couldn't wipe it off my face. As if already a seasoned traveller in economy class, Oscar located his seat, fastened his seatbelt and promptly went to sleep.

Blame it on a bug in the cabin, but with just that one flight, we were hooked. We both developed a very severe case of cabin fever and simply could not get enough of our own on-board entertainment! After enjoying the 'Spooktacular' event with the Helen Woodward Animal Center near San Diego, Oscar and I flew to New York. We arrived at the same time as the freezing weather, so we took a rain check all the way back to the Golden State, just because we could.

There, we visited Muttville, Contra Costa Animal Services and Tony La Russa's Animal Rescue Foundation. We stayed with the inspiring Nancy Janes, founder of the Romania Animal Rescue, which we had visited while in that country. When the clouds cleared over the Brooklyn Bridge, we flew all the way back to the Empire State. We visited NYC Animal Care and Control and went to shake the paw of friendship with Lady Liberty, because 'service dogs' were permitted on Liberty Island too.

From the East Coast we flew back to the West Coast to participate in a Surf Dog surfing competition at Huntington Beach. Oscar was a born traveller, not a surfer, and he had to take second place behind Abbie, a professional surf dog from San Diego.

After drying off, Oscar and I landed in Texas, where we would make a short stop at my old university. I hadn't been back since tossing my graduation cap towards the stars. From the Lone Star State we flew north and south, up and down, left and right, upside down and roundabout. If there had been a flight to the nearest Starbucks every morning, we would have taken that too! When our paws finally touched the ground, we were in Los Angeles, within sniffing range of the greatest pooch stars of all time.

First on our list was tracking down Oscar's childhood hero. Not to be confused with a puny little former planet or a Greek god of the underworld, there was only *one* Pluto, and the press had reported that he would be making a public appearance at Disneyland on the exact same day that we were planning a visit!

When we arrived at the park, every single attendant tried to direct us to the dog kennels – the holding cages where visitors can leave their dogs while enjoying the park. But, as a service dog, Oscar had a one-way ticket to meet Snow White, Cinderella, Donald and Daisy, Mickey, Minnie – and Pluto, of course.

When we did track down Mickey Mouse's dog, Oscar blushed all over. I had never seen him that shy before. He wobbled like glob of jelly in the daunting presence of Pluto. I told Oscar to get a grip and reminded Pluto that, while he may be one of the most popular cartoon characters of all time, he was really just like every other

doggie. Pluto communicated in a series of barks and body movements, and, just like my Oz, he had a very long tongue that spent
more time out in the sun than in his mouth. Both Oscar and Pluto
have large, engaging eyes, two big black ears and a tail. Pluto's tail
was arguably a bit too thin and snaky to quite match his celebrity
status; Oscar's was more like the tip of a Californian palm tree, which
was far too fancy for a previously disadvantaged dog!

During the course of the day, we chased Chip and Dale, discussed
dog adoption with 101 Dalmatians and even caught sight of London
Bridge with Peter Pan, without having to subject Oscar to a six-
month quarantine. We bumped into Goofy, famed for having little or
no intelligence, but Oscar wasn't at all interested in having his photo
taken with this clumsy canine.

Oscar was even asked to sign a few autographs of his own. I don't
know who people thought he was, but, when they asked, 'Winnie
the Pooch' just gave them the paws-up!

No one would have known that Oscar was on a whirlwind tour
of the world. We had had media coverage in every single country
thus far except the United States. When we had been invited to the
Playboy Mansion for a day in October, the *LA Times* had jumped
on the story. But when the playgirls had popped out of their
commitment, so had the *LA Times*. That's America, I told Oscar.
It's only about the rich and famous and the number of diamond
studs in your collar. Money and fame buy you attention, Oz, even if
you are up to no good.

When it came to the who's who of Hollywood, we couldn't
veer off onto Highway 1 for the gorgeous drive north to the SPCA
in Monterey County without parking off first on Hollywood
Boulevard. Over 2000 of the greatest names in the entertainment
business are embedded in the Hollywood Walk of Fame, but we
went on the prowl for just four. Rin Tin Tin and Strongheart had

appeared on the big screen long before Oscar had even been a figment of his great, great, great, great-grandma's imagination, but he knew all about Lassie, having seen a few reruns of the fictional collie dog on TV.

After paying his respects to each of these doggie heroes on the star-studded pavement, Oscar went to find his very own star. When he finally found our fourth hero at number 6721 Hollywood Boulevard, his nose looped right out of joint. 'Oscar' was spelt correctly, but they had got only one letter correct in his last name. Oscar took a seat on top of his star and quickly realised that no one could spot the difference between a Micheaux and a Lefson when his rear end was covering the name!

'Hey,' wagged Oscar to everyone admiring an Oscar in Hollywood. 'Who says a pavement special can't have his fifteen minutes of fame too?'

25

Viva Las Pooches

Oscar had claimed the concrete impression of his name as his own, but now he needed a week off in which to let his head return to its normal size. The drive from la-la land to Carmel-by-the-Sea is truly spectacular, and the destination even greater. Just like my dog, the town of Carmel is a true original. Every house looks like a storybook creation, as if handmade by a gingerbread man in the land of Make-Believe. It's hard to fathom that such a place can actually exist beyond the contrived imaginations of a fairy-tale production, but it does. It has also been voted one of the country's top dog-friendly destinations, so it's heaven for a hound on earth!

Restaurants offer special menus for dogs, and water is often served from a champagne bucket at no extra charge. For those that get thirsty beyond the delights of the doggie dining service, there's always the 'Fountain of Woof' to fall back in – a fountain in the centre of town exclusively for the use of dogs! Most of the quaint shops welcome dogs with bone-shaped biscuits outside their doors, and there's even a gallery named after a blue dog.

Hotels and inns offer pet-sitting services, and at the one that belongs to beloved actress and animal rights activist Doris Day, the guest of honour gets his own blanket and evening turndown service, with a home-made treat on top. Not surprisingly, Snoopy and Charles Schultz also chose to make Carmel their 'kennel'.

No matter what's yappening in town, a dog's best friend in Carmel is without question the wide, wonderful, spanking-white beach that is located just a step away from the centre of town. It welcomes dogs with wild abandon and doesn't ruin all the fun with a law about leashes. I couldn't wait to share the beach with Oscar. As we were spoilt for beaches in South Africa, I knew this would make him feel right at home – not that Oscar was showing any signs of homesickness.

Just when we thought Carmel couldn't get any better, it did. Overlooking the lovely beach is the world-famous Pebble Beach Golf Course and, after a tug of seaweed, Oscar and I set off along its lush green fairways. Around the cliffs of the eighth hole we walked, and then over to the notorious par-3 seventh hole. In the footsteps of the great Nicklaus and Watson, Oz landed in a bunker and walked across the putting surface without catching a birdie.

Almost a year and a half earlier, before Oscar and I traversed this terrain, I had stood at the edge of the green where the rocks and waves meet in a spectacular display of power. It was a rare sunny evening, and as I gazed across the beach into the distance, I thought about my life and where it was headed. I felt so deeply about dog adoption and the sad plight of dogs in shelters, and I desperately needed to find a way to vent the passion surging inside me.

Either that, or face losing what was left of my eyebrows, which I'd started plucking out in my growing frustration with my life. I started imagining a world tour with my dog, and at that very moment vowed that the next time I came to Monterey, my dog would be in my suitcase. Carmel held so many special memories for me; it was only fitting that I shared the town with my dog.

I had actually first discovered Carmel with folk singer John Denver, back in 1995. Although I had grown up listening to John's music, he and I had met in Cape Town on a golf course, on his birthday, at a moment that had already been written in the stars (or so his astrologer told us later). John was a regular participant in the AT&T Pebble Beach National Pro-Am, and a month later he called me up in South Africa, begging me to come and caddy for him. He reckoned I could help him swing like a golfer – and not like a singer – on national TV.

I didn't need much persuading to lug a golf bag around the greatest golf course in the world, rubbing shoulders with the most famous celebs and golfers in the universe.

Golf scores aside, it was one of the most exciting and enjoyable weeks of my life. I hugged Bill Murray, was introduced to Kevin Costner and finally got to tell Clint Eastwood that he looked just like my dad! Best of all, I got to know John better, with the added bonus of having him sing to me every day. This would be the first of many rounds of golf that John and I would share together – usually as a team, taking cash off Clint and co.

Monterey Bay was our favourite place. We lived and laughed there, he sang there, and in 1997, when John accidentally sent his LongEZ aircraft into a downward spiral into the watery view below, I cried there too. A year later I returned to Carmel with my new husband and some bittersweet memories in tow. I thought that the place would never be the same without my Rocky Mountain man, and when my new hubby was more interested in spotting sea otters amongst the seaweed than little white balls in the rough, I knew it to be true.

A decade or so later I returned again, this time with my dad, to celebrate his seventieth birthday over a round of golf at Cypress Point. And so I had shared this place with the three most important men in my life. Now, here I was again, with the mutt beneath my wings. To anyone on the outside, it would have looked like I was downgrading on companions, but from the inside, I knew that Oscar was my winning lotto ticket. We were soul mates and best friends. He couldn't sing or heal a whale, and he hadn't brought me into existence, but he sure could make me happy.

Oscar and I were staying at the Coachman's Inn, an adorable place in the centre of town. Thanks to the manager, we had the best suite in the house, which included a huge fireplace and a bed so big that my dog could run circles in his sleep and not disturb me once.

As I plunged into the featherbed that evening and peeped over the covers at Oz, I started to giggle. This whole scenario I had contrived with Oscar was absurd, but I loved it. I cringed at what my friends would think if they could observe us together. I knew that they would insist that I get checked into a maximum-security mental institution without parole – or my dog – and preferably as soon as possible.

My dog shared my bed. He picked *his* spot, and only then did I find mine. We hugged each other goodnight and kissed each other good morning, even if I had woken up with his nose on mine. I cooked for him and, in return, he cleaned my face. We exercised together, we travelled together and we dined together. We even watched each other go to the bathroom, and while I sat on the loo reading the *Sunday Times*, his face would peer up at me just below the headlines.

We never let each other out of sight, and we never once fought. Oscar was always happy to go with the flow. We were best friends on the worst of days and would give our life for the other without hesitation, should such a need ever arise. Quite simply, we had a relationship that most couples could only dream about.

The only element missing was ... a ring! At that moment, Oscar and I looked at each other, and we each knew what the other was thinking. We were both single and, although we knew that we would never have much of a love life together, the Swiss golf pro had ruined any interest I'd had in sex a long time ago! What do you think, Oscar? I asked. He wagged his tail, and I howled with laughter. If anyone had thought that I was nuts before for undertaking a world tour with a dog, they ain't seen nothing yet!

A week later, Oscar and I landed in the express wedding capital of the world, Las Vegas. We had hit the right location, but we now needed God to help us find a chapel with a wedding official who wouldn't call the police when we arrived to exchange our vows. There were plenty of chapels; we just wanted the one that would say 'we do' to marrying a dog!

We cruised down Las Vegas Boulevard and parked our rented Ford Mustang at the lower end of the Strip. There were more chapels down here than casinos; how could we not get lucky? Our first target would be the Graceland Chapel, a landmark on the Strip. With over fifty years' experience in marrying couples, could they possibly have an excuse not to let a pooch walk down the aisle? They had already married the likes of Billy Ray Cyrus and Aaron Neville. The great Jon Bon Jovi had held a concert in the parking lot for seventy-five couples who all renewed their vows at the same time. Surely the time had come for them to be rewarded with an Oscar? No, not exactly. We moved on.

From the Cupid Chapel to the famous Little White Wedding Chapel and every other chapel in between, we pleaded for someone to give us our paws in marriage. But our extraordinary request usually resulted in us explaining our case to security in the adjacent parking lot. God's servants were inequitably selective. If this was how they treated their brothers and sisters, they were in for a big shock when they got Upstairs one day.

But Oscar and I weren't giving up yet. This was the land of the free, and we had a democratic right to marry whatever would make us happy ever after! A few more chapels down the block, and we found ourselves facing a themed wedding chapel. From its cheap-looking exterior, it seemed likely that whoever was waiting inside would to want to hitch anything or anyone who pitched up.

It was weird. It felt perfect. We rang the doorbell and walked inside. Elvis was standing at the counter. Somehow, I knew he wouldn't decline my request. 'Hello, Elvis,' I said. 'To cut to the bone, will you marry me and my dog?' Elvis dropped his silver shades and looked me straight in the eye. Then he looked down at my dog. He put his shades back on, shook his hip for a brief second and then spat the words right out: 'Baby, this is Vegas. We marry anything here!'

The lights were dimmed, and the beautiful stained-glass windows high above the altar sprang to life. All that had to happen now was the chapel doors to open. I knew my dog couldn't ditch me. I had his passport, and even with his service-dog status, he still couldn't go far without his beautiful bride. Then the doors swung open, the music started playing and, moments later, Oscar was rolling down the aisle in the passenger seat of a pink Cadillac to the sound of 'You ain't nothin' but a hound dog', courtesy of Elvis, who was in the driver's seat. A black bow was fastened around Oscar's neck. I lifted my veil. I couldn't have wished for a more handsome 'husband'.

Elvis read out our vows, and when it came to wishing us a hunka hunka burnin' love for the rest of our lives, Oscar promptly rolled over and went to sleep. But we still got the badge, the certificate and our names up in lights on the billboard outside the chapel. The deed was done.

When the news reached home, my parents were hardly amused at having a *dog* as their new son-in-law. Even my nine-year-old niece Annika phoned me to say that, although she liked me and Oscar very much, she just wanted to let me know that the wedding wasn't 'very cool'. I knew that when she eventually saw the footage of the wedding, she'd change her mind and welcome her new uncle-in-law into the family.

My husband and I took the moment in our stride. Of course the 'wedding' had been all about shooting footage for the documentary – and perhaps there was just the teeniest desire to buck the system, which both Oscar and I thought needed bucking every now and again – but make no mistake, we didn't take our vows lightly. We promised to promote 'pound hounds' around the world until death did us part, or until every homeless dog was adopted, whichever came first. We knew that it would be a lifelong commitment, just as it was for the over 5 000 independent animal shelters that were scattered across the United States.

Before our wedding, and in order to enjoy a combined kitchen tea and stag party, Oscar and I had visited the Animal Foundation in Vegas (established by the Lied Foundation), which was probably the best facility we had seen. For one, there weren't any wire cages. The dogs were kept in indoor facilities, and each enclosure was surrounded by glass and fitted with under-floor heating. The shelter also had one of the best adoption rates in the county. It is estimated that 25 per cent of all animals that enter shelters in the States are eventually adopted.

The public is passionate about promoting dog adoption, so much so that when Vice-President Joe Biden went to buy a puppy, the breeder concerned received so many death threats that the Secret Service and the FBI had to be called in!

One can understand that animal lovers get very sensitive when the figures are added up: conservative estimates reveal that between six and eight million animals enter shelters in the United States every year. Other reports reflect a figure almost double that. Either way, the numbers paint a very sad picture. More than half of the animals that enter these shelters meet their end on the euthanasia table or in a gas chamber – over a quarter of a million animals every month, at least 405 lives every hour, or one life every nine seconds.

And that's only in the United States! These animals aren't bad apples. Each one of them is a healthy, friendly being, just like Oscar, who would have made a wonderful pet and best friend given half a chance.

The biggest challenge faced by the dog-adoption agencies is to educate the public and make people realise that they are each a part of the solution. If people would simply sterilise their animals and choose to adopt instead of buying from breeders and pet stores, the unnecessary killing would stop. Oscar and I had by now travelled the world over, and no matter the country, the culture or the shelter, the solution remained the same *everywhere*.

Back on the Strip, Oscar's idea of a wedding night included a few hands of Coyote Poker at the Tropicana Casino, an early night at Caesar's Palace and a late sunrise over the Grand Canyon the following day. The honeymoon was a whole different story. My first husband had forgotten to take me on a honeymoon, and he had been doomed from that day forth until divorce did us part.

With Mr Lefson, I didn't need one. It was 'happily ever after' just being by each other's side, no matter where we found ourselves in the world. Besides, the groom was traditionally expected to pay for the honeymoon, and my husband was not exactly a sugardoggie. I agreed to consider the remaining mileage of the World Woof Tour as our official honeymoon, if Oscar agreed to a little test at our very next destination.

Now that I was married, I felt it only fair to find out what exactly my husband was. From the day I rescued Oscar from the pound, everyone who ever laid eyes on him asked me: 'What *is* he?' I didn't have a clue, but I would say that he was a 'mix-a-lot-A-LOT'. Intense debates ensued at the very sight of Oscar; it became the discussion point at every dinner table he and I graced with our presence. Oscar, of course, didn't give a hoot.

At the time, neither did I. I wanted a dog. It had to have four legs, a nose, a tail and preferably two ears that *listened*. In return, and without any training, I knew that the dog would always have, hold and cherish me. For better, for worse, for richer, for poorer, in sickness and in health, it would remain by my side. It would always stand by me, forgive me, excuse me, adore me, lick me and love me, no matter what I said or did or whether I woke up with a zit on my nose or not.

Which is *exactly* why I can't understand some people's obsession with buying a certain breed of dog. A dog provides a lifetime of loyalty to humans no matter what it looks like, and with humans always striving to be different, why on earth do they want their dog to look like others of its breed, for goodness' sake? And if the choice is between buying a dog and saving a dog's life, surely the decision is a no-brainer? Anyone who is smarter than a fifth-grader should know as much!

Oscar was a one-of-a-kind canine find. He was a freedom fighter, the centre of attention, my jackpot and a wonderful companion. It was obvious that his mother hadn't been picky and that his father hadn't stuck around long enough to teach his son how to cross a road. But who hasn't had a troubled childhood? My mutt had turned into the perfect dog nevertheless, a class act that breeders could only dream of cloning.

The only reason I now wanted to know the root of his 'tail' was simply because I could. Since arriving in the land of opportunity, a number of Oscar worshippers had suggested I give my adorable dog a DNA test. It was a simple, easy and affordable test and it was available at most veterinarians. Why not, I thought. If something ever had to happen to my husband, knowing his ancestry could save his life!

We flew into Fort Lauderdale, where we met Jack Russo of Bobbi's World Kennels. He had kindly agreed to help us sort out Oscar's export permits for the Caribbean, and an appointment with a veterinarian had already been scheduled. It was impossible not to adore Dr Rudd Nelson of the Bayview Animal Clinic. He had twenty dogs of his own, and was ready to make it twenty-one if Oz was denied entry into Puerto Rico!

Dr Nelson was also a gambler and ready to place a bet on the story of Oscar's tail. So sure was he that Oscar was a cross between a Wheaten Terrier and something else, that he promised to provide the Wisdom Panel DNA analysis for free if he was wrong. Dr Nelson took a blood sample and sent it off to the lab, but when the results arrived in my inbox, Wheaten Terrier wasn't to be found anywhere on the radar screen. Dr Nelson had to swallow a slice of humble pie. He certainly didn't have to feel embarrassed. In the zillions of suggestions I had heard over the years, no one had got even one gene right! Finally, the cat was out of the bag and the miracle of science had revealed some answers.

My unidentifiable furry object wasn't a Muppet, a whippet, the gopher in *Caddyshack* or a clone of Yoda of *Star Wars* fame. Oscar Lefson was a minor mix between a Pembroke Welsh corgi, a German shepherd, an English springer spaniel and a good old basset hound.

At last, the mystery of Oscar's pedigree was finally history, and we could let him just *be*!

26

Canine of the Caribbean

When Oscar and I woke up at the glorious Rio Mar Beach Resort in Puerto Rico, we had already dodged the odds. We weren't separated, divorced or having any post-nuptial remorse. In fact, the only item missing from our registry was a tan, and we were about to take care of that! A private stretch of beach beckoned beyond our balcony, and thirty-six fairways of grass surrounded our bedroom. Hound and wife had indeed arrived in the Caribbean.

Animal welfare in the Caribbean is a relatively new concept, and the seven shelters on the island spend much of their time and resources educating the public about basic pet care. We had the pleasure of spending a day with Gloria Marti and volunteer extraordinaire Cybelle Cartagena of the Save A Sato Foundation. They collect homeless dogs from the streets of Puerto Rico and rehabilitate them, and an impressive 75 per cent of these *satos* are eventually adopted through their sister agencies in the United States.

Gloria founded the charity fifteen years ago and will be the last to tell you that she hasn't taken a day off since! After hearing that, Oscar and I didn't dare complain about our jet lag, demanding travel schedule or dirty laundry; this lady had a level of dedication we could only dream about, lying under our coconut-tree canopies later that afternoon!

After Puerto Rico, Oscar and I were supposed to visit Cuba, even though there weren't any shelters on that island. There was, however, a sterilisation initiative on the go, called the Spanky Project. The only obstacle in our way was Oscar's import permit ... again. To have one or not to have one, that was now the question – and no one could answer us. The Spanky Project couldn't help us either, although they were quick to remind us that Cuba was a long way from Italy, and the Cubans cared more for tobacco leaves than for bleached blondes. Immigration in Cuba was a strict affair, and a blonde rocking up with a hound in her handbag would not convince Castro to raise the white flag.

It soon became clear that no one had ever imported a dog into Cuba, nor had anyone ever smuggled one out, which explained why there wasn't a pet-travel agency on the planet that could tell us what to do!

However, Oscar and I were willing to be the guinea pigs. After all, if nobody knew what we needed, the airport officials probably wouldn't know either. There was still one major problem, though: assuming we got my hound into Havana, how were we going to get an import permit for Costa Rica, our next stop, if there weren't any registered veterinarians in Cuba?

After much deliberation, the decision was finally taken to trade a Cuban cigar for a bow and arrow in the heart of the American Southwest, and for two days that's exactly where we went. Monument Valley is right on the Arizona–Utah border. This is where infamous craggy red buttes punctuate a wide-open frontier that has been immortalised over the decades by countless Hollywood Westerns. This is where John Wayne saddled up and where the Lone Ranger saddled down. It's where the West was won and, unfortunately for Avis car rentals, where their Thunderbird was lost.

We had decided to take our wheels on the scenic 'drive' inside the Monument Valley Navajo Tribal Park in a bid to film a low-budget epic of our own. Instead, we made a strong case for car insurance! We drove that poor vehicle all over the landscape and didn't brake for anything that grew in our way. We were more worried about protecting our uninsured body parts against frostbite – the very first snowfall of the season had decided to bestow its early blessing at exactly the same time as our visit.

We had planned to follow the summer sun throughout our tour and, bar a few cold snaps in the Swiss Alps, our plan had thus far worked perfectly. As we certainly didn't have any space in our bags for winter woolies, being freezing cold was the price we had to pay for the spectacular scenery that surrounded us: the snow-capped buttes and sculpted pinnacles were simply awe-inspiring.

Unfortunately, there wasn't enough snow to cover up all the stray dogs that roam around the Navajo reservations, and one in particular caught my eye while I was having breakfast one day. It was a young black dog that was standing dead still in the vast parking lot behind our hotel, staring at the only car in the vicinity. It was obviously longing for a scrap to be thrown from the car window. The poor thing was homeless, hopeless and hungry.

As the snow gently covered its slight frame, I pressed my cold nose up against the window and watched this pathetic little creature beg for salvation. Eventually the condensation blurred my vision and I went back to my seat. What I had just witnessed would have smudged a hundred picture-perfect landscapes, and it broke my heart. I had seen two people sitting in the vehicle, but after a few moments they had driven away without making even one donation to the tarmac below.

Did this couple even notice the dog standing out in the freezing cold, I wondered. It was impossible for them not to have seen it. How could anyone not take pity on it? I wished for a brief moment that I could understand the thoughts of these people, but realised that I dared not enter their heads for fear of turning to stone. They did not inhabit a world I would ever care to know.

But thinking alone wouldn't save a starving dog. I reached for another plate and began loading it up. By the time I had finished with the breakfast buffet, I had relieved it of enough food to feed a nation. I left no egg unturned – my friend outside was hungry, not fussy.

Careful not to lose a morsel, I opened the hotel door and sank into the snow. A few minutes later, my work for the day was done. Somewhere in the lone spaces of Arizona, a full American breakfast had pulled into an empty parking lot and a little black dog could finally have its day.

After spending the better half of the morning trying to warm up along Highway 163, we drove back down to Phoenix, where we caught a direct flight to San José, Costa Rica, where we were to meet Patricia Artimaña of the El Arca de Noé Animal Sanctuary. Patricia had been planning a huge adoption event for over a year in anticipation of our visit to her beloved country. Despite our amended travel itinerary and mercurial finances, we had miraculously managed to make Costa Rica on time!

The first person to meet us in the arrivals terminal was the latest, and last, addition to my long line of cameramen: Jonathan was a dude from Cape Town. A friend of mine had convinced him to help me out on the final stretch of the tour. He was tall and skinny, and aside from the tuft of fluff growing from his lower chin, he looked squeaky clean, sweet and sincere. Even if he'd sported more hair than a gorilla, I would have been relieved that I had someone to take over the camerawork again.

I had waved goodbye to Inaam in Thailand, from where he had headed back to India in order to obtain a visa for China. He never made it. Immigration refused to allow him to board his flight from Delhi to Beijing. He was accused of carrying a counterfeit visa and of having written a fan letter to the Dalai Lama ten years previously. That basically summed up his brief travelling career, and there was nothing I could do to help him. A tantrum would fail to make anyone quake in their boots half a world away. I had thus been forced to learn how to use the camera very quickly, but had also hired freelance cameramen along the way in order to shoot the necessary footage.

Costa Rica's national news team was waiting for Oscar outside the terminal building. I wasn't expecting anyone to meet us at the airport except for Patricia and Jonathan, and was thus completely unprepared. Oscar, of course, always looked good. He was the star everyone had come to see, but as his official interpreter, I should have been better prepared for my pooch's paparazzi. I had known as far back as Greece that pyjamas never look good on TV, no matter how much make-up you wear in order to try to shift the focus away from your outfit!

Thanks to Patricia's precise planning, Costa Rica would turn out to be one of our favourite destinations. Patricia was a fantastic person, a breath of fresh air bubbling over with enthusiasm. With her huge heart, she was always looking for ways to help us out. She had arranged everything for us for this leg of our trip, and her two entertaining French friends, Alexandra and Valerie, also lent a hand. They were forever calling us up or popping in to make sure that we were comfortable, alive and safe from snakes. Valerie was an eternal pessimist, so much so that it was impossible not to laugh out loud at all her dismal predictions. It didn't matter what we did or didn't do in Costa Rica, Valerie was always in the shadows, reminding us to 'BE CAREFUL' and to watch out for the 'damn snakes'!

I have a serious snake phobia. Valerie's false alarms may have been funny to everyone else, but they scared the living daylights out of me. My life basically revolved around staying out of the paths of snakes. When I was in Texas on the golf scholarship, I even surrendered fifty yards off my drive in order to keep the ball going straight and narrow. Thus, after four years in the rattlesnake capital of the world, I was the only person in the Lone Star State who hadn't ever seen a rattlesnake! I had absolutely no intention of breaking my unblemished record any time soon.

Thanks to Valerie's constant reminders, I never sat on a toilet seat in Costa Rica for fear that a venomous viper would jump up and bite me! As most of the 135 species of snakes in the country are well camouflaged and nocturnal, I had to adapt or die. I always looked under my sheets and turned my socks inside out before going to bed, and I kept the bathroom light on in case I suddenly needed to get out of the room. I also pushed Oscar in front of me wherever we went, and I never fell asleep without keeping at least one eye wide open.

When the day of the adoption event arrived, I decided to wear my favourite, made-in-Thailand T-shirt to mark the occasion: 'Oscar for President' was printed in big, bold letters on the front of the T-shirt. Not even a blind dog could have missed it. Perhaps if I had known then that the president of Costa Rica was also an 'Oscar' I would have opted for a different design!

Seven dog-adoption agencies joined in the festivities. No snakes were sighted, and eleven adorable dogs were adopted during the event. Patricia had hoped for many more adoptions, but the strong media presence meant that the dog-adoption message would be spread far beyond the confines of the event. With any luck, it would also reach the office of the president himself!

For the two remaining days we had in Costa Rica, we decided to give Valerie a dose of her own medicine and be 'very *un*careful'! Oscar and I spent the second-last day of our visit in a luminous yellow gyrocopter high above the Arenal Volcano on the outskirts of San José. Oscar was a chill pill no matter what we got up to, but my fear of heights *and* my fear of flying were surpassed only by my phobia for slithering snakes.

The German pilot tried to convince me that gyrocopters weren't dangerous, as the machine was already in autorotation and could just glide down and land should the engine suddenly fail. Land where, I wondered. I looked left, right, down and all around and saw only a dense rainforest that contained at least 135 species of snakes, with a melting pot of piping-hot lava directly below us.

I switched gears mentally and reminded myself that the weak link in any aircraft is the pilot. The fact that I was facing the back of this one's helmet was a good sign. He had survived for this long as a pilot, and would surely live to see another day – or at least another thirty minutes, while we finished looking at the ozone layer.

Surviving the lean, mean yellow machine meant we could participate in another *Fear Factor*–like episode. This time, though, it would take place a little closer to Mother Earth, at the Turu Ba Ri Tropical Park, to be exact. This was where the World Woof Tour met Superman, and where the hand of God rested on a cable and a very strong hook.

The zip line that we were about to 'fly' across was the longest and fastest in the whole of Costa Rica. As I lay belly-down on the boarding tower, I looked out yonder at the kilometre of cable that would carry us over the forest canopy and, presumably, to safety on the other side. I was attached to the zip line by more cable, which was fastened to a harness that was centred around my back. The very first dog ever to take on a zip line was then fastened to me by a harness that had been made especially for him in South Africa.

At the count of three, Oscar and I had to hold on tight, close our eyes and scream our tonsils out. As we flew over the green blur below us, we couldn't help but feel rather Superman-like. For a superhero, it was nothing to fly over 135 species of snakes! Having been there, done that, we were now ready to grab our life jackets and go fishing for piranhas in the great Amazon River.

We flew into Iquitos, a bustling Peruvian town located in the heart of the Amazon Jungle and accessible only from the air. Within its boundaries is situated an animal shelter accessible only by water! Amazon Community Animal Rescue, Education and Safety (Amazon CARES) was founded in 2004 by American dynamo Molly Mednikow, who admits to waking up each and every morning still wondering how the hell she ended up in the South American jungle with one dog shelter and a thousand mosquito bites! It is incredible what she has been able to create in the most extreme climate and under challenging circumstances. Through a thicket of overgrowth, Molly cleared the way for a jungle shelter that houses between twenty and thirty dogs at any given time. She arranges for volunteer vets from over a dozen countries to visit Amazon CARES five times each year to assist with sterilisation, and they have helped to sterilise almost 4000 dogs since May 2004. Through all of her efforts, Molly has instilled a new perspective on animal welfare in one of the poorest regions in the world. It is simply remarkable, and was just the inspiration we needed to explore the vast region further.

Seeing the greatest river in the world was a dream come true for me, but cruising on it in the most luxurious accommodation the river had to offer was beyond the realms of even my wildest imagination.

The *M/V Aqua* is the brainchild of Francesco Galli Zugaro, founder and CEO of Aqua Expeditions, and while he had never considered catering for a canine on board before, he was amused by my most unusual request and curious enough to give it a try.

Heading towards the origin of the Amazon, we had plenty of time to adapt to our oversized, air-conditioned cabin suite, which boasted an enormous window through which to view the river. One of our favourite pastimes was to snuggle up under the blankets and imagine all the creepy-crawlies in the muddy water and dense thicket out yonder that couldn't touch us. Thanks to Valerie's words of caution, which still haunted me, I had already checked the sealant around the window frame to ensure that there would be no unexpected visitors or 'mutt overboard!' in our room.

A skiff took Oscar to the shore every morning so that he could relieve himself of the few sips of fine wine he'd consumed the night before, and he had over one billion acres at his disposal on which to expel what was left of his fine doggie dinner.

Oscar was totally and utterly obsessed by the diversity of the sights and smells of this pristine wilderness. Kenya may have had the Big Five, but this place had the full nine yards, and then some!

From the mother ship we explored the region from the safety of our nippy skiff, manoeuvring through vast stretches of water as well as dark, damp tributaries that would make even those of the Hunt for the Blood Orchid abandon their mission. Under the very capable captaincy of Juan Tejada, we had the opportunity to see endangered pink Amazon dolphins, three-toed sloths, fuzzy orange and chic black howler monkeys, black jaguars, a vast array of vibrant bird species, and even a Homo sapiens or two inside their dugout canoes.

Fortunately, the only item we couldn't tick off on our 'naturalist' checklist was the largest species, and my greatest fear – the legendary

230

anaconda. Ye Olde European explorers of the South American jungle had recorded giant boas that measured up to 100 feet in length. Juan claimed to know where we could find one, but somehow my body wasn't in the mood to be coiled, squeezed, suffocated, crushed and then swallowed whole, thank you very much. I didn't have to ask for my hound husband's vote of confidence either. In this case, the wife ruled the roost!

There are actually more than 175 snake species in the Amazon Basin, and for the first time in Aqua Expeditions' history, we didn't see *one*! Admittedly, we had excused ourselves from the jungle walk, where passengers voluntarily chop their way through virgin Amazon terrain. We had barely let our boots touch land. On the rare occasions that we had, it had indeed been a rewarding experience.

Meeting some of the indigenous people who live in the Amazon and within the vast Pacaya-Samiria National Reserve was a privilege bestowed upon only a fortunate few and, now, a dog. Oscar and I visited a few jungle schools and handed out Rogz collars to the locals, who put them on their own dogs. It was also a good excuse for Oscar to challenge the local children to a game of soccer. I watched in wonder as a few dozen kids chased a foreign dog and a muddy, half-inflated ball across a clearing in the Peruvian jungle.

How incredible is this, I thought. I knew I would remember this unusual and inspiring moment for the rest of my life. I took it to heart, and, with tears flowing, I thanked everyone on the *Aqua*, in the Amazon and in the heavens who had afforded us this unforgettable experience.

When it was all over, Team Amazon and Oscar convinced me to join them for a swim in *the* Amazon River to cool off. The lengths of the Amazon and the Nile have been locked in a tight battle for the title of the world's longest river, but it didn't matter right then. Whichever way the cookie crumbled, Oscar had dived into both. As for me? Well, I was just praying that a strange new strain of bacteria wouldn't chew off my fanny before it could go on the Inca Trail!

27

Muttchu Pittchu

We were on the prowl for the Lost City of the Incas, but we weren't going to have to hunt hard. It being the biggest tourist attraction in Peru, locating it was going to be more like trying to find a haystack in a needle. One ninety-minute flight from Lima to Cusco, then a train followed by a bus and, with any luck, we would arrive at the cherry on top.

From a modern human perspective, the route was embarrassingly simple. From a dog's point of view, it would call for every last trick up MacGyver's sleeve! The Incas never stuck to the beaten path, and getting to their rather inconvenient location high up in the Andes mountains required a substantial amount of time and expense. The last thing we wanted was to trek all the way up there and be told that my pooch could not enter. In order to avoid any doggie disappointment, I had made a number of inquiries months before our planned visit. I contacted a dozen hotels in Cusco, but those that bothered to reply made it clear that no dogs were allowed.

I contacted PeruRail, but I couldn't get an answer from them either. I figured we could probably hire a car to get from Cusco to

Urubamba Valley if the train was fussy, but the bus from the station to the famous ruins was linked to PeruRail. If we could get on the tracks, we could get on the road, and if we could get onto both, we would land right outside the entrance gate to the ancient ruins.

The possibility that red tape would ruin our plans would still exist then, with less than 100 metres to walk. As I didn't want to shatter any of the sensitive dry-stone walls with a high-pitched tantrum, I contacted the Ministry of Foreign Trade and Tourism to get the scoop, but, again, I did not receive any answers.

We needed help from a local travel agency, which would be able to make all the right calls in Spanish and then turn our question marks into exclamation barks. I explained to the agency that Oscar was a service dog and that we were in Peru to film the greatest documentary ever made. I figured that perhaps these two factors would help the agency to twist a few arms.

As it turned out, all it did was help the agency to confirm some accommodation in Cusco and a 'no dog!' everywhere else. I didn't have to remind them that they were dealing with a determined brat of psychopathic proportions; they knew that already. I had never learnt how to accept no for an answer, and my attitude had served me well thus far. We were at the Jorge Chávez International Airport, ready for our flights to Cusco, and there was no way we would turn back now. The word 'yes' was non-negotiable. The agency would find a way for us to see Machu Picchu, or I'd sue them before they could say, 'Here come the Spanish'! Fortunately for them, I was about to uncover the secret solution to all of Oscar's travel troubles.

No one in South America had the faintest idea what a service dog was, and we had an aeroplane to catch. I had tried to get Oscar permission to fly in the cabin, but it was impossible to explain the North American Disabilities Act in English with a South African accent to a Spanish-speaking employee. How would I get my hound on board without a demotion to the hold? Sending Oscar back down into the depths of the aircraft would be the surrender of a service dog's rights!

Besides, Oscar was now a seasoned cabin junkie. He had grown accustomed to walking down the aisle and placing his doggie bag under the seat in front of him. He knew where to sit, he knew when to stay and he could hold out for a bathroom break over a sixteen-hour period. He provided free entertainment and a pleasant distraction, and he never got irritated when everyone on board lined up to pat him when he was trying to read the in-flight magazine. He was, in fact, the perfect passenger. Every cabin crew wanted his kind on board on every flight! To take the cabin away from Oscar now would only damage his confidence, for which I would never be able to forgive myself; it also wouldn't be fair to all his fans on board.

It was time to think outside the box. Even a fifth-grader knew that guide dogs were allowed everywhere – even in Malaysia! The only potential problem was that I wasn't blind. Or was I? If I didn't have to be physically disabled to qualify for my mental rights under the Disabilities Act, did I have to be physically blind to have a legitimate visual impairment? Could my blindness perhaps be more about my ignorance in seeing what was going on in the world around me?

Put it this way: I wasn't recycling at the moment, I had bought products from China and my global footprint was expanding with every flight I was taking. *Of course* I was blind – blind to the negative impact my behaviour was having on the world around me. I couldn't believe that I hadn't thought of this before we had taken off from Cape Town International Airport!

The possibility was so bright that I would now *have* to wear shades – but we had to remain calm. There were just a few more things to consider before we proceeded to the check-in counter. No one in their right mind was going to grasp the concept of mental distortion, and even with a severe case of myopia, anyone would see our story coming a mile away. To make the situation easier for everyone to understand, it would be simpler to play out the part as if I had a physical impairment and worry about the technical explanation later, should one of us get arrested. I would put on the shades, hold on to my dog for dear life and fall over anyone who got in my way.

As luck would have it, I had just bought an el cheapo pair of very dark, oversized sunglasses in Iquitos. I called up my doctor in Cape Town and asked him to do me a favour ... a very *big* favour. Within ten minutes, I had the ammunition I was looking for in my inbox – a carefully scripted letter stating that Oscar was my pair of prescription glasses!

Now I needed a dog who was ready to take the leading role. In theory, Oscar was already a guide dog – he'd made me follow him across five continents! It was just the formal training that was missing. He hadn't had the good fortune of growing up in a privileged environment that had afforded him the opportunity to study for a degree in 'guiding lights', but he did have medical science on his side. Although he was not one of the three most common breeds used as guide dogs, Oscar's DNA test proved that he came from the right stock – among his ancestors had been at least one German shepherd.

On top of that, Oscar had an orange jacket, which I had specially ordered for him when we were in Florida, with the words 'service dog' on it. For all intents and purposes, the locals might translate it as 'guide dog'.

Now all I had to do was to act blind, whatever that meant. Drama was the only subject I had ever failed at school, but now, presented with a cause greater than a grade, perhaps I could produce an award-winning performance.

I closed my eyes, grabbed my dog's lead in one hand and Jonathan's arm in the other, and headed for the check-in counter. Oscar had his 'tall tail' up and was trotting along like a born leader. When our time came to check in, I could feel my heart skip a few beats. This tour of ours was getting crazier by the hour, and I vowed that I would check myself into a clinic the day I landed back in Cape Town – assuming we ever found our way back there!

Jonathan took care of the ticketing and the luggage, while Oscar and I stood staring into the abyss. A few conversations were exchanged between the staff members, but half an hour later we were on board and on our way to Cusco … along with an unexpected business-class upgrade!

One obstacle down; two to go. A woman from the agency met us at the airport and checked us into our hotel. PeruRail had denied our request to take Oscar on board: when we'd informed them that he was actually a guide dog, our previous correspondence had given the game away. They knew Oscar was only a guide in disguise. The answer was a flat 'NO'.

The woman from the agency strongly recommended that we leave Oscar at the hotel and take the train to Machu Picchu the following day, or face the unfortunate reality that we had come to the region 'for nothing'. Because of a recent mudslide and subsequent road closures, it was impossible to hire a vehicle, and there were no more permits available to tackle the Inca Trail on foot.

Still, there was no way in hell we were leaving my dog behind. Oscar was the reason we were here. If he could convince as a guide dog, he could also play the part of a suitcase. The meeting was over. The entire team would assemble the following morning at seven and take the arranged transport to the train station!

Just before arriving at San Pedro Station, we stopped to give Oscar a quick bathroom break. This would be the last drop zone before our arrival at Machu Picchu four hours later. When Oscar was done, I popped him into my shoulder bag, covered his head with a sweater and hoisted all twenty-two kilograms over my right shoulder. We were ready to take on our next challenge.

Jonathan led the way, and I followed closely behind him. We handed our tickets to the ticket master and then proceeded to the railway car. We had paid for the Vistadome – the most spacious compartment that any train in the region had to offer. The Vistadome had the added advantage of being fitted with large side and overhead windows, allowing for panoramic views of the Andes – and providing the perfect distraction from a stowaway dog!

The train was full, but there was plenty of legroom and breathing space for our doggie bag! The professional staff on board served refreshments and snacks throughout our journey, but my bag never blinked so much as an eye. Aside from my dislocated shoulder, everything seemed to be going along nicely. Although ... something was starting to smell not quite right ...

Within seconds the smell was so bad that I was expecting oxygen masks to drop from the overhead locker above our seats.

Admittedly, it was all my fault. I had included a boiled egg in Oscar's dinner the night before, and I knew that a suddenly altered diet had the potential to upset his stomach. But this was more like an atomic explosion! This was the kind of gas that could fuel an economy, ignite a war or make a Himalayan camel retreat. Oscar was on a roll. One after the other, he just kept on producing the goods. And I couldn't tell him to stop for fear of exposing his presence. I couldn't take him outside and I couldn't bend over to stick a plug in his sink!

There was no mistaking where the sulphurous aroma was coming from, and with Oscar being invisible, *everyone* was now staring in absolute disgust at Jonathan and me.

It was good to get off the train at last, to put it mildly. Now that we were all free again, we could release the culprit back into fresh air. It was time to stick the sunglasses back on my nose and start tripping over everything – as a convincing performance was crucial if we wanted to get on the bus with Oscar and make it to the sacred Inca landscape. But, we needn't have worried, since we boarded the bus without any problems. Twenty minutes later we were standing outside the entrance to our prize. I gripped Jonathan's arm tightly as we proceeded to the ticket booth.

Immediately, the guard sounded the alarm. 'Dog forbidden!' I felt like a Colombian drug lord discovered with enough marching powder to keep an army going. Goodness, my dog just wanted to sniff out an old ruin, not a new coke plantation! I readied the mace in my pocket. If I had to use it in order to get that one snap of my pooch at Machu Picchu, I was willing to go for it!

But then Jonathan stepped forward and calmly stated that Oscar was a guide dog and that I was blind. If the Peruvian guard had spoken better English, I'm sure he would have asked me what the hell I was doing on a remote mountain peak when there was nothing for me to see. Instead, he just grunted and allowed me to go through the gate. Getting the camera through security wasn't so easy, however: filming inside the site is also strictly forbidden. Over the course of the next ten minutes, Jonathan, by some miracle, managed to convince the guards that the oversized camera was just a cellular phone, albeit one on steroids.

The masterpiece of architecture perched on top of the dramatic mountain range exactly resembled the images I'd seen in magazines. Spectacular. Being able to see it with my dog smiling in the foreground was, however, nothing like the magazines. It was simply unbelievable! There were security guards everywhere, and they were understandably very suspicious, watching our every move. We tried to keep a low profile despite having half a dozen llamas follow around the most unusual tourist, with his very fine yet foul smell, ever to visit the site.

Whenever I saw the possibility of a great picture, I would rip off Oscar's orange jacket, throw down my sunglasses and click away. We were like monkeys in a theme park of opportunity; once I'd taken the pics, I would put on Oscar's jacket and my glasses again, grab Jonathan's arm and head off to the next viewpoint, where we would proceed with another photo shoot. We knew that at any moment we could be arrested and kicked down the mountainside. Even the most gullible person would have known we were playing blind-man's bluff.

Incredibly, nothing of the kind happened. The guards just kept watching us and talking to each other through their walkie-talkies. After three hours of snapping pics, we finally called it a day. Although it hadn't been the simplest of operations, mission impossible had been made possible.

We re-enacted the entire scenario in reverse the next day, until we finally got back to Cusco. We were met by the agency staff and they couldn't believe that we had managed to pull off such a 'stunt'. For us, it had just been business as usual. Only the Taj Mahal and the Parthenon had got the better of us, although we had been able to take a photo of the Taj from the outside and had found a suitable replacement for the Parthenon.

We decided to take a well-deserved break that evening. I ordered a massage for both Jonathan and me. Afterwards I packed my clothes and wrote on my blog, which I had fallen behind with ... and then the phone rang. It was the manager. He was in an absolute state. *Of course* he had made an exception by allowing a hound in his hotel, but he hadn't been expecting a humungous chocolate log to be soft-served on the second floor as a token of our appreciation! Furthermore, there was a group of thirty students from South River High School in Maryland staying in the hotel and the tour operator was so upset over the incident that he was threatening to take his business elsewhere. I was ordered to make an appearance in the dining hall *immediately* to apologise to everyone.

In all my years with Oscar, he had never, ever made a blunder. Perhaps one of the students had forgotten where the bathroom was? I decided to investigate further, and I didn't have to look far. When I opened my door, I knew that we were guilty as charged. It was the identical aroma that had almost suffocated the occupants of carriage number 3! I would have to eat humble pie on Oscar's behalf downstairs.

I walked to the dining room, hung my head in shame and began to apologise to the students who were seated in front of me. But when Oscar walked in a few seconds later, it was all over bar the screaming. It was as if one of the Beatles had just appeared. Everyone immediately jumped to their feet and ran towards Oscar in delight. I was soon to learn that all of them had watched, with great amusement, as we'd dodged the llamas and security at Machu Picchu the day before; the students even had photographs of our escapade on their cellphones!

They begged for Oscar's autograph and promised that, in exchange for a group photograph with him, Sir Oscar was welcome back on the second floor *any* time!

28

Rio to almost finito

Oscar and I were expecting an Academy Award for all our perfectly executed and convincing performances. Flying back to Lima and then on to Rio de Janeiro with a business-class upgrade was the cherry on top. While everyone battled for legroom in the back of the Airbus, Oscar was eating caviar and mayonnaise in the comfort of his oversized seat. As per the usual, every flight attendant wanted their turn to have their photograph taken with my hospitable guide dog, and when it came time to satisfy the captain's request, no one made a peep when I made a boob and took off my goggles by mistake in the cockpit!

Muslim territories aside, South America is probably the least dog-friendly place on earth, and the sprawling city of Rio is no exception. I had given up trying to find a hotel that would accommodate us in the city, but now that I knew I had an Oscar-winning showpiece in my midst, I didn't care. If they wouldn't take a guide dog, we always knew that we could wheel in a farting suitcase. In addition to visiting Dr Bianca of the ARCA Brasil Humane Society's compassionate veterinary team, we wanted to catch a Brazilian tan on Copacabana Beach, catch a tram to Sugarloaf Mountain, meet Christ the Redeemer and hang-glide over all of it when we were done.

Unfortunately the rain had other ideas, but through a miracle of nature it lifted just in time for us to visit two of our desired attractions. Months before our arrival in this carnival town, at a time when I was still dumb and ignorant, I had contacted Rio Tourism to try to arrange permission for my pooch to meet Christ the Redeemer. God had created Oscar too, and all he wanted to do was to pay his respects like any other grateful servant.

They had emailed me back to inform me that the Catholic Church owned the property and I would need to contact them directly. I wasn't holding my breath. When the Pope finally answered my email, the Vatican revealed no surprises. It was, as expected, 'No! NO! NOOOO!' The fact that he was an under-aged boy didn't earn him any points either.

However, now that we were considerably wiser, getting to the top of Corcovado Mountain to kiss the Redeemer's stony feet was sure easier than confession.

Once we had made peace with Christ, we thought we were ready to jump off a cliff. Hang-gliding over Rio is rated as one of the 1000 things to do before you die, and after having completed the other 999 things on the list over the past eight months, why not take our chances? If we had managed to dodge crocs, the police, a border patrol *and* the aircraft hold, could acting like a condor do any harm?

The experience would also give the term 'exposure' a whole new meaning. This was the kind of event that kids dig to watch. If they wanted to get a cool dog one day, they would think back to Oscar barking above Rio and head straight to a shelter.

We met Ruy Marra, founder of the largest free-flight company

243

in Latin America. Ruy was entertaining, smart and, from what I could tell, still alive, as were the other 30 000 passengers he had hang-glided with in tandem since starting his business, Superfly, twenty-five years earlier.

Oscar and I sighed with relief; the guy obviously knew what he was doing! All I had to do now was to calm down. Since John's accident, flying had become a nightmare for me. In fact, from that day the music died until fairly recently, I hadn't been able to board a flight unless I was totally inebriated. If I could fly today without as much as a seat beneath me, I could fully proclaim, 'Freedom from my phobia, hallelujah!' and let the angels sing.

Ruy talked us through some basic safety procedures in his office, and then a van transported us to the top of Pedra Bonita Mountain. Along the way, Ruy could sense I was beginning to get a little anxious, to put it mildly, so he tried to get me to think positive thoughts. To settle my nerves, he asked me to imagine a joyful time when I was much younger. Daisy the butterfly came to mind and Simba made a brief appearance, but then Valerie from Costa Rica arrived to ruin what was fast becoming a happy childhood. '*Be careful*,' she said in my imagination: 'BE *CAREFUL*.'

My survival instincts went on red alert. Was imminent death the reason why hang-gliding hadn't become as popular a pastime as golf, I started to wonder. I remember reading somewhere that, in the 1970s, roughly one in every 2 000 hang-gliding flights ended in a funeral, and of the forty entrants in the first US championships, half were dead within three years. I had written a will before we left on the tour, but if I was going to be dispersed across Copacabana Beach, pieces of Oscar would also be close by. Without Oscar in the world, I figured it didn't really matter who picked up my scraps. And I had done a great job of spending most of the content of my final will and testament over the past eight months anyway.

By the time we reached the top, I was dizzy and ready to fake a faint. Ruy had informed us on the way up that he had flown his own dog on many occasions, so while Oscar couldn't claim to be the first dog to glide over Rio, he was certainly in experienced hands. While Ruy and his team arranged all the ropes and cables, Oscar and I walked around and watched a few flights take off. By pure accident, I overheard a guy tell his buddy that only one in every 116 000 hang-gliding flights was doomed.

I had just watched three disappear over the edge of the cliff 'successfully'. Suddenly, our odds were now worse than they had been just minutes before. What goes up must come down, but was there perhaps another way to get to the bottom without losing face? Before I could consider any options, Ruy appeared and started to prepare us for the flight. He ran through a few basics, but they all boiled down to one key factor: Running!

Ruy made it very clear that once we had committed to taking off down the short, sloped ramp, there was no stopping halfway and no turning back. Oscar's legs weren't long enough to contribute to the run, but if mine suddenly froze up, Mr Nice Guy Ruy would have to carry on running and, Redeemer willing, we would all live to fight the muscle spasms later!

From the discussion we'd had in Ruy's office, I'd learnt that it wasn't uncommon for Rio's warm thermals to propel us much higher than our take-off of 1 600 feet. But I had made it very clear that we were aiming for the shortest, safest route down. We didn't need height or scenic detours. All we needed was the Noddy badge and a beating heart after our feet touched the ground.

Quite understandably, Ruy was beginning to worry about my state for the task ahead. He gripped my shoulders and talked me through a few respiratory exercises, which only made me hyperventilate more. But Ruy had seen it all before, and he wasn't going to give up on me. He was a master at mind control, a motivational speaker, and an accomplished author on the subject of facing one's fears and reaching for heights far greater than those you ever thought possible. He sounded like a verbal sequel to *Jonathan Livingston Seagull*. Richard Bach's book had been my childhood bible. I was beginning to find my faith.

Ruy continued to talk about how powerful it was to have the courage to challenge those debilitating belief patterns from your past that inhibit you from living a full and complete life. Having the courage to leap off a mountainside, despite feeling fear, meant you would have the courage to face any of life's obstacles.

This was the kind of stuff I had studied in sports psychology. Hang-gliding was just another conduit to helping me break free from the negative limitations that would slowly weigh me down over time. With minutes to spare, I started thinking about Oscar's life. When he was stuck in the shelter six years ago, he probably had less than a 25 per cent chance of ever finding a home; or, rather, he had a 75 per cent chance of dying before someone like me came knocking at his door. If Oscar had known and believed these odds, would he have given up? Would he not have bothered to come out, tail wagging, from the corner of his cage when I arrived at heaven's gate? Would Number B5 ever have become the best-travelled dog in history?

And then I thought about my own life. Would I have been here if I had listened to everyone who told me, because of the economic recession, what a terrible time it was to go on a tour with a ... er ... *mutt*? I stared into the distance and took a deep breath. I realised that there was nothing I'd rather do than take this leap of faith. This wasn't about my doomsday; it was about living beyond my wildest imagination. I could stay fixed to the ground and wait until I was too old and grey to take flight, or I could do it while I was still young enough to know that I get only one chance to soar in flight. I did not want to live my life regretting opportunities I never embraced, no matter what the risks.

You *bet* we were ready to take flight, and when Ruy blew the whistle, we seized the moment with all our might! I sprinted down that runway in a dash of speed that would have made Forrest Gump cheer. Ruy couldn't keep up, so I ran for all three of us. I ran for my life and I ran for my best little friend, who was calm and collected at Ruy's side. I ran for every dog who had never felt the kind touch of a human hand. I ran for the homeless, the hopeless and the hungry, and for all the other underdogs. I ran for the kids of Cambodia, the pigs in China and for little black dogs that beg in parking lots.

Then, when the wind beneath our wings left me running in space and the safety of land was behind us, the realm of possibilities seemed endless. We soared far and high above the earth in a vast, glorious expanse of sky, and I believed, at that moment, that one day all beings would defy their own predicaments and come to see the beautiful beings that they already were.

When we finally landed on São Conrado Beach, Oscar and I had made it further than most people had ever believed possible. As for Ruy, he suggested that I return to Rio for the 2016 Summer Olympics, where a gold medal would surely be waiting for me in the 100-metre sprint!

On a personal note, I had definitely seen the light, but with two flights still on our radar, I had to remain focused on the task at hand.

As we picked the last grains of sand out of our hair and fur respectively, all our social obligations for the World Woof Tour were officially over. All that remained now was to catch a flight to Buenos Aires and to get Oscar's paperwork finalised for our arrival in South Africa. In a sublime state of denial that our tour was rapidly drawing to a close, we made a last-minute detour to visit the magnificent Iguassu Falls.

We arrived in Buenos Aires a day later than planned, and the pet travel agency Las Lunas, which had been expecting us the day before, was not amused by our tardiness. South Africa has strict quarantine regulations and, although Dr Jyotika Rajput and her accommodating team at the South African Department of Agriculture, Forestry and Fisheries had kindly waived the thirty-day quarantine for Oscar, 'dogplomatic immunity' was valid only if all the papers were in order. Arranging this was a time-consuming process that, under normal circumstances, would take at least four weeks to complete.

Needless to say, we had arrived only twenty-four hours ahead of our expected departure, but with the sweetest of smiles on our faces! It seemed like an impossible task to get everything arranged on time, but we had no alternative. Malaysia Airlines was the only airline flying directly from Buenos Aires to Cape Town, and there were only three flights a week. Missing ours would mean arriving two days later than expected, on 12 December. This would spell disaster for us. Oscar may have been excused from being subjected to thirty days of isolation in quarantine, but he still had to swing by for an inspection immediately after landing in Cape Town ... and the quarantine offices were closing for the Christmas holidays on 11 December. If we arrived a minute too late, there would be no other option for Oscar but to 'celebrate' his homecoming all by himself in the concrete confines of a quarantine cell until the offices reopened a month later!

Getting the papers organised would be a miracle of epic proportions. Thanks to Christelle at home base sending 'good luck' e-cards to the office every second, Manuel Leunda and his formidable team were prepared to give it a shot. Knowing that it took two to tango,

Oscar and I figured that it was only fair to get out of their way. While the team got to work, we headed for the popular tourist district of San Telmo for a bit of sightseeing.

With the advent of a new day, we still didn't have any guarantee that the paperwork would be completed on time. Manuel was running around like a madman at our Buenos Aires base, while Christelle in Cape Town had destroyed her manicure without leaving enough keratin on which to have another. As for me and Oscar, we had our first opportunity in over eight months to sleep in, read the newspaper and enjoy an in-room breakfast service!

As the afternoon approached, hope prevailed. It looked like a 'green for go'. Oscar had to be at the cargo terminal of Ministro Pistarini International Airport five hours before the flight, and we were soon ensconced in the taxi and on our way. Since there was no other option, we had to fly on the national airline of Malaysia and, not surprisingly, they allowed pets to travel only as cargo – guide dogs included.

As it was to be our last flight, Oscar was prepared to take it like a man in the hold. We met a rather stressed-out Manuel and his loyal assistant Luciano at the terminal. They had managed to turn worry into wine, and Oscar and I were most grateful for the trouble they had gone to. All that was left to do was to pay Manuel for his services and fly home, but when I saw the invoice, I almost choked over the dogbox. I knew Manuel and his team deserved a bonus, but at a rate of $3 400, I could have hired illegal transportation to haul us across the Atlantic and we could have cleared ourselves through immigration on a remote beach just north of Cape Town. This gave crying for Argentina a whole new meaning!

Seeing my reaction, Manuel carefully pointed out that he had provided all his services for free. I looked at the breakdown of costs, and he was right. The agency had gone the extra million miles because they believed in our mission. The greedy sod was Malaysia Airlines. Clearly not in the spirit of wanting dogs on board unless they justified their weight in gold, their rate for flying Oscar was just shy of $3 000, with the paperwork making up the balance of the tab! The most we'd ever paid to fly Oscar was on Air France, from Paris to St Petersburg, and that had cost $1 000, which was still $500 more than we'd paid on any other flight. With all the taxes included, my ticket cost just $467.

I went red with rage. I could fly a couple and their eight point eight kids for the same price as Oscar, *and* they would get served on board! How dare they do this and expect to get away with their petty little prejudices beyond their country's borders? Manuel tried to calm me down, but smoke was already streaming out of every cavity. Supporting Malaysia Airlines would be even more criminal than supporting Chinese products. If I was serious about remaining true to my principles, there was no way that Oscar and I could take this flight!

There had to be another way home, even if a different airline flew out only thirty days later. How bad could a month in the Patagonian wilderness be? Oscar could hang out with the world's biggest Magellanic penguins and, with $3 500 in my pocket, I could buy the whole damn rookery as his amusement park for his Christmas present! Better yet, we could sail back to Cape Town via Antarctica. That possibility was squashed when I learnt that the Antarctic Treaty had banned canines in 1993, when evidence emerged that canine disease distemper was spreading to Antarctica's seals.

At this point the cargo staff was calling for my precious cargo. I didn't know what to do, and Manuel was beside himself trying to understand how the hell such an indecisive team had managed to make it this far! I thought about missing Christmas with my family.

We always played golf, and inevitably one of us always lost the round with a golf club over our head. It was family feuding at its best, and I knew I would miss it. Then I thought of all those tins of Pedigree that I had been forced to waste on narrow-minded Malaysian hotel owners to prove to them that a dog had indeed 'blessed' their dingy businesses! In that moment, the decision was made. We would boycott the bastards and not fly back to South Africa on Malaysia Airlines.

There wasn't another flight from Buenos Aires that could get us to South Africa by 11 December, so our focus turned to the southernmost part of South America. It didn't come without a guilty conscience. With the change in date and airline, the reams of paperwork that Manuel had been so proudly holding in his hands during the deliberation would now be of little use to anyone, except perhaps to a schizophrenic blonde and her 'mascota' looking to fuel a campfire in Patagonia.

I wholeheartedly apologised to Manuel for the about-turn in arrangements. I also tried to get hold of Christelle in Cape Town, but she had already fainted in her office. By the time we made it back to the hotel, the intensity of the past twenty-four hours had settled somewhat and Manuel was beginning to see the humour in the most ludicrous situation he'd ever dealt with in his business's history. We chatted about all the activities Oscar and I could do in Patagonia, and then the conversation went a bit deeper.

Manuel may not have been envious of how 'loco' Oscar and I were, but he did admit to being a little jealous of our flexibility. With a young family at home, he couldn't even begin to imagine himself deciding, on the spur of the moment, to extend a holiday by another day, let alone a month.

I had often wondered why I hadn't followed a more 'normal' route in life, like having kids and a husband who paid all my bills. I didn't necessarily want a normal life; things had just never worked out for me that way. Manuel and I called a very long day a night and agreed to meet in the morning to make the necessary arrangements for the month ahead and the subsequent flight home.

Little did we know that the plan was about to change ... again!

29

Home, sweet bone

Manuel may have had a family to take care of, but I had my mother to deal with. As soon as I got to my hotel room, I phoned her to tell her that we would be arriving a month later than expected. There was a moment of silence on the line, and then I could have sworn I heard her curlers explode through the ceiling, taking the gutter and chimney along with them!

'Joanne! You take your dog around the world and leave us all to worry about you for eight months. You call only when you're broke, have been arrested or are walking down the aisle with a dog. Now you're phoning to tell me that you've missed your flight and are heading into the wild south. Do you think this is a joke? Enough is enough!'

There was no mistaking what she was saying: it was the next flight ... or my inheritance. At the rate that I was blowing bucks, I didn't have much of a choice. It was too late to catch up with Malaysia Airlines, and it was way too late to make it Manuel's problem. I sat down and composed my thoughts. If we could defy the odds and travel via Rio, I knew we would find a way to get home before

D-Day. If I could just find a flight the next day – even if it went via Timbuktu – we would make it home just in time.

I went online and checked out what was available. Not surprisingly, I found just what I was looking for. There was indeed a flight back to Cape Town. South African Airways flew via São Paulo and connected through Johannesburg. Oscar and I would have to go all the way back to Brazil, but we would arrive on 11 December. We would have to have Oscar's check-up done in Johannesburg, and we would be back in Cape Town to paraglide off Lion's Head that same afternoon. Better yet, guide dogs were allowed in the cabin of SAA aircraft and, as always, at no additional charge. There was one seat left on the flight, and before Oscar could bark 'yelp', I had clicked on the 'purchase' button.

I sent an email to Christelle, knowing she would handle the latest update. Manuel, on the other hand, was beginning to believe that he was a stand-up punchbag on Comedy Central. When he saw my confirmed booking, however, he gamely started making the necessary arrangements. Best of all for everyone concerned, and with the exception of a few minor changes only, we could use the same paperwork.

The team at Las Lunas was sad to see us go, but Manuel wasn't crying quite yet. He'd seen and heard all of this before, and we were still in town! When the aircraft finally took off for São Paulo, Oscar and I knew that the World Woof Tour and all our adventures were almost over.

We still had to bluff our way onto the trans-Atlantic aircraft, but this feat we would manage to achieve after sweating it for a full hour while the duty manager for our flight went off to further 'investigate' my 'blind' status. We didn't get a business-class upgrade, but Oscar was right beside me in a bulkhead seat and sitting just as pretty as he had been in the private jet on our very first flight together.

I always bumped into someone I knew on a flight back to South Africa, but this time I was relieved when no one appeared on the other side of my shades. Unless I wanted to be kicked off the aeroplane mid-flight, I couldn't be seen watching movies or reading the in-flight magazine. I waited until the cabin lights were turned off before fumbling my way to the bathroom.

There was nothing to do for the next eight hours except reflect on the journey behind us and on the road ahead. After all our adventures, how on earth would we cope when we'd finally crossed the finish line and had to slam on the brakes? Even the thought of sleeping in the same bed for longer than two nights in a row was unthinkable ... but how to imagine waking up in the same city day after day, and not having to hide my dog in a bag and leopard-crawl our way into another hotel or train? It was unfathomable.

For the better half of the past two years, my routine had encompassed cranking on my computer, drinking barrels of coffee, and keeping my dog happy and healthy enough to play the lead role in our self-made travel documentary. I had managed to squeeze in the odd shower, but my existence had revolved around connecting with various organisations around the world, trying to source the worst hotels at the best prices and find the cheapest cars on the most wheels.

I knew that Oscar was ready to smell the sweet, sweet grass of home, but would I cope with the comfy cocoon of suburbia without a wake-up call every morning? Thankfully, I didn't have a choice; the crew had already begun to prepare the cabin for landing.

After touching down at OR Tambo International Airport, a wheelchair welcomed me at the exit as Oscar and I disembarked. I collected our suitcases and Oscar and I approached custom control, where the quarantine officer took us aside. He had a very careful look at our paperwork, which read like a novel. It even included laboratory work that had been done on my dog long before we'd started on the tour. Things seemed to be going rather well. The officer could see that Oscar had a doctor's appointment scheduled at the quarantine station, but nowhere on the paperwork did it mention that said patient was a guide dog.

Not knowing quite what to make of the situation, but understanding that the polite and sweet smiling lady in the filthy jeans needed her dog to help her find the exit, she decided to let us through. Only one short connecting flight stood between the beginning of a dream and the end of a tour. I could almost see Table Mountain in front of my shades and feel the cool southeasterly breeze gently drying the laundry on the line.

After touching down in the Mother City, our aeroplane taxied past the private hangar where we had boarded the private jet back in May. Once everyone had disembarked, Oscar and I were assisted to the gate, where my 'bank manager' was delighted to wheel us out of the last tricky moment of our tour. My mother was ecstatic that we were home safe and sound, and she had brought along her adopted dog Jessie, which I had given her as a farewell 'present', to welcome us back.

We headed straight for Lion's Head, where Pete from Wallend-Air was waiting to paraglide us down to Camps Bay beach. Oscar and I were extreme-sports junkies by now, and nothing but a few wind vectors, sand sprays and familiar faces would get in the way of our next 'fix'.

It was a glorious day, and we landed on the beach to the warm welcome of our key supporters. I had wanted our return home to be an intimate affair, one where Oscar and I could have a celebratory moment with the handful of people who had believed in us and supported the project when nobody else would take us seriously. When all the hugs and congratulations were over, Oscar and I returned to our pad. I had sold my property near Noordhoek Beach to fund the WWT, but I was still renting the small cottage where I had lived before.

Coming home was a moment I'd thought about many times on the tour. After spending 221 nights in 116 different beds, I wondered how Oscar would react when he finally got back to a cabin without any pressure and didn't have to go anywhere but to his king-sized mattress. A very familiar place, simply called 'home'.

I watched Oscar closely as we entered the garden. He took a few sniffs on the grass as he had always done, and then waited for me to open the front door. As we walked inside, I was expecting a reaction of sorts. Perhaps a tail wagging at 100 beats a second, or a 'thank-you' lick for the greatest honeymoon adventure ever? That would have been a nice bonus.

But this was Oscar, the coolest, most laid-back pooch on the planet. He took a few casual slurps of water and then went to sit at the front door. Then he looked up at me as if to say, 'Where to next, babe?' That was Oscar; so comfortable in his own skin – as long as I was close by. If he hadn't suddenly taken off to chase the neighbour's cat as if he hadn't chased one in nine months, no one would ever have known that he had left home.

Over the course of the next few weeks, we settled into our new routine and our old habits. We'd take the top of the car down and speed down the highway with the wind blowing past our ears. We'd cruise through the centre of town and Oscar would startle motor-cyclists at traffic lights. He would disrupt the peace with constant barking all over the place. It was if he wanted to say, 'And where the hell have *you* all travelled to lately?'

Needless to say, it wasn't long before everyone knew we were back in town. I even got a call from a psychologist I used to visit. I had already called up my favourite head doctor to thank her for her help in obtaining a service-dog certificate in the States, but the others just wanted hear about our journey. The tour was a milestone indicating how far I had travelled inside. I didn't necessarily want to write or talk about it – it was just a personal revelation that made me weep with immense gratitude.

Over the previous years, these professionals had all tried to help me find purpose in my life. Passion was never my problem; I just needed a cause on which to focus all my energy. In trying to find the answers, the professionals and I had talked about many things. What did I love, who did I hate and what would I change if I had a magic wand for just one day? What made me tick, what made me sick and what was this affinity I had for shelter dogs all about?

Had Daisy been the culprit who had started it all off, or had it originated in my own personal experiences of sometimes feeling lonely, rejected and unwanted? Was that why I felt so drawn to the plight of the shelter dogs, and why I could relate to their pitiful predicament as if it were my very own? I never really got the answers to my questions from the shrink sessions, but, as I later learnt, the answer has an uncanny way of showing up in the most unlikely of places when you least expect it.

After all the head-shrinking and head-scratching, who would ever have thought that a mutt on the verge of extinction would be the answer to everything I had been looking for?

Over the course of the next few weeks and months, the 'tail' of 'Phileas Dog' and his picture-perfect poses before some of the world's most famous landmarks hit newsstands around the world. Readers *everywhere* adored the story, but most of them were convinced that it was all a hoax. Bloggers thought the tour was a great idea, but commented that it was a pity that quarantine laws would prevent it from ever happening in 'real life'.

Readers were also convinced that the cute pooch had been created in cyberspace, or at least had undergone some major cosmetic surgery in PhotoShop to look *that* good. I had studied a course in professional photography a good few years before the tour, and my dog was a *supermodel*; we took that 'criticism' as a *major* compliment! When the story made the front page of a prominent Cape Town newspaper, it sparked such an outcry from suspicious readers that the editor called me up to tell me that their reputation was on the line. Was there any way for me to prove that Oscar was indeed the 'real deal'?

As word spread and I began working through the footage and sharing our story at local schools and special events, all disbelief was laid to rest. Oscar was becoming a bit of a celeb around town, and occasionally a motorist would shout out his name or try to take a photograph of him on a cellular phone while still driving at full throttle. Even the homeless drunk in the city park had read about him in yesterday's news.

Oscar and I made a few trips to Johannesburg to honour some engagements, and of course my loyal pooch was right beside me on the aircraft all the way. A number of passengers were already aware of the real story behind Oscar's orange jacket and my shades, but I really started panicking on one flight when the flight attendant informed me that the captain wanted to see me and my 'guide dog' in the cockpit *immediately*. We had just boarded a flight from Johannesburg to Cape Town, and I knew that we were in trouble. After a flawless record, it seemed that our moment of truth had finally arrived, and we prepared ourselves for immediate ejection.

Oscar and I walked into the cockpit to meet the captain. I could hardly believe it when he leant over and gave Oscar a big pat on his head and a good scratch on his back.

'Sorry for disturbing you, Joanne,' he said, 'but I just had to say hello to Oscar!' I lifted my dark glasses and winked at him. 'It's an absolute pleasure, captain.'

My paparazzi-friendly pooch handled fame just as casually as I had handled cash over the past eight and a half months, but we never lost sight of the master plan. We always knew that the end of the tour would, in many ways, be just the beginning; the start of using Oscar's epic journey as a vehicle to educate and inspire people.

Oscar had earned the public's recognition. We had flown around the world in order to get it, and we couldn't waste the opportunities now available to us. We would use every one of them to point out the connection between Oscar's humble beginnings and the millions of 'Oscars' that were still out there, dying to write a chapter of their own in a great adventure. We started putting together the documentary about our experiences straight away, and began planning a national tour for late in 2010.

I wanted people to know that my dog was no better than any of those who are facing a bleak future in a cage at a shelter; Oscar was just a lot luckier than most of them will ever be. He'd never had to prove his worth to me by doing anything other than being himself. Now that Oscar had all the mileage under his collar, he and I were still a team; to everyone else, though, he was now an extraordinary tale.

Oscar was the ultimate ruff to riches story that everyone loved to love. He was the underdog who had defied mammoth odds to become the face of a cause. He gave value and credibility to every shelter dog, and was a shining example of the potential that exists within all homeless dogs if they are given a chance to be adored.

Still, whenever somebody came up to acknowledge my dog for his achievements, I thought of those waiting at shelters around the world, dying for someone to come along and rescue them. My emotions always gathered in my throat when I thought about it. Every time. The adoration that was pouring out for my little Oscar

I wished on every shelter dog in the world. Dogs in shelters don't need a fan club or a ticket to fly; they just need kind, gentle hands, a modest home and a little bit of loving attention to make them feel like they have flown to the moon and back.

I look at Oscar and I have to pinch myself when I realise just how far he has come. From being a confined canine whom no one wanted, he was now a borderless freedom fighter whom everyone would take home in a heartbeat. When all his fans want a piece of him, I'm always in the background, explaining that I'm not about to slice him up, but that I know *exactly* where they can find their own 'Oscar'. I also remind them that Oscar is one of a kind. His kind of appeal cannot be purchased from the pet shop down the road or sold by a breeder. A class act like Oscar could *only* have come from a shelter.

Oscar had known how to roll over and say, 'Take me, take me!' and he had known how to use his big brown eyes to attract his blue-eyed girl. He'd instinctively known that I had thrown him a life jacket, and if he hadn't, he'd sure known how to fake enormous gratitude.

I cannot say for certain whether another adopted dog will ever have the opportunity to lift its leg on the Great Wall of China or make a splash in the Trevi Fountain. It may never dip under the lily pads in the great Amazon Basin or, God help us, smell a constipated camel near the border of Pakistan. It may never see Moscow, or Manhattan, or Pluto, or Paris. With any luck, it will *never* have to howl a hunka hunka burning tune with an Elvis impersonator in the front seat of a plastic pink Cadillac. An adopted dog may never become your better half, but I guarantee you that it will be the link that will make your daisy chain complete.

Oscar is just like every other shelter dog. Unless a cat crosses his path, he will stay by your side forever, and he will think you are beautiful, even if you don't brush your hair for eight months. If, for some crazy reason, you decide one day that you want to embark on a journey to find the beginning of the rainbow, he will be your guiding light all the way. He will lick the blisters from your feet and use his paw to protect your eyes when passport police poke a torch in your face. He will put you on a pedestal when the world weighs you down, and when you've blown all your bucks, he will sleep with you under a starry, starry night.

He will make you stop and smell the roses, and give you a reason to keep going when the world's sadness gets in your way. He will catch the flies that irritate you and crunch the mosquitoes that want to bite you.

You can stick him in a doggie bag or a dogbox and he will always emerge with a wagging tail, as if you had given him an upgrade to business class. He'll be your clear-seeing eyes when you think you've lost the plot, and your beacon of hope when you think you're going nuts. A shelter dog will be the wind beneath your wings when the mountain crumbles beneath you, and when the day is done, he will be your pillow to rest upon … without asking for anything in return.

When you wake up and the colours of your rainbow have faded, you will realise that your pot of gold was always the dog that walked beside you. You will wonder how you ever lived without him, and how you could live on if you lost him. You will bless the day that you found him, and know that, without you, he wouldn't have taken a journey at all.

Only then will you understand why your adopted dog was always the constant sun that warmed your way and the beacon that made your journey that much brighter for having shared it with you.

In the greatest chapter of my life so far, it was Oscar who made every breath worthwhile.

Epidogue

So, with almost 75 000 kilometres and a whole lot of fascinating experiences and close encounters of the canine kind under our collars, had it all been worth it? Had all the time, expense and effort warranted such an extraordinary mission?

Ah, that's an easy question to answer: *You bet your bottom dollar!*

How many people get to travel around the world with their best friend for a cause they both feel passionate about? With the exception of my mother's wedding day, the night we had to sleep under the stars and were bitten to smithereens by mosquitoes, there wasn't a moment when we would have wished ourselves elsewhere. As long as Oscar was with me, he was up for every challenge; as long as I had him by my side, I was inspired to keep moving forwards without ever looking back. The tour was a once-in-a-lifetime opportunity, and we are, to this day, still immensely grateful that we were able to experience it while still young – and wild – enough to survive it!

Was it Oscar's destiny to travel around the world and become a role model for the cause? Could any dog have completed this journey, or is Oscar that one-in-a-million mutt who has the natural ability to charm his way around the world? On the journey, he assumed various guises, from a dead suitcase to a guide dog, a lap dog, a laid-back passenger in a gyrocopter and a sophisticated business-class traveller. Would any other dog have been so multi-talented and adaptable?

Well, I like to believe that the universe has included dog adoption as a priority on its to-do list, and that Oscar was the pup with a purpose the universe had summoned to help me with the cause. I'm not saying that any other adopted dog couldn't have done it too, however – and here's why. Despite what everyone may think, Oscar was never trained to do anything prior to the World Woof Tour. My dog's inherent ability to play the leading role perfectly under all circumstances was not due to training. He was simply a product of all the good stuff that makes everything sparkle. Let me use my deceased tomato plant as an example.

When I was married and bored, I couldn't cook or look after a garden. (I still can't, but that's another story altogether.) Despite my lack of domestic skills, I decided to start a vegetable garden, so off I went to the nursery. I chose a tomato plant with which to kick things off, as the store manager told me that it was literally *impossible* for a tomato plant to die. A tomato plant always grew up strong and produced the red goods, no matter what. He was so sure of the plant's ability to survive that he guaranteed it.

When I got home, I stuck the plant into the ground and went to the gym. Knowing that my baby couldn't desert me, I let the clouds water it and the soil feed it. When it was ripe, I planned to eat the fruit of no labour! Within a week the plant had withered away. One tomato had managed to make a brief appearance before the vine died, but it wasn't much bigger than a peach pip. I got my money back, and my vegetable patch never got off the ground.

A tomato may not look like a dog or grow on Oscar's unusual family tree, but we all need the same stuff to grow up strong. With love and care, that vine could have helped to feed my husband for a whole week. Without those two elements, it withered and died, despite its enormous potential. Thankfully I am a much better canine keeper than I am a tomato reaper, and with all the right elements, an ugly duckling called Number B5 became an unlikely prince named 'Oscar'.

I never trained my royal highness to be anything other than my best buddy. We did everything together. I loved and adored him. I showered him with affection and a few good strides in the forest each day. I encouraged him to be a dog, and told him he was worthy of his name. I let him sniff other dogs in all the right places, and I allowed him to chase squirrels in the day and fireflies at night. I let him beat little boys at beach frisbee and allowed him to hit a few golf balls when he wasn't digging down a mole's hole.

He slept inside and out – wherever he felt comfortable. I fed him all the right stuff and let him dream upon a wishbone every night. Somewhere in all of this 'training', he developed a strong sense of confidence in himself and an unwavering trust in me as his guardian and queen. When all of his fine attributes were refined to pooch-perfection, he had arrived with all the 'right stuff' to become the first dog in history to take on the world.

As for playing the role of a blind person with a guide dog, what on earth was I smoking? It was never my or Oscar's intention to buck the system, although we would both be lying if we said that we never took advantage of it. I have a tremendous amount of respect for the South African Guide-Dogs Association for the Blind and the incredible work that they do. But the World Woof Tour was an extraordinary mission that barked out for creative improvisation at every twist and turn. Without it, we would have lost our minds (what was left of them, anyway) and Oscar would not have been as comfortable, which would have impacted on his overall well-being.

Every brick wall that we were able to demolish was done in the spirit of this worthwhile cause. That is not to say that I don't think some of these walls *shouldn't* be broken. Why an animal must endure any form of quarantine when its medical records can prove that it is of absolutely no threat to society is beyond me. It is also worth asking why a well-trained animal is not allowed to share public transportation. Why must it be treated like a dog?

Without a doubt, Oscar was one of the best-behaved passengers on board every flight and, given the choice, I can guarantee that every passenger would have preferred Oscar on board rather than a screaming toddler disrupting the peace at 35 000 feet! Be that as it may, I certainly don't think that the airlines have to worry about a sudden influx of blind passengers with untrained hound luggage when this book is published. I am also not suggesting that buying an orange jacket will be your one-way ticket to a business-class upgrade. Less than 10 per cent of countries actually have quarantine, so what I do want to tell you is that travelling with your dog is indeed possible – and certainly kinder than hanging it out to dry in the backyard while you are on holiday.

As far as the objectives of the World Woof Tour are concerned, was it a success? If one dog was adopted as a result of the WWT, I think our days on the road were well spent. After all, if my dog's life depended on my travelling around the world, of course I would do it! His life is precious – as is every other life – and going the extra mile to save it will always be worth the effort.

Almost half of the 'Oscars' chosen at the shelters were adopted, and we constantly receive emails from people who have heard Oscar's story and have adopted or will be adopting a dog as a direct result. However, as long as there are shelters, our work will not be finished. A cage is no life for any animal, and many no-kill shelters are no better than those that practise euthanasia. In many cases, they can actually be a lot worse, as they become overcrowded hoarding grounds where staff refuse to allow any of the dogs to be adopted – as was the case with Zara, the dog we wanted to adopt in Romania, but whose 'owners' would not release her.

The funds to keep these frustrated and despondent dogs alive could be put to far better use in a sterilisation project.

Was the tour fun, or was it a real 'mission'? Well, we had a rather large dose of both. If we're talking about sleep, laundry and personal grooming, it was an absolute disaster. As for Oscar, what dog wouldn't get a kick out of smelling over 7000 years of scents at the bottom of a camel-thorn tree? As with any worthwhile mission, there were both enormous highs and incredible lows.

We met over 15000 shelter dogs on our journey, and each one of them could just as well have been Number B5; given another set of circumstances, one of them would have been mine. Instead, most of these dogs will now either be dead or in exactly the same cage right now. Many of them had been burnt, stabbed, raped or poisoned, and all of them had been abandoned; many of them were either sick or starving.

I saw a dog who had never known a life beyond its cage for all eleven years of its existence. But we also met dogs who had survived the most atrocious situations. We saw disabled dogs that had learnt to 'walk' in specialised harnesses with wheels. We met dogs like Mango at KAT in Nepal, who had defied such tremendous odds that he'd become the shelter's proud mascot!

Behind every story was someone who, at one time or another, had decided to effect the changes that they wanted to see. I wonder at all the people in the world who have financial wealth and influence but do not help or support any worthy cause or think beyond their own selfish interests. Then I think of individuals like Jan Salter, Jean Gilchrist, Patricia Artimaña, Nancy Janes and the Dalleys, to name just a few, and my faith in humanity is restored. They are the uncelebrated stars who are the deserving recipients of every Oscar.

As for the moral of the story, well, that's when things get really emotional for Oscar and me. Let us wipe away the tears and sum up the tragedy as clearly and quickly as possible. There are simply too many dogs on the planet and not enough homes to go around. For every dog that has a home, three do not. There are two main reasons for this tragic state of affairs. The first is irresponsible pet owners who do not have their dogs sterilised and allow them to produce yet more unwanted animals, which just promulgates the cycle. Just one unsterilised female and her unsterilised offspring can produce 67 000 puppies in six years.

The second reason? Many people who want a dog buy one from a breeder or a pet shop. Please, let me be blunt here, seeing that millions of lives are on the line: breeders are not in the game to make puppy love. They are in the business of *manufacturing*. They produce puppies for money, no matter what they tell you, or will try to have you believe. Breeding dogs or supporting dog breeders is the main reason why millions of shelter dogs have to be destroyed. Every time another puppy pops into the world, no matter how cute and adorable it is, another home is snatched away from a shelter dog – a dog that has already been born and will now never get a second chance.

When I see a cute puppy, I see just another black garbage bag containing a dead dog. I have seen dogs being put down, and let me tell you, it is undoubtedly one of the saddest things you will ever see in your lifetime. The sight of a beautiful dog, alive the one moment and motionless the next, is an image that will haunt you forever.

The blame cannot rest on the shelters or on those who have to do this dirty work, as they have limited space and resources at their disposal. I blame the ignorance of those who do not consider the dire consequences of buying or breeding a dog.

I could write about the depressing statistics of the thousands of dogs who are destroyed every day and how many millions they tally up to at the end of any given year. I am not going to do that here, however. The internet is an invaluable tool, and all the facts and figures are there for everyone to see. For those of you who find it impossible to believe that dogs like Oscar are being put down every single second, I encourage you to research the subject further or visit a few of the websites that I have listed at the back of the book.

Let me rather leave you with some really *good* news. Finding a home for every pet is not a dream. It is an attainable goal. The solution is *so* simple that it's actually hard to believe that euthanasia is still necessary in our society today.

If you want a dog, adopt one from a shelter. If you have a pet, sterilise it.

It is that simple. So, are you going to save a life, or are you going to silence a shelter dog's bark forever? Will you stand up and effect the change you want to see in the world?

Whether you like it or not, your choice will be either a measurable part of the solution, or an integral contributor to the tragedy. You are *in* the equation. There is no middle ground and there are no exceptions.

The best news of all is that you now have Oscar's story in your paws. Surely his tale must be all the proof you will ever need to realise that when you adopt your dog from a shelter, not only are you saving a great animal, but it will also be the beginning of the greatest journey that both of you will ever take.

Watch dog

SOCIETIES VISITED

Amazon CARES, Iquitos, Peru: www.amazoncares.org

Animal Foundation, Las Vegas, Nevada, USA:
  www.liedanimalshelter.org

Asociacion Animales de Asis, San José, Costa Rica:
  www.animalesdeasis.com

BIM Khoteichi Shelter, Moscow, Russia: www.moscowbim.ru

Botswana SPCA, Gaborone, Botswana: www.spca.org.bw

Brigitte Bardot Foundation, Paris, France:
  www.foundationbrigittebardot.fr

Bulgarian Society for Animal Protection and Preservation, Sofia,
  Bulgaria: www.bulgariadogs.com

Care For Dogs, Chang Mai, Thailand: www.carefordogs.org

Contra Costa Animal Services, Contra Costa, California,
  USA: www.co.contracosta.ca.us

Friends of Animals Kos, Kos Island, Greece:
  www.animals.cos-island.info

Grassy Park SPCA, Cape Town, South Africa: www.spca-ct.co.za

Greek Animal Welfare Fund, Athens, Greece: www.gawf.org.uk

Group Initiative for Animals, Sibiu, Romania: www.gia.org.ro
Helen Woodward Animal Center, Rancho Santa Fé, New Mexico,
    USA: www.animalcenter.org
Humane Society of Broward County, Fort Lauderdale, Florida, USA:
    www.humanebroward.com
Kathmandu Animal Treatment Centre, Kathmandu, Nepal:
    www.katcentre.org.np
Kenya SPCA, Nairobi, Kenya: www.kspca-kenya.org
Langkawi Animal Shelter, Langkawi, Malaysia:
    www.langkawilassie.org.my
Leh Dog Sterilisation Project, Leh, India: www.vetsbeyondborders.org
Mayor's Alliance for NYC's Animals, New York City, New York,
    USA: www.AnimalAllianceNYC.org
Muttville, San Francisco, California, USA: www.muttville.org
Ndola SOCA, Ndola, Zambia
Nea Filadelphia, Athens, Greece: http://www.friendsofanimals-nf.com
PACDOC Orphanage, Siem Reap, Cambodia:
    Email: potlongngo@yahoo.com
Penang SPCA, Penang, Malaysia: www.spca-penang.net
Rescue Centre, Koh Samui, Thailand: www.samuidog.org
Romanian Animal Rescue, Livermore, California, USA:
    www.romaniaanimalrescue.com
San Francisco Animal Care and Control, San Francisco,
    California, USA: www.sfgov.org/acc
Sanctuary for Sick and Old Donkeys, Leh, India:
    www.donkeysanctuary.in
Save A Sato Foundation, San Juan, Costa Rico: www.saveasato.org
SCAD/Soi Dog Rescue Bangkok, Bangkok, Thailand:
    www.scadbangkok.org
Second Chance Animal Aid, Shanghai, China: www.scaashanghai.org
Shelter for Abandoned Animals, Zagreb, Croatia:
    www.zagreb.hr/Skloniste.ns

Society for the Protection of Animal Rights in Egypt, Cairo,
    Egypt: www.sparelives.org
Soi Dog Foundation, Phuket, Thailand: www.soidog.org
Sonadi Charitable Trust, New Delhi, India: www.sonadi.org
SPA Shelter, Paris, France: www.spa.asso.fr
SPCA of Monterey County, Monterey, California, USA:
    www.spcamc.org
St Petersburg SPCA, St Petersburg, Russia: www.sp-animal.spf.ru
Sunrise Children's Village, Siem Reap, Cambodia: www.scv.org.au
The Beijing Human & Animal Environmental Education Centre,
    Beijing, China: www.animalschina.org
The El Arca de Noé Animal Sanctuary, San José, Costa Rica:
    www.arcadenoecr.com
The Rescue Train, Los Angeles, California, USA:
    www.therescuetrain.org
Tony LaRussa's Animal Rescue Foundation, Walnut Creek,
    California, USA: www.arf.net
Windhoek SPCA, Windhoek, Namibia: www.spcawindhoek.org.na
Yedikule Animal Shelter, Istanbul, Turkey:
    www.fatihbelediyesiyedikule hayvanbarinagi.com
ZESPA, Zanzibar, Tanzania

SUPPORTERS OF THE WWT
4roues-sous-1prapluie, Paris, France: www.4roues-sous-1parapluie.
    com
Achilleas Hotel, Athens, Greece: www.achilleashotel.gr
Animal Travel Services, Cape Town, South Africa: www.animal-travel.
    com
Aqua Expeditions, Lima, Peru: www.aquaexpeditions.com
Belvedere Guesthouse, Windhoek, Namibia: www.belvedereguest-
    house.com
Big Sky Lodges, Windhoek, Namibia: www.BigSkyNamibia.com

Bobbi's World Kennels, Fort Lauderdale, Florida, USA: www.bobbis-worldkennels.com

Chedi Hotel, Milan, Italy: www.thechedimilan.com

City Sightseeing, Athens, Greece: www.citysightseeing.gr

City Sightseeing, Cape Town, South Africa: www.citysightseeing.co.za

City Sightseeing, San Francisco, California,USA: www.city-sightseeing.us

Coachman's Inn, Carmel, California, USA: www.coachmansinn.com

Crown Relocations, Dar es Salaam, Tanzania: www.crownrelo.com/tanzania

David Livingstone Safari Lodge & Spa, Livingstone, Zambia: www.dlslandspa.com

Dream Hotel Bangkok, Bangkok, Thailand: www.dreambkk.com

Dynamic Air Cargo Co, Bangkok, Thailand: www.dynamicaircargo.com

EU Rail: www.eurail.com

Fumba Beach Lodge, Zanzibar, Tanzania: www.fumbabeachlodge.com

Gaborone Sun, Gaborone, Botswana: www.suninternational.com/DESTINATIONS/HOTELS/GABORONESUN

Hotel Cristallo, Assisi, Italy: www.hotelcristallo-assisi.com

Jungle Safari Resort, Chitwan, Nepal: www.junglesafariresort.com

JW Marriott, Bucharest, Romania: www.jwmarriott.ro

Karen Blixen Coffee Garden, Nairobi, Kenya: www.karenblixencoffee-garden.com

Kenya Airways: www.kenya-airways.com

Lifestyle Portraits, Cape Town, South Africa: www.lifestyleportraits.com

Livingstone Adventures, Livingstone, Zambia: www.livingstonsadventures.com

Michaelangelo Lodge, Ndola, Kenya: www.michelangelocafe.com

Moivaro Lodge, Tanzania: www.moivaro.com

Nepal Guide Trek, Kathamandu, Nepal: www.nepalguidetrek.com

Nepal Himalaya Trek, Kathmandu, Nepal: www.nepalhimalayatrek.com

Nice Equipment, Cape Town, South Africa: www.niceequipment.com

Pedigree South Africa: www.pedigree.co.za

Plaka Hotel, Athens, Greece: www.plakahotel.gr

Plan Tours, Istanbul, Turkey: www.plantours.com

Red Capital Ranch, Beijing, China: www.redcapitalclub.com.cn

Rio Mar Beach Resort and Spa, San Juan, Costa Rica: www.wyndhamriomar.com

Rogz, Cape Town, South Africa: www.rogz.com

Safpar, Livingstone, Zambia: www.safpar.net

Sappho Travel, Athens, Greece: www.sapphotravel.com

Sheraton Hotel, Iguazu Falls, Argentina: www.starwoodhotels.com/sheraton/property/overview/index.html?propertyI=1152

Sossusvlei Lodge, Sossusvlei, Namibia: www.sossusvleilodge.com/

Superfly, Rio de Janeiro, Brazil: www.riosuperfly.com.br

The Imperial Hotel, New Delhi, India: www.theimperialindia.com

Turu Ba Ri, San José, Costa Rica: www.turubari.com

UPS South Africa: www.ups.com

Vision Holidays, Las Vegas, Nevada, USA: www.visionholidays.com

W Hotel, Istanbul, Turkey: www.whotels.com/istanbul

Wallend Air, Cape Town, South Africa: www.wallendair.com

Wisdom Adventures, New Delhi, India: www.himalayas-travel.com

USEFUL WEBSITES

www.abandoned.co.za: a site dedicated to dog adoption in South Africa

www.animalethics.org.uk: a site that addresses animal rights

www.aspca.org: a site dedicated to the safety and well-being of animals in the USA

www.earlings.com: a site that explores man's dependence on animals

www.goveg.com: a site that focuses on a vegetarian lifestyle

www.humanesociety.org: the USA's largest and most effective animal-protection organisation

www.ifaw.org: a site that addresses animal-welfare matters and animal cruelty around the world

www.peta.org: a site dedicated to the safety and well-being of animals

www.petfinder.com: a site dedicated to dog adoption within the USA

www.spcai.org: an internationally represented site dedicated to the safety and well-being of predominantly domestic animals

www.worldanimal.net: a site dedicated to dog adoption in the USA

www.worldwooftour.com: a site dedicated to Oscar's journey around the world

www.wspa.org.uk: a site that addresses animal-welfare matters and animal cruelty around the world

Do you have any comments, suggestions or
feedback about this book or any other Zebra Press titles?
Contact us at **talkback@zebrapress.co.za**